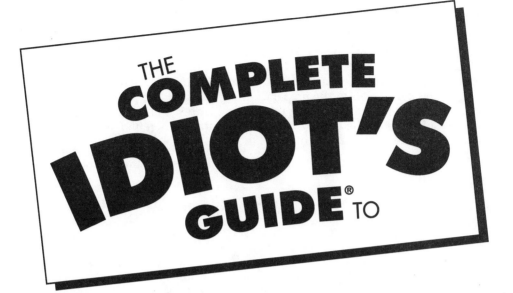

THE COMPLETE IDIOT'S GUIDE® TO

Performance Appraisals

by Adele Margrave and Robert Gorden

alpha books

A member of Penguin Group (USA) Inc.

Publisher
Marie Butler-Knight

Product Manager
Phil Kitchel

Managing Editor
Cari Luna

Senior Acquisitions Editor
Renee Wilmeth

Development Editor
Deborah S. Romaine

Production Editor
Billy Fields

Copy Editor
Rachel M. Lopez

Illustrator
Jody P. Schaeffer

Cover Designers
Mike Freeland
Kevin Spear

Book Designers
Scott Cook and Amy Adams of DesignLab

Indexer
Tonya Heard

Layout/Proofreading
Terri Edwards
Donna Martin
Gloria Schurick

Contents at a Glance

Contents

Foreword

"How'm I doing?" Everybody wants to know how they're doing on the job, and every manager has an obligation to let his or her people know this. Yet, when managers are asked what they like least about their jobs, the first is "firing people," and second "conducting a performance appraisal." Why do supervisors feel this way? It's no problem when the appraisal is good, but most people find telling somebody they are not performing up to standard is an unpleasant and often stressful situation.

But performance appraisals have to be given in most companies. And it doesn't have to make either the appraiser or the person being appraised uncomfortable. It can be conducted in a meaningful, and stress-free manner that will lead to productive results.

This is the theme of *The Complete Idiot's Guide to Performance Appraisals*. Adele Margrave and Robert Gorden have written an engaging "how-to" manual that is not only a prime training tool for new supervisors, managers and team leaders, but also a reference guide to all staff members that are faced with conducting periodic performance reviews.

There are several reasons for conducting performance assessments. They include determination of salary increases, evaluation for promotional consideration, identification of training needs, obtaining feedback on effectiveness of operations, compliance with government regulations, and documentation in the event that it becomes necessary to demote or terminate an employee based on inadequate performance.

In this book, readers will learn how to prepare for the assessment interview. It will show how to overcome the common practice we've all experienced where the supervisor just tells the employee what was done well and what was performed below standard. The appraiser will learn how to make the assessment a cooperative exercise in which both the assessor and the assessee participate in the discussion

Managers will learn how to deal with employees who break into tears, get angry, react negatively, or even violently when the appraisal is not to their liking.

In addition, the book recognizes that in most companies, the appraisal system is already established and supervisors must comply with it. It describes the most commonly used programs, such as "check-the-box" and "fill-in-the-blanks" and offers suggestions on how to get the most value from them. It also provides guidelines on constructing an evaluation program, designed to meet the special needs of your organization.

Another interesting feature of this book is an entire section devoted to how the reader should react when his or her own performance is being reviewed. It outlines how to prepare for that review and how to deal with a boss when you disagree with the appraisal.

The book is loaded with examples and anecdotes of good, bad, funny and sometimes tragic results from real life performance appraisal experiences.

The performance appraisal process, if properly managed, can be a highly stimulating experience for both the employee and the supervisor. *The Complete Idiot's Guide to Performance Appraisals* provides an easy-to-read, pragmatic, easy-to-apply road map for every manager, supervisor and team leader who conducts performance reviews.

Arthur R. Pell. Ph.D.

Dr. Arthur R. Pell, a long-time consultant, lecturer, and writer in the human resources field, is the author of 46 books. Among his most recent books are *The Complete Idiot's Guide to Managing People, The Complete Idiots Guide to Team Building, The Compete Idiot's Guide to Recruiting the Right Stuff,* and *Winning the War for Talent.* Over 250,000 people in the United States and Canada have attended his lectures, workshops and seminars.

Introduction

Lots of business people we know would do anything—short of jumping off a cliff—rather than give or receive a performance appraisal. What is it about this common business practice that makes the hair on the back of your neck stand out straight? Certainly the confrontational aspect of doing a performance appraisal can be rather off-putting. But more than that, we believe that most people rarely have had the experience of giving or receiving a constructive, productive, and yes, even motivational performance appraisal. Impossible, you say? Not at all—it's highly possible and worth the time and effort to do your homework to get it right. *The Complete Idiot's Guide to Performance Appraisals* can show you how!

The real purpose of a performance appraisal or evaluation is to help the person being appraised to do better, accomplish more, and get motivated to work toward making your company more successful. It also can be used to acknowledge a job well done, a way of showing that you actually notice and appreciate the personal commitments many of your employees make. It's one of those win-win propositions. If need be, you can use performance reviews to help a poorly performing employee see what it would take to succeed, and try to find out what that employee needs to do so. Why is it, then, that so many managers use an appraisal as a way to exert their power and control and keep employees "in their place?" What those kinds of managers are missing is that when you put an employee down by criticism, you could hurt productivity for a short or even a long while. The days of the coach beating a good performance out of the team are over.

A well-written performance appraisal can jump-start a so-so performer, and increase the loyalty and excellence of your all-star performer. Those appraisal documents—and the way they are delivered—are uniquely powerful. Don't underestimate the positive effect they can have on your business and company morale. It doesn't happen magically, however. It takes thoughtful preparation and advance planning. It also takes warmth, honesty, and sincerity. This book will show you how to turn your most dreaded management task into your most effective motivational business practice.

How to Use This Book

We tried addressing the topic of appraisals from different aspects, including the manager's as well as the employee's perspective.

Part 1, Love 'Em or Hate 'Em, (Almost) Everybody Needs 'Em, explains what performance appraisals are or should be, who is involved, and how you know if you need them. The legal aspects of proper appraisals are explained, and you'll learn how to stay out of court. We go into the advantages of feedback, and help you choose your philosophy and style of appraisals.

Part 2, Let's Start at the Very Beginning, goes into who should be involved in creating the company's appraisal system. We talk about the homework necessary to complete before you undertake appraisals including writing job descriptions, how to do an appraisal with or without a form, and how to focus on what is most important: motivation and improvement. We also cover how to introduce a new appraisal program to your staff.

Part 3, What's My Line: What to Say and How to Say It, takes the manager into the actual appraisal meeting. We cover how to take care of yourself and your environment, and give you a heads-up about what NOT to do during the meeting. You will learn how handle the classic appraisal meeting and also learn how to handle or gracefully exit a potentially dangerous appraisal situation. Then we will help you navigate the period after an evaluation.

Part 4, When It's Your Turn to Receive, examines the employee's (the person being appraised) perspective. We go into how to be equally or more prepared than your boss, how to handle a classic appraisal, and even how to handle an appraisal with a difficult boss. Not only that, you will also learn what recourse you can take if everything goes badly.

Part 5, Building a New Performance Appraisal Plan, walks you through the construction of a formal performance appraisal system for your company. We discuss style, timing, and how to roll out a new program so that employees will buy in. We also go into the more sophisticated kinds of appraisal systems, such as performance management and 360-degree feedback.

Part 6, Measurement Matters: Types of Appraisals, describes the pros and cons of the different styles of appraisal forms—from the most basic "fill-in-the-blank" type to the most complex format. You will get advice on how to choose what is right for your company, and we will show you a sample of completed forms to illustrate various styles.

Extras

To help make the text a little more easy to read and user friendly, we've added valuable tips and advice in sidebars throughout the book. You can't miss the shaded boxes that will highlight the information we don't want you to miss!

Close Up

These boxes bring you up close and personal with terms you might not be familiar with or that might be used in a different context.

Empowerment Zone

In these boxes, you'll find practical management suggestions and observations.

Wise Counsel

These bits of information provide cautionary tips or advice to keep you out of trouble.

Just the Facts

These boxes provide factual examples and information to add to your expertise.

From the File Cabinet

The longer stories in these boxes are real-life experiences that either Adele or Robert has had, which help illustrate key points.

Acknowledgments

We want to thank the many people we worked with over the years who provided us with examples of how to, and how not to, do a performance appraisal. We especially want to acknowledge those mentors who model the motivational management style that we promote.

Certain people deserve special thanks for their support and encouragement during the writing process: our wonderful agent, Andree Abecassis (of Ann Elmo Agency); the staff at Alpha Books including Renee Wilmeth, our acquisitions editor; Debbie Romaine, our development editor; Rachel Lopez, our copy editor; and Billy Fields, our production editor.

Our sincere appreciation to our colleagues in the human resources field for their contributions: Melissa Ridlon and Valerie Roberts of Children's Hospital, Oakland, CA; and Harry Joel. Thanks and hugs go to Betty Becker, SPHR, for her technical expertise and ongoing advice and assistance. And we would be remiss if we did not thank our loving and understanding families for putting up with us while we worked on this book: Adele's husband, Jon Ivanish, and Robert's wife and children, Jean Shimozaki and Kayo and Mikio Gorden.

Special Thanks to the Technical Reviewer

The Complete Idiot's Guide to Performance Appraisals was reviewed by an expert who double-checked the accuracy of what you'll learn here, to help us ensure that this book gives you everything you need to know about performance appraisals. Special thanks are extended to Betty Becker, SPHR. With 20 years of expertise in all aspects of human resources, Betty is certified as a Senior Professional in Human Resources Management and is a member of the Society for Human Resource Management and the Sacramento Area Human Resources Association. She is currently director of human resources for Western Contract, a business and home interior design and furnishings company in Sacramento, California.

Trademarks

All terms mentioned in this book that are known to be or are suspected of being trademarks or service marks have been appropriately capitalized. Alpha Books and Penguin Group (USA) Inc. cannot attest to the accuracy of this information. Use of a term in this book should not be regarded as affecting the validity of any trademark or service mark.

Part 1

Love 'Em or Hate 'Em, (Almost) Everybody Needs 'Em

Whether you are on the giving or the receiving end of a performance appraisal, if you are like most people, you don't look forward to the experience. Almost every business needs performance appraisals to make compensation and promotional decisions, as well as to just find out how people are doing in their jobs. But the process of delivering a performance appraisal often is procrastinated endlessly. Adding to the stress are the possible legal consequences if a performance appraisal is challenged—another good reason (you might think) to drag your feet before doing one. What can you do to make this necessary evil more appealing?

This section helps you do the necessary preparation before undertaking an appraisal. You need to be very clear on what you and your company believe in and what defines successful performance. Without that roadmap—one that has been clearly communicated—appraisals might be perceived as just one more unclear message delivered differently, if not sporadically, by every manager in your organization.

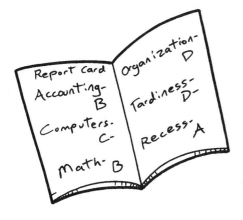

Report Cards for the Working Class

It's safe to say that every company we have ever worked with over the years has had problems with performance appraisals. Painful for the appraiser as well as the person being appraised, performance appraisals seem to be the most widely dreaded of management practices. Why are these feedback instruments so often hated?

Maybe it's because most companies aren't very good at performance appraisals. They don't know how to design them and most of all they don't know how to deliver them. From the dark ages of the industrial revolution the belief has hung around that performance appraisals are a method by which a boss can "power trip" the employees and keep them in their place. Employees rightfully resent this treatment and give such bosses a hard time. In this environment everyone is negatively affected—you might call it a lose-lose situation.

Why not change that paradigm by learning to do it right? Done correctly, performance appraisals are a powerful tool that can motivate workers to improve not only themselves but their company as well. It takes a bit of work to adequately prepare for them, but once you've done your homework, performance appraisals might be something that you and your employees actually look forward to.

The formal performance appraisal has become one of the most important management tools around. It is used for motivation, promotions, raises, layoffs, and assessing training needs, among other things. And *anything* that is so important involves many legal and financial implications. Nowadays you can't afford to use a poorly defined performance appraisal.

Measuring Performance

Broadly paraphrased from *Webster's Dictionary*, to appraise someone's performance is to estimate the quality of (someone's) execution of work. Seems simple enough at first glance—so why does the mere mention of the term make most people's palms sweat?

Managers often feel they don't have the time to do performance appraisals, or maybe they can't deal with that much confrontation. And in today's litigious society, a poorly done performance appraisal can be likened to a ticking time bomb in someone's personnel file. No wonder performance appraisals are considered a dreaded but necessary evil.

Performance appraisals can have similarly stressful effects on the workers who receive them. Your chances of being promoted are based on your boss's opinion of your performance. Whether you get a raise—and often how much that raise will be—depends on that appraisal. And in most cases, your self-esteem can be built up or torn down by what's written on that important document known as an appraisal.

Empowerment Zone

How many people do you know who really take or give criticism very well? Some managers probably would rather hide under their desks than approach an employee directly, especially if the encounter could be unpleasant. Anything that affects a person's well-being (money for basic needs, self-esteem, relationships) is a big deal, whether positive or negative.

In the Good Old Days

When the concept of reviewing an employee's performance first was considered, the majority of employees probably accepted the opinions of their supervisors. They might not have liked it, but 50 or more years ago, it was not a common practice to question the boss. Bosses enjoyed that kind of treatment and grew to expect it from all employees. A boss's written estimate of an employee's performance, as subjective as it might have been, was final.

There still are many employers who expect that same kind of blind respect and acceptance. But in recent years, employees have become more vocal and now might question or challenge their supervisors or employers. Employees will ask questions such as

➤ Just *who* is giving this evaluation?

➤ Has the appraiser really observed the execution of the work?

➤ Has the appraiser communicated any expectations about the quality of work?

➤ Who established the standard of quality?

➤ Does that person understand the work at all?

➤ Does the appraiser know anything about the person whose work is being appraised?

➤ How long has the appraiser observed the work?

➤ Is the appraiser biased or favoring some employees over others?

In Today's World

Twenty-first century bosses and managers will have to be able to respond to the preceding and many other questions from their direct reports. And if you can do this without being defensive and by using clear, jargon-free language, so much the better.

Performance appraisals can be formal or informal—it all depends on your company and its size, complexity, and philosophy (and possibly on your industry as well).

The trend today is to use more sophisticated techniques and new formats in appraising such as

➤ Self-appraisals.

➤ Peer-to-peer appraisals.

➤ 360-degree appraisals.

➤ Continuous feedback.

➤ Management by Objectives (MBO).

We'll go into all of these in greater detail in later chapters.

Wise Counsel

There are many so-called experts out there who recommend cookie-cutter techniques for responding to all your problem employees, or motivating others. Nothing tends to make employees angrier than formulaic sayings or the trend-of-the-month consulting movement. Try to keep feedback direct, honest, objective, and sincere.

One for You, One for Me

Anyone who is working for anyone else should get a performance appraisal; how formal it is depends on factors we will cover later (see the chapters in Part 2). Employees at all levels within an organization should be told how well they are doing their jobs, whether they are doing their jobs correctly—or if not, how so.

Close Up

Discoverable describes information that is considered evidence which can be used in a legal case. A performance appraisal frequently is sought during the investigation or formal discovery process prior to a trial or hearing.

Once you begin a performance appraisal system, it must be handled fairly and equitably. A labor attorney would love to find out that only certain employees received documentation regarding their performances. So don't think you can be selective about this process. Discriminatory policies can get you into lots of hot water. Performance appraisal documents are *discoverable* in a court of law.

Should the higher-level staff get appraisals? Of course they should. Even the CEO of a company should be given an appraisal by the board of directors. Every day in the newspaper you can read about CEOs of major corporations suddenly being removed from their offices because they didn't meet performance expectations. Maybe one of the reasons such large severance packages often are paid out is because some of the executives were not given timely, accurate feedback.

Who Gives Performance Appraisals?

The person who directly supervises another person normally gives the performance appraisal. If you are the boss of a small company and everyone reports to you, *you* should do an appraisal for each of your employees. In larger companies, you usually follow the management hierarchy on an organizational chart to find out just who evaluates whom. A supervisor evaluates a staff person, a manager evaluates a supervisor, a director evaluates a manager, and so on.

Here is a very simplistic organizational chart showing a typical "chain of command." Normally you would be appraised by the position (or title) directly above yours.

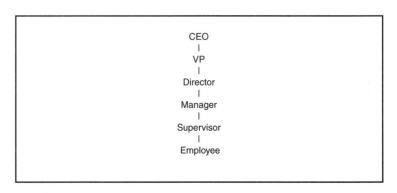

```
CEO
 |
 VP
 |
Director
 |
Manager
 |
Supervisor
 |
Employee
```

There might be times when you don't strictly follow the chain of command. It is crucially important that the person giving the appraisal supervises or has direct knowledge of the performance of the person he or she is evaluating. Sometimes input will be gathered by more than one person. This might be important if the supervisor travels and isn't in daily contact with the worker or vice versa.

The person who has communicated expectations about how a job should be done is the most appropriate person to do the appraisal. We'll talk about special circumstances later in the book (see Chapter 13, "Potential Problems and Difficult Situations"). In today's world, only someone who has observed a person's work can give a credible appraisal. Without direct knowledge of an employee's performance, you are not qualified to give an appraisal.

The Same By Any Name

The document by which we estimate another's execution of work can be named a variety of things; among them are

> ➤ Performance appraisal.
> ➤ Performance review.
> ➤ Performance evaluation.
> ➤ Performance assessment.
> ➤ Performance update.
> ➤ Performance management report.
> ➤ Performance survey.
> ➤ Performance summary.
> ➤ Performance rating.
> ➤ Appraisal instrument.

Just the Facts

A recent U.S. Labor Board survey which interviewed 1,000 companies asked why employees stay at their jobs. The top six reasons:

➤ Feel valued

➤ Recognition

➤ Challenging job

➤ Career opportunities

➤ Relationship with manager

➤ Friendships with colleagues

Empowerment Zone

Should you put the appraisal in writing? By all means! If you plan on using your evaluation for promotional purposes you will need to document who was the strongest and most qualified candidate.

What you want to call your method usually is a matter of personal preference or philosophy. Some companies actually form committees to design and name the document. There have been times when attorneys have been brought in to choose the most accurate and least legally questionable name. Obviously, a popular choice—and the one that we embrace—is performance appraisal.

The law does not dictate what you name your document. However, in keeping with non-discriminatory practice, it's probably a good idea to use the same name throughout the organization.

You might need to schedule a training session to make sure you cover in detail the way a performance review form is to be used and the company's philosophy about doing them. We will cover some of these topics in detail in later chapters.

Empowerment Zone

Consequences are most effective when they closely follow the behavior they are meant to reinforce. Catching people doing things right is a more positive stance toward managing people than trying to catch people doing something wrong.

Appraisal, review, evaluation, assessment—whatever you call them, if you picked up this book you must have some curiosity about the topic. Depending upon where you are in the working world you might have, or are expected to have, a more intimate knowledge of these management tools. You might have received one or more or delivered them to others. Chances are good that receiving or giving the document was not the most pleasant experience. If it was pleasant, congratulations—you might want to review what made it so and incorporate those details into the process you are involved in now. If it was not, read on.

From the File Cabinet

A team leader at a company we worked with utilized an instant feedback instrument that she called "Caught You Doing Something Great." If she saw or heard of one of her team members performing in an exemplary manner, she would complete the document in handwriting and give it to the employee on the spot. The form itself had a colorful design and was meant to be hung on the wall of the employee's cubicle.

Sure Signs That You Need Them

Take the following management quiz to determine your need for a formal performance appraisal system. Respond to the following by circling Y for yes and N for no:

1. The number of employees in your company is greater than ten.   Y N

2. Your company has been in existence more than a full year.   Y N

3. You have employees who report directly to you.   Y N

4. Someone recently has asked, "How am I doing?"   Y N

5. Do you like the idea of paying by performance?   Y N

Empowerment Zone

It's also a good idea to get all staff familiar with the name of the instrument. Many people are unfamiliar with the term "assessment" and fear that it means something negative. You will be much more successful with a performance appraisal system if you consistently refer to it in a positive manner.

6. Has an employee ever hit you up for a raise?   Y   N

7. Has an employee asked you about promotional opportunities?   Y   N

8. Has an employee given you the impression that he or she is looking around for another job?   Y   N

9. Has an employee inquired about a performance review?   Y   N

10. Do you have employees who are interested in other opportunities for advancement?   Y   N

11. Do you want to know how work is done in your business, department, division, or other area?   Y   N

12. Do you care about developing your employees' skills?   Y   N

13. Do you want to increase communication among your staff?   Y   N

14. Do you want to forge better relationships with your employees?   Y   N

15. Do you want to have a legally defensible method of awarding promotions and raises?   Y   N

If you answered yes to two to four questions, it's a good idea to consider a performance appraisal system.

If you answered yes to five to seven questions, it's advisable that you implement a formal performance appraisal system.

If you answered yes to more than seven questions, what's taken you so long to implement a formal performance appraisal system? Get going! And if you answered no to 12 or more questions—this book may not have a lot of relevance for you today, but maybe you'll need it in the future!

The Least You Need to Know

➤ It's possible to do performance appraisals in a manner that motivates employees.

➤ Poorly done performance appraisals can have expensive legal consequences for companies.

➤ Performance appraisals, like report cards, can have a big influence on people's behavior.

➤ Everyone in an organization, at every level, should receive a performance appraisal.

➤ An employee's direct supervisor who has observed the employee's work should be the one who completes an appraisal.

➤ Most companies with more than ten employees need to have a formal performance appraisal system.

Chapter 2

To Appraise or Not?

In This Chapter

➤ Should you do appraisals or not?

➤ What do the experts say?

➤ Why you can't afford to not use them

➤ What should be on every manager's To-Do list

If you are a manager or are running your own company, you already have more than enough to do. We can bet you don't spend a lot of time sitting around wondering what to do next. On the contrary, you might have problems completing everything during regular working hours. So if you are not currently doing performance appraisals, why in the world would you want to add another time-consuming task to your To-Do List?

Whether they are first or last on your priority list really depends on what you believe performance appraisals will do for your employees and your company. If you believe they can improve your employees' performance and ultimately improve the profitability of your company, you might give the process a higher priority. But if you think they are only as useful as your old 386 computer, obviously you would rather sort paperclips or eat stale crackers than write performance appraisals.

The Pluses of Performance Appraisals

The benefits of implementing a performance appraisal system are many. But there also are reasons you might not feel the need to enter into this new project. If your company is small enough that you are able to have frequent conversations with your  *direct reports* you might not feel the need to have a more formal process for feedback. You might even have a feeling that a formal written process would take the genuine, personal quality out of your dealings with co-workers.

If you truly have the time for regular conversation with all of your workers, good for you! We would not want any system to hinder that kind of communication. That kind of open communication in the working place is highly desirable and often seems a rare commodity. So if it is present in your business, keep up the good work, by all means. Regular feedback through an appraisal system will be easier to implement in such an environment.

> **Close Up**
>
> **Direct reports** are employees whose primary reporting relationship is with you. You probably hired them, and at the very least you directly supervise them.

What's Good for Your Company ...

A performance appraisal system can be very beneficial to the company as well as the individuals being appraised. Below we have listed some of the advantages that come to mind.

Performance appraisals can

➤ Increase employee loyalty to the company.

➤ Protect your business from discrimination suits.

➤ Guide you and your employees toward what needs to be done to refine their job skills.

➤ Encourage your team to develop and improve the way your business does business.

➤ Assist you in making promotional decisions.

➤ Assist you in making compensation decisions.

➤ Provide you with quality communication time with your employees.

➤ Give you opportunities to explain your vision of the business and where workers fit into it.

... Can Be Good for Your Employees

Employees need evaluations to move forward in their careers—even if that means they are ready to move to other companies. We can safely assume now you are saying to yourself, "Why would I want to help a good employee go to another job?" Well, let's face it: Most employees will eventually end up working someplace else, especially if they have better opportunities or other needs to explore. If you treat them as valued workers and help them to develop their skills while they are with you, they could bring you a lot of business in the future.

Just the Facts

The average worker in today's world changes jobs seven times during the course of his or her career. In some fields, such as high tech, the number of job changes might even be higher.

From the File Cabinet

What you give often comes back to you in unexpected ways. Take Lynn, for example. She worked hard to learn different aspects of the business and how to supervise projects and other co-workers. Lynn's boss, the owner, really valued her and had promoted her as much as he could. Lynn left the copy store to advance her career, but she remembered what her former boss had done for her. In her new position as an office manager at a lobbyist's office, Lynn brought a lot of business back to her old workplace because of the relationships she had developed there.

Safeguarding Your Business

Performance appraisals truly can protect your business from needless litigation. What would you rather have when the time comes to prepare for a wrongful discharge allegation: your memory of three years of events against those of your employee, or three years of detailed employee evaluations that showed continued performance problems? Sadly, in many companies, any sort of communication typically is lacking.

Too often managers who make little time to communicate with their employees can run into problems they didn't anticipate. They assume that their staff knows what they want in terms of performance. But very few people can read subliminal

messages—they need explanation and understanding of expectations. Without communicating and documenting your feedback with employees, it is your word against theirs that they ever received clear instruction.

What happens if you have to fire an employee for poor performance? How will you prove to a jury of this employee's peers that you were justified in firing her if you can't prove you clearly communicated your expectations? We have learned from experience that the courts are sympathetic to employees in these sorts of cases.

With clear documentation of ongoing counseling of poor performance, your decision to fire someone is more strongly supported. This ongoing written documentation is often called a paper trail. It can help you and your company immeasurably if you ever have to go to court to defend an employment decision.

No Time to Talk

You could blame lack of communication on the lack of time for conversation, or on our modern age of the technological superhighways where life moves too fast to take time to talk. But because this problem has been going on for decades and probably centuries, there must be other reasons.

We have worked with managers who seem too busy to even say "Good morning" to their staff when they arrive in the morning. Does that mean the manager was too busy for common courtesy? Saying "Good morning" takes about a second or two. Managers who are reluctant to say even that much to their employees might have a very difficult time giving regular feedback. And without feedback, how will they accurately evaluate performance? Such managers leave themselves wide open for potential trouble from employees who might feel disrespected.

Fear of Confrontation

It is an unfortunate quality of human nature: Many of us have a difficult time confronting others. Not only do we find it difficult to give negative feedback; we find it hard to give any feedback at all. It is easy to get wrapped up in everything else there is to do at work without including conversation with those who report to us. Giving a performance appraisal can be looked at as a confrontational kind of meeting. You are, in fact, confronting someone when giving an appraisal. If the conversation proceeds professionally, with the right motives and adequate preparation, there should be no fear of negative confrontation.

Part of the problem might be that we anticipate a conflict when we have to give any kind of corrective feedback. The single most common reason for not being assertive is the fear of negative responses. In Chapter 10, "Prepare and Practice," we'll cover ways to work on reducing your anxiety in this type of situation.

The Value of Communication

Giving a performance appraisal might be the only time a supervisor spends any "quality time" with each of his or her employees. It can be a time that you close the door and give one-on-one attention to an individual. If you are sincere in your intentions, and really listen to the conversation, this time can be invaluable in motivating an employee through communication. You might give this person the opportunity to realize how their efforts can contribute to the success of the company. The employee might give you insights into the job that you would have no other way of learning. This might be a touchy-feely result of a performance appraisal, but it is an extremely powerful one. People's feelings do count when it comes to their work, especially when it comes down to deciding whether to look for other work or not, or whether to contribute value to your business. Employees who feel comfortable about communicating their ideas at work are usually loyal to the company and more personally invested in its success.

Wise Counsel

If you're not talking directly to your employees, you better believe they are talking about you behind your back.

Empowerment Zone

Since research has shown that people tend to overestimate the reaction they will get from giving corrective feedback, use that knowledge to help yourself be more assertive. You can be tactful and assertive at the same time.

What the Experts Think

People tend to be very opinionated about performance appraisals. Consult any management guru and you will find yet another opinion. Either someone thinks they are the greatest invention since the toaster or they think they are ludicrous and unnecessary. And there is probably every theory in between the two extremes.

Give Praise "In the Moment"

Ken Blanchard of *The One Minute Manager* (William Morrow & Co., 1982) fame believes you should praise in the moment. The minute you see an employee doing something good, give him or her on-the-spot praise. The closer reinforcement follows

Close Up

Vertical feedback is from the top down, for example from a supervisor level down to a staff level in terms of giving an appraisal. **Horizontal feedback** means getting appraisals from your peers or co-workers at your same level.

Just the Facts

Deming's ideas are interesting in that they were so effective in Japan, where workers are not known for individual initiative. In fact, companies in Japan are looking to the United States for ways to encourage individual initiative and entrepreneurial spirit. Japanese companies are, however, very good at eliciting information from workers to each other and to management. Workers really do believe someone in management is listening to their suggestions to make work flow better.

a behavior occurring, the more powerful and effective it is. When you are trying to help someone acquire a new skill, you want to praise them when they are doing something that approximates or looks like the behavior you ultimately want them to do. This is what psychologists call shaping a behavior. However praising in the moment and shaping behaviors as they occur does not replace a more thorough type of review, which should happen at least once or twice a year.

"Tell Me What You Think"

Steven Covey, who wrote *The Seven Habits of Highly Effective People* (Simon and Schuster, 1989), thinks we should have performance agreements in which the feedback can be more *horizontal* than the typical *vertical* method. That also might be useful but it doesn't take into account that people naturally respond to their place in a group's hierarchy and want to know what the "top monkeys" think of them.

"Fuhgeddaboutit!"

W. Edwards Deming is one of the most famous naysayers about using performance appraisals. Deming, renowned for his transformation of Japanese business philosophy, thinks that performance appraisals are not only unnecessary, they are downright dangerous. In Deming's way of thinking, the ratings nature of performance appraisals actually kills initiative and causes workers to be competitive with each other rather than be concerned with the success of the company.

Deming's management theory, known as the System of Profound Knowledge, provided a rationale to improve every aspect of life. Deming consulted with businesses worldwide as well as serving on the faculty of the Stern School of Business at New York University for 46 years. His theories met with much greater acceptance in Japan than in the United States, until the 1980s.

From the File Cabinet

One manufacturer that we worked with was concerned about product waste costs going up. Previously they had tried to lecture the employees on the importance of this with no effect. This time they made a contest among the different shifts. Wasted product would be measured after each of the three shifts. This technique helped people to cooperate better on the different shifts, which had been one of the problems they'd had. There was a cash incentive tied to this campaign and most of the workers thought it was a lot of fun. The rewards were given every two weeks so there was always another opportunity to achieve. The cash rewards were more than paid for by the savings produced from the reduction in waste costs.

And a poorly constructed performance appraisal system might do just that. Unfortunately, it seems the majority of companies use performance appraisal approaches that encourage such criticism. With a well-designed program, the competitive aspect can be reduced, and the motivational component emphasized.

Legal Considerations

The intent of this book is not to scare you away from doing appraisals. On the contrary, we believe companies *must* have performance appraisal systems in place if they want to enjoy sustained success in today's competitive business environment. But there are important legal caveats you need to be aware of. If you choose to implement performance appraisals, it's crucial that you do them fairly and consistently. Without fairness and consistency you may be accused of discriminatory practices.

We who live in the United States are blessed with many advantages, but we also live in possibly the most litigious country in the world. Employment law has become a hot issue, with discrimination being expressly forbidden by not just one but a number of laws including

> ➤ **Title VII of the Civil Rights Act of 1964** prohibits in virtually every employment circumstance discrimination on the basis of race, color, religion, gender, pregnancy or national origin, age, sex, marital status, physical or mental disability, medical condition, sexual orientation or any other characteristic made unlawful by federal, state, or local laws.

17

Wise Counsel

When the EEOC files a claim against your company, they will require the company to either admit guilt or provide evidence to the contrary. And the EEOC typically chooses to represent employees whose cases seem strong. Win or lose, being investigated is time-consuming, costly, and not very much fun. And if you lose the case, you could have to pay substantial penalties.

Empowerment Zone

Be sure that your comments are made about documented performance—some objective way of gauging how the performance was done. Specific examples—with dates and details—will help illustrate that the behavior was observed and documented. Making broad generalizations can and will be challenged.

➤ **Age Discrimination in Employment Act** prohibits discrimination against workers age 40 and over in any employment-related decision.

➤ **Americans with Disabilities Act (ADA)** prohibits discrimination against qualified individuals with disabilities.

➤ **Uniformed Guidelines on Employee Selection** addresses use of employee selection tools and their impact on discrimination based on race, color, religion, sex, or national origin.

➤ **Fair Labor Standards Act** and its amendments provide guidelines on employment status, child labor, minimum wage, overtime pay, and record-keeping requirements.

Such legislation has come about because of discriminatory behavior on the part of employers somewhere, at some time or another. Which ones you are subject to depend on the size and type of company you have. The Federal government investigates claims of discrimination largely through the Equal Employment Opportunity Commission (EEOC).

What Do Performance Appraisals Have to Do with Discrimination?

Maybe nothing, maybe everything. You might truly believe you are reviewing employees on the performance they have exhibited to you. What if employees compare their appraisals and salary adjustments with those of other employees who are a different age, race, gender, color, orientation, or some other legally protected difference? And what if there is a large discrepancy in performance ratings and raise in salary? Unless you have concentrated solely on documented performance issues, you could have a problem. Good intentions are not enough in these sorts of situations. We go into behavioral language in more detail in Chapter 11, "Script or Ad Lib?"

A Tale of Two Perspectives

What happens if an employee accuses you of discriminatory practices? "Not me," you protest, "I haven't got a discriminatory bone in my body." Unfortunately, as careful as you think you are being, your actions could lead someone to accuse you. Consider the saga of Harriet and Kimberly.

Harriet started working as a clerk in the hospital's billing office when she was 40 years old. By virtue of her tenure, not her performance, she eventually was promoted to the position of clerical supervisor, a position she held for four years. Now age 57, Harriet was looking forward to finishing out 20 years with the hospital and retiring to collect her pension. During her eighteenth year of employment, her department was reorganized under a young (late twenties) director named Kimberly. The first thing Kimberly did was split the department into three teams and hire two more supervisors who also were much younger than Harriet. After several months, it was apparent that Harriet's team was way behind the other teams in productivity.

So Kimberly decided to do performance appraisals on all of the supervisors who reported to her. Nan and Kelly received high praise for their first six months on the job. Harriet's appraisal was not as complimentary. Communication between Kimberly and Harriet went from bad to worse. Kimberly wanted to fire Harriet, but when she reviewed her personnel folder, she found that all of Harriet's previous performance appraisals had been good—not outstanding, but acceptable. It seems that Harriet's former supervisors had given Harriet acceptable performance appraisals because they liked her as a person, not really because her performance merited all acceptable ratings. Their reluctance to be more honest with her hurt Harriet because she never received the constructive feedback that might have helped her improve. And this less than honest feedback would have unfortunate consequences for the hospital as well.

A few months later, financial concerns forced the hospital to lay off 10 percent of its staff. Kimberly thought this was her golden opportunity and she laid off Harriet, using poor productivity as the reason for her choice.

Claiming age discrimination, Harriet filed a lawsuit against Kimberly and the hospital. Through a series of depositions, Harriet's personnel folder was subpoenaed and reviewed. The fact that she had 17 years of good performance appraisals and only one not-so-good appraisal weighed heavily in Harriet's favor. The relative youth of the supervisors who kept their jobs did not help the hospital's case. Ultimately, the hospital settled out of court and Harriet was awarded an amount equal to five years of her previous salary.

One could argue the merits of the actions of any of the parties. But one thing was very clear: Age discrimination was probably far from Kimberly's mind when she chose to lay off Harriet. To Kimberly, this was clearly a problem of poor performance; Harriet's age was beside the point. However, in Harriet's mind—and in the mind of the judge who reviewed the case—this was a matter of discrimination. The story of Harriet and Kimberly can and does happen to many supervisors who have the best interests of the company in mind.

Reviewing past performance appraisals is necessary before taking any action, positive or negative, regarding an employee. If you have never reviewed an employee's history before, ask for help from your supervisor or a human resources professional. As unfair as some discrimination charges might seem, they can happen even in the most "fair" of workplaces.

Close Up

Retention means keeping employees at your company. When unemployment is low, as it was in the United States in the late 1990s, there is an overabundance of jobs and a shortage of workers at almost every level and industry. Using effective retention strategies has become critical in keeping companies staffed.

Empowerment Zone

Separate personality from performance. Just because someone's personality is more like yours does not necessarily mean his or her job performance is the strongest.

Compensation Issues and Promotional Decisions

How will you determine who should get a raise—or who should be promoted to a higher level? The dart board approach might have its appeal in certain arenas. But if you want your company to do well, and you want your good employees to stick around, you will need to consider raises and promotions as effective *retention* devices.

Performance appraisals can be very useful in determining who is the strongest performer. Of course, that means that people must be evaluated fairly and equitably. The same criteria should be used to compare people doing the same job. This is no time to play favorites.

If one employee receives a promotion or raise that another employee thinks is not merited, there could be trouble. An unhappy employee potentially is a very expensive employee. Your well-documented performance appraisal might be the most effective documentation for helping your company avoid a discrimination charge.

Here are some performance appraisal **DON'Ts**:

➤ Don't use an appraisal to discipline for past performance.

➤ Don't focus on personality issues.

➤ Don't make gender-based statements.

➤ Don't make vague generalizations.

➤ Don't use subjective language.

➤ Don't use language you might regret later.

➤ Don't use labels.

Here are some performance appraisal **DO's**:

➤ **Do** focus on performance.

➤ **Do** use specific performance examples.

➤ **Do** communicate sincerely.

➤ **Do** listen to the employee.

➤ **Do** be objective and use objective language.

➤ **Do** be as clear and concise as possible.

➤ **Do** use examples or behaviors you can observe, count, or graph (such as sales volume, yelling at customers, number of double shifts volunteered for, or number of sales calls made).

What Should Be the Boss's Priority?

Many managers we have known have procrastinated doing performance appraisals for—in some cases—years. It's pretty disconcerting to review the personnel file of a long term employee only to find out that he hasn't been appraised in five years. Invariably these managers will say they are just "too busy" to take the time to complete an appraisal. In other words, they look at a performance appraisal as a low priority compared to their other responsibilities. We strongly disagree with this judgment of what is most important on a boss's To-Do List.

People or Paper?

What do you consider to be your most important responsibilities as a manager? Depending on the business you are in, your priorities might be unique, but it seems most companies see profitability as their highest goal. Along that vein, many managers cite financial goals as the top items on their goal-planning lists. Things such as effective budgeting and keeping income high and expenses low are chief priorities. Submitting accurate financials is so important that it keeps many managers tied to their computer screens crunching numbers the better part of most days. Their method of communicating with their staff is through a series of e-mails. Some days, the employees hardly see their manager. Their manager is doing the things that he or she thinks are the essential functions of their job as a manager.

Without People, Who Needs a Manager?

A manager manages people. The nuts and bolts of the job generally are performed by people—at least until robots are perfected. A manager is needed to lead these people, to motivate them, to teach them, to coach them to better performance. Shouldn't the people who are part of the manager's job be the most important function? If you are good at leading and motivating people, the rest of the job will get done. People need feedback. They need to know how they are doing, whether their performance is acceptable, and what they need to do to improve. They need praise, encouragement, and constructive—not destructive—feedback.

In an ideal world, this is what we think should be on every manager's daily To-Do list:

Empowerment Zone

It's difficult, if not impossible, to lead people by spreadsheet or from behind a computer screen. Your computer and math skills might make you a terrific technician, but maybe a very poor manager of people. If you need help with this, get consultation, mentoring, or training.

➤ Communicate daily with employees (and remember that communication goes two ways).

➤ Create and share a vision with staff.

➤ Reward good performance when it happens and don't use lame or trendy ways of saying it.

➤ Listen to staff and share insights and ideas.

➤ Keep staff informed about company news and progress.

➤ Lead by example, and exhibit a positive attitude.

➤ Give constructive feedback sensitively.

➤ Celebrate small and large victories.

➤ Help employees align personal goals with company goals.

➤ Treat others with respect.

➤ Achieve business goals by implementing the preceding 10 steps.

If you keep in mind that your employees are your most important asset and responsibility, doing performance appraisals will become a task you will do regularly with pride and without fear. Regular communication will ensure that the appraisal contains no surprises and is simply an extension of that communication.

The Least You Need to Know

➤ Employees need feedback and performance appraisals in order to feel connected to the company.

➤ Lack of communication with employees can lead to much bigger problems, and bigger problems can be very expensive.

➤ We live in a legislation-heavy country with many laws enacted to protect employee rights. Careful, sensitive feedback might do much to avoid a discrimination claim.

➤ Managing people requires good people skills, including feedback and communication.

Chapter 3

Everybody Needs a Little Feedback

In This Chapter

➤ The advantages of using feedback

➤ The disadvantages

➤ When should you evaluate?

➤ Bizarre but true stories

Feedback is commonly known as that annoying screech you get from a microphone if it is held too close to a speaker. In the world of business and management, feedback should have anything but an annoying reputation. A dictionary definition of feedback, in the business context, might read something like this—the act of transmitting evaluative or corrective information to the original source about an action, event, or process.

Feedback is a means to evaluate and make corrective comments. It's the response to that question, "How am I doing?" It can motivate or it can destroy—it all depends on how you use it.

The Advantages of Using Feedback

A performance appraisal is a formal approach to giving feedback. There are many less formal methods of feedback—for example, just having a casual conversation. Any time you take the time to ask someone how they are doing on their job and exchange comments, you are engaging in feedback that can help build and strengthen a working relationship. Some people need to use a formal structure such as a performance appraisal meeting in order to give feedback. Those that are able to give more frequent feedback through conversation probably have more trusting relationships with their staff. It also helps to guide people to know when they are meeting your expectations, and when they need to change the way they are doing things.

People Who Need People

Human communication requires feedback. When a person asks a question or makes a statement, he or she expects a response. This is not rocket science, but basic common sense. And when feedback is given that is positive, or at the very least helpful, a good result should occur. In the working world, workers tend to work better and more efficiently if someone—you, perhaps—gives them constructive feedback about the job they are doing. It's difficult to work in a vacuum.

Empowerment Zone

The most common complaint of those people who opt to work alone from home is the lack of human feedback. It's difficult to be motivated all day without the sociability of conversation with another person. Not many people can work for a long period of time without interaction or feedback from others. The phone alone is oftentimes not enough.

Great Expectations

If you manage other people, those people will expect—and require—feedback from you. You will be a much more effective manager if that feedback occurs more than once a year. Saving all your feedback for an annual performance appraisal makes the event much more formidable—both for you and the person you are appraising.

There Shall Be No Surprises!

We will say it throughout this book: There should be no surprises in a performance appraisal. If you have been too busy or too scared to say something to an employee when some behavior or problem is first observed, what makes you think that it will be easier to save it for their performance appraisal? It won't be easier—it will be much, much harder.

The Advantages of Regular Feedback

Obviously we advocate giving more frequent feedback to your staff. There are many reasons we think this is good management practice and we've listed some of them below.

➤ You will know each other better.

➤ You might even learn to trust each other; through trust comes loyalty.

➤ Expectations will be clear. Your employees will do a better job because they understand what you want—and what you don't want.

➤ Your employees won't be afraid to talk to you.

➤ You will learn from the insights of your employees.

➤ Your employees will feel like you are treating them like mature adults who can handle direct feedback.

➤ You will learn of problems before they become catastrophes.

➤ You will be able to discover what's bugging them before they bail out for another job.

And we're not just talking about endless positive feedback. There are diplomatic ways to offer constructive feedback as well. We'll give you lots of suggestions for this in Part 3, "What's My Line: What to Say and How to Say It."

When Feedback Can Hurt

We're not going to lie to you. We believe in feedback and that its good points far outweigh any negatives. However, feedback can be given inappropriately—the wrong news at the wrong time—and there could be negative consequences as a result.

Hold the Emotions

We all have times when we say things we regret. If you are in a bad mood—for any reason: you had a fight with your spouse that morning, your son wrecked the car, your boss put you down—this might be an inappropriate time to give feedback to another person. It's not advisable (or fair) to punish someone else for your own bad mood. And it happens all the time. If you yourself have a pretty thick skin, you think what you had to say is no big deal. But a sensitive employee will never trust you again.

"Never trust? Never is a long time," you rationalize. "It can't be that bad." With those sensitive souls, oh yes, it can be that bad.

Empowerment Zone

As Dale Carnegie said, "Any fool can criticize, condemn and complain—and most fools do."

Empowerment Zone

During our years of dealing with employee relations issues, we always have been amazed at the number of occasions employees would tenaciously cling to the painful memory of an offhand remark made by a supervisor. For some employees, the wrong words cause deep hurts that they will never forget. Don't underestimate your influence as a supervisor.

For example, let's say you know you have a short fuse and your temper sometimes gets the better of you. And due to the stress of the moment, you give feedback of some sort to a sensitive employee. Your inability to control your outburst of temper could turn a performance appraisal or any other conversation into an event so damaging that you will be unable to salvage the relationship.

Timing Is Everything

Another example of unfortunate feedback might be a time when you have scheduled an appointment for a performance appraisal an hour before you are leaving for a well-deserved, two-week vacation in Hawaii. You can feel the sun and taste those mai tais already. In walks your employee for an appraisal. This is the most important appointment of her year—her merit increase is dependent on this conversation. But you are more focused on finishing quickly so you can start your vacation. You speed through the conversation, making light of her comments and postponing answering some of her questions. You send her on her way after only 30 minutes instead of the hour she was expecting. She'll recognize the bum's rush and may well be on her way to finding a new job before your vacation tan fades.

Wise Counsel

If feedback is rushed or insincere, don't think you're going to fool anybody. Most employees will know they are getting the bum's rush and think that their appraisal is not very important to you. Even feedback that is corrective in nature is important to deliver with the sincere desire to help the employee succeed. Taking your time to really watch and respond to your employees' reactions is important to their believing you really want to work with them.

Badly timed, poorly prepared, or thoughtless feedback is certainly more harmful than no feedback at all. Think about what you're going to say and to whom you are going to say it. Once those words bubble out of your mouth, there is no way to take them back.

Lay Off the Sarcasm

As a boss or manager, your feedback is critically important to your employees. Although an offhand remark might seem a small thing to you, your words impact their livelihood—or at the very least their satisfaction with their jobs. And even though your staff might act as if they are laughing it off, there's a good chance they are holding their real feelings back. You can unintentionally be sowing the seeds of dissent. Kind of sounds like Captain Bligh in *Mutiny on the Bounty*. You might avoid a mutiny, but you are not going to build a loyal team with sarcastic, overly negative, or thoughtless feedback. In other words, think before you speak!

From the File Cabinet

The controller of a company we worked with, Mr. Quincy, prided himself on his "in your face" sense of humor. He seemed to always have a witty but uncomplimentary remark to say about anyone and anything. As he was a close personal friend of his boss, the CFO (Chief Financial Officer), he felt free to say what he pleased, since his boss would never correct him. Unfortunately, he carried his sarcasm even into performance evaluations with his staff. One of his direct reports, an accountant named Barry, told us that during his appraisal meeting, Mr. Quincy made comments such as, "I might consider promoting you next year, that is, if the company stays solvent that long." Mr. Quincy continued to make such disparaging comments about the company that Barry immediately started looking for another job, fearing the company was about to go out of business since the Controller, who would know about the solvency of the company, was making these statements. In reality, the company was in no danger and the comments were Mr. Quincy's attempt at humor.

Examples of off-hand sarcasm could sound something like this:

➤ "You must be new at this job, you still care."

➤ "Everyone knows the company would just fall apart without your daily suggestions."

➤ "I appreciate your interest but I'm the boss here. I'll let you know when I need your opinion."

➤ "What do you think? That we run a democracy in this department? Well, you're wrong."

What's Enough?

Good question. There are lots of different theories out there. We like the *One Minute Manager*'s philosophy of frequent, timely feedback. This will entail your being around to observe what's going on, of course. Instead of waiting for them to ask you, why not ask your staff regularly, "How are you doing?" Engage them in a conversation. It doesn't require a formal meeting; it could happen at the water cooler. If the question

Empowerment Zone

Giving conversational feedback is more difficult if you are naturally reticent. It will become easier with practice. Some managers force themselves to walk around their departments and practice making conversation with employees for a short period each day. If this comes easily to you, you are fortunate and are well on your way to forming closer, and in the long run, more trusting relationships with your employees; if it doesn't, it will become more natural the more you work at it.

Wise Counsel

The key here is sincerity. Most people are pretty good at spotting it in a second when you are not sincere. "Hello" he lied.

(Don Carpenter quoting a Hollywood agent.)

comes from you directly, your staff will feel you are sincerely interested in how they are doing, and they will probably respond positively to that.

A Case Study in Communication

An extremely effective people manager we know is the CEO of a large insurance company. (We'll call her Carla.) Her job is incredibly busy, with every minute of her calendar booked weeks in advance. With responsibility for operations in several states, she travels a good part of each week.

Despite her whirlwind schedule, whenever Carla visits the administrators of a claims processing service center, she schedules "walking around time" on her calendar. During this time, she walks up and down the aisles of the customer service department and makes contact with each customer service representative. Spotting the nameplates on their cubicles, Carla will address them by name and ask a question such as, "How are you doing?" Her manner is genuine and warm. If an employee asks her a question she can't answer, she makes a note of it in her day planner so that she can find out and get back to the person with a personal note or e-mail.

The employees look forward to Carla's visits, are flattered by her attention, and are impressed that she is an approachable human being. She makes them feel good about their company.

Carla makes all of this look quite easy. And yet she is naturally an introverted person. Being outgoing is an acquired skill for her—one that she has worked hard to master and practices continuously. Talking with employees might seem like a relatively unimportant portion of Carla's job as CEO. However, she sees it as one of her most important duties. Watching her success in building a loyal team, she must be right.

Frequent feedback is a skill worth practicing. It doesn't have to take a long time. A few minutes each day will get you started. Then practice, practice, practice.

Timetable for More Formal Appraisals

How frequently you require managers to give feedback is a personal choice. We have seen various schedules used. It really depends on your company and the dependability of your managers to comply.

Happy Anniversary

The most common formal performance appraisal is done annually. Anybody who has been in the working world for any length of time typically expects to receive an appraisal once a year—usually at the anniversary of his or her date of hire. A year's interval is an appropriate amount of work time to expect an evaluation.

Employees expect to receive an appraisal as close to their *anniversary date* as possible, especially if an increase is tied to the appraisal. People expecting raises generally want to get a raise sooner rather than later. So it's advisable to start thinking about the appraisal in advance of the anniversary date.

Keeping a tickler file—manually or by computer—is a good way to set up a reminder that an appraisal is due—maybe a month in advance of the due date.

Same Month, Every Year

Some companies have adopted the practice of evaluating all employees during the same month of the year. This usually is done for budgeting purposes—all raises can be anticipated during one month instead of scattered throughout the year.

If your company is small enough, this might work for you. However, in larger companies, if you and your managers have more than a handful of employees, this system could set you up for failure. One company designed such a program without considering supervisors in production units that

Close Up

The **anniversary date** is commonly defined as the date of hire, typically the first day actually worked. However, it also could denote the anniversary of a job change or promotion, so an employee might have more than one anniversary. It's important to have a clear policy stating which date will be used for appraisals.

Wise Counsel

Late appraisals can cause a lot of hurt feelings and resentment—especially if tied to a potential salary increase. When you are extremely busy, you might feel that completing an appraisal form is not your first priority. But to your employee it is the first priority. If you give them the impression that you forgot, are too busy, or just don't care enough, you could lose good employees.

had 30 to 40 people reporting to them. Completing 30 to 40 appraisals all in the month of February was virtually impossible, considering the amount of time the supervisors had to spend completing the performance appraisal form and then making individual appointments with so many people.

Making a List, Checking It Twice

Some companies opt to do performance appraisals twice a year. This might be because there is a compensation plan in place that utilizes step increases. Step increases are typically used for line staff and frequently are seen in union environments. Giving salary increases every six months is very generous and, depending on the size of the company, might require lots of administration.

Getting to Know You

Introductory appraisals are done within the first 30 to 120 days after an employee starts work. After an employee receives a probationary appraisal, he or she changes in status from a probationary employee to a regular employee.

Bizarre But True ... Stories from the Trenches

No matter when you decide to appraise your employees, it's important to do a professional job. Try to put yourself in the place of the person being appraised. Respect, thoughtfulness, and caring will go a long way toward making the session a pleasant experience for both of you.

Unfortunately, not all employers have supplied a fair amount of caring in their methods of appraising employees. Many of us have had rather painful experiences relative to the topic of performance appraisals. Viewed by many as a necessary evil, managers have been known to drag their feet, protest, and procrastinate as long as possible before doing them, if they do them at all.

While surveying colleagues before writing this book, we found that most rolled their eyes when we broached the topic of performance appraisals past. Here are a few of those stories. You might even be able to add a few of your own.

The stories we are sharing all represent negative performance appraisal scenarios. Of course, many people also have pleasant stories to share. But the negative ones always seem more unforgettable to the participants. All the names have been changed to protect those involved.

"You Still Have a Job, Don't You?"

A bright and ambitious program analyst named Nancy had worked for more than a year under Mr. Farber, the Director of Information Systems of a large company. Nancy was thorough and detail-oriented in her work, had established positive relationships with the departments she supported, and was eager to get feedback from her manager. Of course, she also anticipated an annual increase which had been promised her when she was hired. The days and weeks passed; still there was no word from Mr. Farber.

Finally, two months past her anniversary date, Nancy approached him and asked whether she was going to get a performance appraisal. Barely looking at her, he gruffly said, "You still have a job, don't you?" She stared at him disbelievingly. "If you still have a job, that means your performance is okay." When she also asked about an increase, Mr. Farber mumbled unintelligibly and walked away. She did receive an increase some weeks later, but was never granted any kind of performance appraisal.

Try to imagine the loyalty this employee had felt—and lost—toward her manager. When another opportunity presented itself, Nancy bid him farewell with no regrets. The event took place years ago, but she'll never forget it.

The moral of the story: Simply retaining the position is not an indication of a positive evaluation—or a positive performance.

The director should have

➤ Engaged in regular, frequent feedback throughout the year.

➤ Set mutually acceptable performance goals.

➤ Made sure to give timely appraisals and timely salary increases.

➤ Treated a valued employee with respect and communicated with that employee considerately.

How Not to Win Friends and Influence People

Jim changed careers and finally obtained an entry-level position in a company he had dreamed of working with. His boss, Katherine, recently had been promoted to management. Jim was patient and supported her loyally during his first year of employment. When it came time for Jim's annual performance appraisal, Katherine was fairly timely. She met with him privately and gave him an excellent appraisal. Then shaking his hand, Katherine ended the conversation saying, "You really have done an

31

outstanding job, and if you'd done a better job negotiating a salary a year ago, you'd be making more money. But you didn't." Jim was stunned into silence. And smiling, she showed him out of the office.

Ms. Manager ruined a fine conversation with what must have seemed like a clever witticism to her. But Jim felt no more loyalty to this person. He also shared the story with whomever would listen.

What was wrong with this picture? She should have

➤ Kept her comments to herself.

➤ Maintained professional behavior during the appraisal.

➤ Treated the employee with respect.

Laughing All the Way to Court

The CEO, Mr. Barnes, interviewed and hired Barbara to be the Human Resources Director of his medium-sized firm. He told her he needed someone with strong training and employee relations skills and Barbara felt this was a good match for her skills. Approaching 50 years of age, Barbara was a seasoned professional and confident she could make a difference.

A short time after Barbara was hired, Mr. Barnes hired a Chief Operating Officer, a young woman in her thirties named Marian, and changed the reporting structure so that Marian was now Barbara's boss. Marian had a completely different idea about what she wanted in Human Resources—she wanted the focus to be on recruiting alone, and had little interest in training or employee relations. Things were off to a bad start. Communication between the two women was strained, to say the least. After a number of months, the two painstakingly agreed upon goals for the Human Resources Department. These were the goals upon which Barbara would be evaluated.

The relationship between Marian and Barbara continued to decline. Marian couldn't resist making ageist jokes from time to time. She pointed out to other associates how amusing it was that when Barbara was a sophomore in college, Marian was only in the third grade. She would also make comments at staff meetings referring to Barbara as "from the older generation."

Finally, after six months of working together, Marian grew impatient with Barbara's different style. She decided to give her a performance appraisal and made her own form, listing a completely different set of goals from the ones that had been discussed with Barbara. She documented that Barbara was failing in all these new goals—goals that Barbara was unaware of. And since she lacked the courage to deliver the appraisal personally, she left it in Barbara's mailbox.

Tempted to see an attorney first, Barbara went to see the CEO. Given the circumstances, he offered her a financial settlement rather than go to court.

Moral of the story: Putting false statements in writing can get you in a lot of trouble. Don't use a performance appraisal as a weapon—the tactic often backfires.

Close Up

A **separation agreement** basically is a contract to terminate the employment of a staff member under mutually agreed-upon circumstances. Frequently there is a financial agreement in exchange for confidentiality of the terms and other negotiated concessions.

➤ Some issues are better not handled within the context of a performance appraisal. That is, don't use a performance appraisal as a weapon.

➤ Issues concerning personality conflicts or other serious performance disagreements should be handled with separate meetings outside a formal performance appraisal.

➤ In a situation like this one, the basic situation was a serious difference in personalities and job approaches. There were other methods of dealing with this kind of mismatch of personalities and styles. A couple of things that could have been considered were

1. A transfer to another location, under a different supervisor, or

2. A separation agreement with a financial settlement—which typically will cost much less than a financial settlement arrived at between angry parties.

Don't Be the Next Bizarre but True Story

There are many, many more horror stories about the giving and receiving of performance appraisals. That's why giving them is looked upon negatively by many people. But if you really look at the preceding circumstances—and many other situations— the management errors involved were obvious. Don't underestimate the feelings or the intelligence of your employees. You are fooling no one but yourself. If you approach the responsibility of performance appraisals with tact, sensitivity, and honesty, you will be much more successful. And your employees will have more respect for you in return.

The Least You Need to Know

➤ Regular and effective communication with your staff will make you an effective and successful manager.

➤ Be careful to time your feedback appropriately. Don't let your bad mood taint an employee's performance appraisal.

➤ Annual evaluations are the most commonly used appraisal intervals, often on the anniversary date.

➤ Put yourself in your employee's place when giving him or her an appraisal: You expect respect, and so do they.

Chapter 4

What's Your Style?

In This Chapter

➤ Identifying your corporate philosophy

➤ Why determining a corporate philosophy is important

➤ Understanding common corporate philosophies and management styles

➤ Interacting with your boss's management style

What difference does style make to a performance appraisal system? It makes quite a bit of difference if the truth be told. We don't know how many different styles of appraisals are being used at companies all around the world, but we can bet it is a very large number. Why don't companies all use the same format? It's a question of style.

When we talk about style, we mean the way or manner in which something is done. And there are as many distinct styles as there are people and personality types. Companies adopt their own styles—their own manner of doing things. Some are formal and probably everyone wears suits and ties, and some are informal where everyone wears jeans and T-shirts. Style also shows up in the kind of performance appraisal system that a company implements. Style is more of a physical statement or reflection of a company's philosophy.

Move Over, Aristotle

You read the last sentence and you're probably saying to yourself, "Give me a break—what does *philosophy* have to do with performance appraisals? Don't tell me I have to study highbrow philosophers before I can do an appraisal?"

Close Up

Your **philosophy** is the set of general principles or laws of conduct you use for practical purposes—that which makes up your system of ethics.

Don't get excited about the word philosophy—we're not going to refer to Aristotle or Kant or any of those other guys. We're talking about philosophy from a business point of view.

If you are the owner or CEO of a company, it's appropriate that you determine what your corporate philosophy is or will be. You are able to set the tone, adopt the policies, and choose the management team that will reflect your philosophy. Your method of evaluating your staff should reflect your philosophy. For example, are you a stern taskmaster, or do you let members of your staff find their own creative ways to function in their jobs? There are many styles or reflections of various philosophies, and we're going to describe several of them to help you identify your own.

Pick a Style, Any Style

There are probably hundreds of different management styles out there in the working world. We're not going to suggest that only one style is the right style. To the contrary, we believe this is one of those areas where the saying "different strokes for different folks" really plays out. People are incredibly different in so many ways, both obvious and not so obvious. This includes philosophical differences. The way that you like to be managed, talked to, and treated might be very different from the way someone else wants to be managed, talked to, and treated.

Empowerment Zone

There are several techniques you can learn to try to understand personality types that are different from your own. The Myers-Briggs Type Indicator is a type theory that breaks personalities down into 16 recognizable types and helps you learn to deal with types different from your own.

Try to See It My Way

We human beings tend to judge other human beings according to our personal standards, expecting people to see things and hear things exactly the way we do. Reality check! It just doesn't work that way. Many times two people will go through the same experience at the same time, and yet their descriptions of the situation will be vastly different. We see the world through our own *filters,* which are developed through the course of living our lives—being raised as children with different families and cultural backgrounds, experiencing the world in our own unique ways.

My Values or Yours?

Values often differ widely. This is seen frequently in the workplace. The reasons people work might be quite different depending on their values. Sure, lots of people work for that paycheck alone. But many people choose work that allows them to follow their passions, or to make a difference in the world by caring for others, or to follow their dream to create something entirely new. People who have strong values about their work might be quite different to evaluate from those who are working for money alone. However, even someone who is just there for money can still have strong emotional reasons for being there, such as survival or to further their family or children's dreams for a better life. The work itself might not be important to such an individual, but the reasons for being there make the job important.

What Values Do You Value?

What are your values when it comes to work? If you are a no-nonsense, nose-to-the-grindstone kind of person, your management style will be far different from the Southwest Airlines style of having fun while you work. Unless it is blatantly abusive, there is no wrong style. There's a place for everyone. But it's important to know which is your style in order to go forward with this management tool known as a performance appraisal.

Close Up

A **filter** is the manner in which an individual perceives the world after being influenced by factors including ethnic background, family dynamics, environment, education, and others.

Just the Facts

One company well known for its pro-employee policies is Southwest Airlines. The company has a philosophy about making work fun, and you can see it reflected in its staff. The airline calls its human resources leader the Vice President of People.

Here a Style, There a Style

We have encountered a number of different management styles over the years. We felt more comfortable with some than others, but that a certain style was not right for us didn't make it wrong. It just wasn't a good fit, philosophically speaking. People tend to work better and more happily in an environment that supports and affirms their personal values.

Empowerment Zone

Some companies manage to put profit *and* people first. It not only works, but it also creates a successful company that makes money while retaining an excellent, loyal staff. We are convinced that when employees feel that they count, they tend to pass this on to the customers.

If the Style Fits …

An altruistic person whose goal is to help others is a bad fit for a company that worships the bottom line. The reverse also is true. Someone whose guiding principle is "profits, not people" would not be a good fit in an idealistic company that puts people and societal concerns ahead of all other goals.

A Match Made in Heaven?

How can you tell if you and a company are a good match. Just like a good pair of shoes, when you work for a company that is a "good fit" it feels good. You feel comfortable and appreciated, your communication style seems to be in synch. But when the fit is bad, it can be really painful.

Determining whether a company is good match for you should be handled during the interview process. Don't be afraid to ask what the company philosophy, mission, and vision are. Typically you'll learn a lot about a company's style from how they articulate things like philosophy. And of course the best way to find out about a company's philosophy toward its employees is to talk to its employees. Ask them about feedback—how it's given, if it's given, etc. No matter how good a job sounds, no matter how good the salary, a bad match will not do you or the company any good.

Companies Need People

No business runs without people—either customers or employees—so it would benefit you to consider your employees' feelings about how the company does business, as well as about the way they are managed and evaluated. It's important to figure out just what your style might be.

Theory X

Douglas McGregor, a management theorist, wrote that there are basically two types of managers, which he indicated with the letters X and Y. Theory X managers believe that workers are inherently lazy, and they must be forced to work and closely monitored to keep them working. This conjures up visions of the ancient Egyptians flogging the slaves to keep them hauling huge stones in order to erect the pyramids. An extreme analogy, you say? Then you haven't worked at some of the companies that espouse Theory X.

From the File Cabinet

Douglas McGregor (1906-1964), was a popular management theorist who influenced many other great American writers on the topic of management, including Tom Peters who has authored many best-selling books on the topic. A professor at Harvard, Massachusetts Institute of Technology (MIT) and Antioch College, McGregor is still respected by current experts in the field. His early death limited the number of his publications, but most management theorists agree that a lot of current management thinking goes back to McGregor's teachings. Probably his best known work, *The Human Side of Enterprise,* published in 1960, supports a belief we share—that employees will contribute more to an organization if they are treated as responsible and valuable.

There are many *autocratic* Theory X managers out there. Because this is an old school theory, we thought they might be from a previous generation. But some of them are quite young (under 40) and still cracking the whip at workers at any level, and there are many people who are acclimated to and feel comfortable working in such an environment.

Close Up

Autocratic is the state of being extremely authoritarian and possessing absolute power. It is the opposite of democratic, in which the population participates in decision making.

Theory Y

Theory Y managers believe workers seek work that is meaningful to them. If such employees are committed to the goals of the company, they will exercise self-direction and be motivated by the satisfaction of achievement.

These managers don't have to *micromanage* their employees. They trust that their employees will do their jobs because of their own sense of responsibility. Theory Y managers are also known as democratic managers.

From the File Cabinet

Grace was a manager at a communications company. Over the years many of her employees complained of her repeated pattern of calling them stupid, incompetent, and disloyal, then turning very sweet and even giving them flowers or taking them out to lunch. Grace's boss tolerated this behavior because she had a similar style. This pattern of behavior is common in people who are abusive. It is never acceptable behavior, but sadly it takes place all too often. Some people will take it, some will leave when the opportunity comes along, and occasionally someone will challenge the pattern. Most employees will take a very safe course and try to avoid this type of boss, and will not take much initiative to generate change.

Close Up

To **micromanage** is to closely supervise and monitor employees to the point of always looking over their shoulders while they work. Micromanagers have little trust in the employees' ability to work without constant supervision.

Which Should It Be?

Confused about whether you lean more toward autocratic or democratic? Consider the following:

➤ Some people really don't mind leaders who are straight with them about wanting things their own way.

➤ If you choose to be autocratic, employee participation in goal-setting for a performance appraisal might be unnecessary.

➤ If you really are not democratic in style, don't pretend to be. One thing that a lot of employees dislike more than an authoritarian style is an authoritarian who pretends to want feedback, then goes ahead and does what he or she wanted all along.

Take Me Out to the Ball Game

Sometimes you need to look only as far as your favorite sports team to see theories become practice. Those that rack up the most wins typically are those whose management teams respect their players and trust them to give 110 percent in every game. These are the Theory Y leaders.

In the year 2000, the teams in the National Basketball Association (NBA) finals were the Los Angeles Lakers, coached by Phil Jackson, and the Indiana Pacers, coached by Larry Bird. Both Jackson and Bird have taken their respective teams farther, faster than many other coaches in the game's history. Phil Jackson has had one year with the Lakers, who have struggled since 1991 to get to the finals. He took the Chicago Bulls to six titles in almost as many years. Bird took the Pacers to the finals after only three years of coaching. Neither coach yells or screams at his players or at the referees. It is reported that Jackson is even somewhat reluctant to call plays once the game is underway. They both use encouragement, positives, trust, and hard work to help their teams succeed. They focus on developing each individual player, while encouraging them to act as a team, not as individual hot shots.

We also could point to Pat Reilly, coach of the Miami Heat, who's gone to the NBA playoffs each year since he started coaching there. The guy is cool, calm, respectful—and a snappy dresser to boot. Or look at Dusty Baker, one of the top managers in baseball, another gentleman cut from the same cloth.

Empowerment Zone

Managers who falsely ask for input, never intending to use it, cause distrust and resentment. This goes back to our often-repeated theme of sincerity and honesty being the bedrock of the appraisal process.

Great leadership does not have to come with harsh, brutal, bullying tactics. Perhaps this is starting to be a more accepted style of management, even in the rough and tumble world of professional sports, where it has long been accepted for coaches to "abuse the best out of you."

A Gallery of Styles

There are managers that fall somewhere between Theory X and Y. Then there are others who try to be Theory Y but just can't let go of some of the Theory X that has been drilled into their heads—perhaps by their fathers, mothers, scout leaders or at a previous job. It is unfortunate but sadly common that some managers are familiar with the respect that comes with Theory Y but feel that they will relinquish control if they go to far in that direction. So they speak Theory Y language while tenaciously clinging to Theory X beliefs.

"I'm the Manager and You're Not"

These managers revel in the power of being a manager. Usually they talk a good line; they know all the right things to say during an interview to make a prospective employee believe they are modern and enlightened. They use words like "teamwork"

Empowerment Zone

It's important that you as a manager set the example for being accountable for your performance. If you consistently take responsibility and deal with it honestly, admitting mistakes as well as accomplishments, you are a role model for your staff to do the same.

Wise Counsel

If you tend to think of and treat your employees as if they are children, they will increasingly tend to act like children. It's one of those self-fulfilling prophesies.

and "accountability" and give employees the initial feeling that they will be treated as adults. After employees are hired and working for this manager, they feel more like they are being treated as children.

The "I'm the manager and you're not" style of manager

➤ Tends to be hyper-critical; accomplishments seldom deserve praise—something always could have been better somehow.

➤ Enjoys correcting his or her employees publicly, preferring to have an audience when chastising a worker for a shortcoming.

➤ Rarely compliments without adding a subtle, or maybe not-so-subtle, put-down.

➤ Lives by the philosophy, "spare the rod, spoil the employee" and believes too many positive comments will give the worker a swelled head.

➤ Goes out of his or her way to find something to criticize when giving a performance appraisal, even if the criticism has to be made up.

If your manager's face comes to mind when you read this list, here are some tips for how to deal with your encounters:

➤ Be prepared (even more prepared than your manager is likely to be).

➤ Write down what you want to say, such as a list of your accomplishments.

➤ Be prepared for a cool reception, and don't take it personally.

➤ Use positive affirmations (mentally compliment yourself) to boost your self-esteem before and after the conversation.

➤ Imagine your boss as an amusing cartoon character—say, Elmer Fudd—and have your own private jokes while he or she whines about you.

➤ Picture a huge cloud of cotton floating between you and Miss (not) Manners to absorb the words and sounds she is endlessly spewing at you.

➤ If your manager makes something up, ask for specific details such as dates, witnesses, and examples of written work. In other words, tell your manager it's time to "show me the facts."

➤ If you are sensitive and find yourself becoming de-motivated or demoralized, look for another job where the manager will show appreciation for the quality employee you are.

Status Quo

The *status quo* manager is happy enough with the way things are now. This manager's major goal is to not rock the boat, and he/she lives by the philosophy "Why fix it if it ain't broke?" Perhaps this manager has a staff that has been in place for a long time. The employees are meeting their productivity goals, and there is minimal conflict between them. For this manager, life is good just the way it is.

Because many people have a difficult time making changes, there are many people who are quite comfortable with this style of manager. These employees clearly don't want to set the world on fire. For the most part, they want to put in their day's work and collect their paycheck every two weeks.

The "status quo" manager

➤ Tends to be a pleasant enough person.

➤ Rarely exhibits emotional behavior of any sort.

➤ Doesn't feel the need to get terribly involved with employees and their lives.

➤ Feels comfortable with known solutions to problems and is averse to trying anything new.

➤ Expects all employees to do things the way they have always been done.

➤ Is decidedly not a risk-taker.

➤ Doesn't stand up for employees if it will put him or her in a confrontation with another manager.

If you picture your manager when you read this list, these tips might improve your working relationship:

Close Up

Status quo is a Latin term meaning "the existing state or condition" or, in other words, leave well enough alone.

Just the Facts

Change often is stressful. Stress occurs when a demand is made that exceeds the current resources of the system. Some people are unsure of their abilities when faced with unknown demands. Stress often happens when a new situation is introduced or when cumulative demands "break the camel's back."

➤ Realize that your performance appraisal will have a comfortable sameness about it.

➤ Consider whether it is worth it to rock the boat and complain—after all, your appraisal will be positive already.

➤ Be aware that it is very difficult, if not impossible, to change such a person's style.

➤ Be prepared with examples of any outstanding accomplishments that may or may not be mentioned.

➤ If you are frustrated with this kind of "white bread" approach to feedback, maybe it's time for you to look for work elsewhere.

The Team Player

The manager who adopts the team player style tends to be very supportive of his or her employees. This manager understands that it takes many different types to make an effective and strong team. Like a coach on a sports team, this manager will always be looking for individual strengths and finding ways for employees to utilize them.

The manager who is a team player

➤ Finds things to appreciate within each member of the team.

➤ Tends to be an impartial mediator if differences of opinion come up on the team.

➤ Is good at bringing the team back together after a conflict has arisen.

➤ Knows what's going on, but doesn't get involved unless necessary.

➤ Looks for a strong level of trust between manager and employees.

➤ Manages negative personal emotions appropriately and expects others to do so as well.

➤ Is able to encourage—and elicit—a positive and creative approach to the work.

Wise Counsel

Don't play favorites! It's natural to gravitate toward people who are more like us. However, showing obvious preference for one employee over another can lead you into a discrimination charge. Try to show equal attention and respect to all of your employees.

When your manager is a team player, these tips can help to keep your interactions smooth:

➤ If you're meeting for your performance appraisal, try to be as prepared and involved as your manager. Your performance appraisal will be a two-way conversation.

➤ Recognize how the strengths and accomplishments of your co-workers can affect your performance.

➤ Show respect for all of your co-workers.

➤ Be an active participant in department meetings.

➤ Think in terms of blending your goals with team goals and company goals.

Mentor

To be a *mentor*, a manager must believe in the potential of his or her employees. Most often, a mentor has benefited from being mentored during his or her career. Imparting the skills of being a leader comes naturally to this person. Employees who work directly for a mentor are very fortunate. Sometimes a mentor can be someone who is not a direct supervisor, but who nonetheless has an interest in guiding others along the path of leadership.

When your manager is a mentor, he or she

➤ Encourages employees to reach beyond the ordinary.

➤ Is extremely supportive of employees and represents them proudly to others.

➤ Coaches on—rather than shows—employees how to reach their goals.

➤ Models leadership behavior.

➤ Tends to macromanage, that is, takes a big-picture approach and gets involved only when employees request it.

These suggestions can help you be ready when it's time for your performance appraisal meeting with a manager who is a mentor:

➤ Be prepared to be challenged (in a positive, constructive way) during an appraisal.

➤ Be ready to discuss accomplishments and how they can be continued and strengthened.

➤ Set personal goals that make you reach beyond your comfort zone.

Close Up

A **mentor** is someone who acts as a wise, trusted advisor or counselor to another person. A mentor typically shares a wealth of experience, as well as lessons in leadership with those he or she mentors.

Empowerment Zone

Although the mentor style sounds attractive, not all employees respond well to a mentor. There are many employees who do not aspire to leadership and are quite happy maintaining the status quo. A mentor will have to know his employees well enough to know who needs which approach.

45

➤ Utilize the mentor's experience to identify areas of growth.

➤ Don't be satisfied with the status quo.

➤ Don't idealize your manager; he or she is still human. Otherwise, you will be crushed when your manager slips up, and you might not try to work things out.

Your Turn to Choose Your Own Management Style

These are only a few of the management styles out there. Perhaps one of these resonated within you. Or perhaps you are a maverick with a style all your own. As we tried to point out, each style affects the kind of performance appraisal that will be right for you and your company. One size most certainly doesn't fit all in this area.

The Least You Need to Know

➤ A corporate philosophy determines the kind of policies and systems your company will have.

➤ Your corporate philosophy should be incorporated into your performance appraisal system.

➤ Make sure your corporate philosophy is more than words on printed paper— that it does in fact include deeds and actions.

➤ The management style your managers exhibit should be a reflection of your corporate philosophy.

➤ Be honest with yourself when you identify your own management style.

Part 2

Let's Start at the Very Beginning

Okay, you've decided you need to do performance appraisals. So where do you start? A lot will depend on the size of your company. Larger companies might have several people involved in designing a program. But if your company is small, the responsibility might fall to you and you alone. Large company or small, however, performance appraisals need to be delivered correctly. The intention is to motivate and inspire—from the strongest to the weakest employee.

The chapters in Part 2 will take you from the preliminary planning stages right into a performance appraisal meeting. Whether you use an informal system or a more formal program with custom forms, you need to take care in your delivery—and with the people who are going to hear it.

Chapter 5

Casting Call: What's My Role?

In This Chapter

➤ Who should be involved in designing a performance appraisal system?

➤ When to ask for help

➤ The pros and cons of the committee approach

➤ Reasons to include employees in the process

➤ Remember why you are doing this

The previous chapters were written to help you do some preliminary thinking before you embark on a major performance appraisal project. Now you're ready to get started on the project itself. Performance appraisals are an invaluable management tool, but depending on your role and title within your organization, you might approach the process from a different perspective.

In this chapter, we address the different people and positions that might be involved in putting together a performance appraisal system. You might fit into one of the categories or you might span more than one. But wherever you fit, it's important to look at all the perspectives. No man or woman is an island—so it's said—and this is one of those projects you might not want to tackle all by yourself—in fact, we don't recommend that you go solo on this.

Although you might be of the school of thought that "if you want something done well, you should do it yourself," there are compelling reasons to include others in this process. We're not saying you absolutely have to include others, but we feel strongly that you will be more effective if you do. The more complicated the work process, the more important we feel it is to get input from those who do the work. And we have plenty of suggestions about where you might find help in putting it all together.

Who Draws the Short Straw?

Okay, you've determined that you really should have a performance appraisal system in place. But it sounds like an awful lot of work. You look around asking, "Who can I delegate this to?" That's a very good question. And the answer depends on the size and complexity of your company.

Larger companies frequently punt this project to *human resources* or personnel departments, if such departments exist. Performance appraisals are commonly thought of as falling under the scope of human resources. However, whether you have a human resources department or not, you might want to include others in the planning process. This chapter will help you decide which people in your organization should be involved.

The Top Bananas

If you are an owner or a chief executive at your company, you are instrumental in establishing the philosophy of the organization. Your style should be reflected in the tone of the performance appraisal system you design. But once you share your personal style, do you need to get more involved with the process? You are busy leading the company—this can't be something that you have to actually get into "hands on," can it?

Size Matters

The size of your company can play a part in this decision. If you are the CEO of a start-up company and your staff is relatively small, you probably will have to be closely involved with the process. Your staff might not have grown to a point at which you can punt this project to someone else. The proverbial buck known as performance appraisals is going to stop at your desk. Naturally, your company size (and possibly the industry in which you work) also will dictate how formal your process will be.

Even if your company is small, a performance appraisal system can serve as an effective retention tool to keep talented employees working for you instead of your competition. People want feedback and need to know they are making a contribution. Your leadership in establishing an evaluation system can give you a competitive edge over companies that either don't use them or have a system that just doesn't work. They are also useful when trying to decide on promotions and in many companies are tied into issues of compensation. Many companies use performance-based criteria to decide bonuses.

An example of this was pointedly brought up by a client recently who was able to show how response time to customer complaints was cut in half while the number of calls that needed to be made back to the customer after their initial call was reduced by sixty percent. These criteria had been identified as goals for the Director of Customer Support. They had also been tied into his yearly bonus package in advance. In this company, the company performance, especially in sales, was down, but the support services improved dramatically and were measured separately from overall product success.

From the File Cabinet

During the late 80s we worked with a large company that was advised by its consultants to cut costs. The billing department lost key staff in the downsizing. Others left the company after getting poor evaluations, unfair in their eyes, that did not reflect the additional work added to their loads. Another problem was the new director, installed by the consultants, did not talk with the existing staff to see what work goals could be accomplished. Some of the new managers thought this was good because they could start fresh with new people. However, this left no one who understood the complexity of the accounts and billing systems. Millions of dollars of outstanding billing would never be recovered.

Calling All Managers and Supervisors!

What role should others have in the appraisal system? The managers and supervisors who work closely with the staff have the best opportunity to know what constitutes excellent performance.

Why include managers and supervisors? As your management team, these are the people most "in the know" about your company's everyday operations. An effective management team should know

➤ How to motivate the people they supervise.

➤ What might de-motivate employees.

Just the Facts

Recent surveys have shown that in a tight job market when jobs are plentiful and wages are competitive, employees are much more likely to leave a company if they feel their supervisor's management skills are poor. Employees expect meaningful feedback and direction. Without that, there is little that will keep them from jumping ship and joining another company where management appears to be stronger.

Close Up

Productivity measures are the standards used to compare the quality of work among staff members in a certain area of your company. For example, each employee might be responsible for turning out *x* number of widgets per hour with waste and error below five percent.

➤ The strengths and weaknesses of their existing staff.

➤ The kinds of people that are attracted to and will thrive in that particular environment.

➤ The best ways of gauging the productivity of their staff.

➤ What measurement factors to use.

Hooray for Human Resources!

If your company is large enough to warrant a human resources (HR) department, or at the very least, a human resources professional on staff, you might feel that all others in the organization are off the hook when it comes to performance appraisals. It's true that human resources departments often are given the assignment of designing a system. If you have an HR department, you certainly will want to involve them in the process.

Here are some of the benefits of using HR in the performance appraisal process:

➤ HR traditionally has authority over the programs that affect employees.

➤ The HR department typically recommends retention tools. So it seems quite appropriate that it be involved in designing a performance appraisal process.

➤ HR professionals might have experience with formats that have worked well—or not worked well—in the past. They might have sample forms to get the process started.

➤ Depending on how long they have been with the company, HR professionals should be familiar with the company's philosophy. Indeed, a dynamic company philosophy might be what HR professionals use to attract new employees to your company.

➤ The HR department often is familiar with the *productivity measures* used by other departments within the company. That's why it's a good idea to have them consult with each department manager and ask for their assistance in building an evaluation plan. And there is no substitute for at least asking direct line employees what they want in the way of meaningful feedback.

Asking for Outside Help

It's great if you have staff to whom you can confidently punt the responsibility of designing a performance appraisal system. But if you do not have such staff, all is not lost. There are a large number of outside consultants who would be happy to help you with this assignment.

You are likely to benefit from outside help in designing your company's performance appraisal system if

➤ You are completely new to this process.

➤ You have no human resources expertise.

➤ Others in your company have no real experience in doing appraisals.

➤ You cannot conceptualize how to form objective, measurable, and meaningful ways to give feedback.

Working with a Consultant

There are highly skilled, professional consultants who will be glad to help you. You won't have to add them to your staff; they work on a limited project basis. They are hired as *independent contractors* to research your company and its philosophy, and to design a system that meets your company's goals.

When you hire an independent contractor, you can negotiate a price for designing the project. Some consultants will give you an hourly price for their time. Others will evaluate the size of the job and quote you a price for the whole project. This can vary depending on the size of your company, the number of jobs, locations, and other factors. Naturally, your input will be necessary and the consultant will have to spend a good deal of time interviewing you and reviewing progress with you.

Close Up

An **independent contractor** is a professional with specialized expertise who is not an employee, who is hired to do a specific task for an agreed-upon price, and who can retain the right to control the manner in which he or she completes the job.

Empowerment Zone

In designing a performance appraisal system, we definitely advise going for the latter method—project pricing. Given the number of people that might be interviewed for the project, the hours could rack up quickly and the bottom line might be more than you anticipated.

Wise Counsel

The Fair Labor Standards Act (FLSA) administered by the Department of Labor closely scrutinizes independent contractor working relationships. If you dictate the working hours and other working conditions (in other words, treat the consultant like an employee), the FLSA might require you to hire this person as an employee, complete with payroll taxes and benefits. Get advice from the IRS if you are uncertain.

Key managers, if not all managers, also will need to spend time with the consultant to share their insights on the project.

Design by Committee

Some companies that we have worked with in the past have formed committees to design a performance appraisal system. Before you start moaning about yet another committee, consider that this is not a one-person job. Input must be sought from a number of people within the company in order to design an effective program.

Potential members of a performance appraisal committee might include

➤ The CEO, as the chief policy maker.

➤ Managers who manage people.

➤ A human resources professional, if available.

➤ Some regular employees, perhaps some of the your company's stronger performers, or those who welcome new opportunities.

You can call your group a committee or a task force, whichever you prefer. Whatever you call this group of people, their responsibilities will be to take a well-rounded look at the company, establish the reason for instituting a performance appraisal system, and identify the type of employees who will be impacted by this program.

Your employees might have the best ideas in terms of planning this system. If they have been with the company for any length of time, they have an intimate knowledge of what is good or not-so-good performance in their own departments. In doing an evaluation of how to give meaningful feedback, you also might learn some of the systemic issues that prevent employees from performing as expected. They also might have a better idea of what it takes to motivate improved performance in their co-workers.

Do You Know What Your Employees Are Doing?

This isn't a facetious question. Do you really know what your employees do every day? You might have the big picture view of what you expect the job title to be responsible for. But do you really know the day-to-day nuts and bolts—all the tasks and duties that go into their jobs?

If the answer to that question is yes, congratulations! Maybe you've actually done the job yourself and know all the ins and outs. But if the answer is "not exactly" it might be more difficult to evaluate an employee whose job—how it is done and what might interfere with the job being done—is not somewhat familiar to you. Your lack of knowledge also can contribute to employees feeling that their managers really don't care about the quality of their work.

There are a number of great reasons to include employees in the planning process:

1. Employees are intimately acquainted with all of the tasks that make up their jobs, and all of the things that impact their ability to do those jobs.

2. Employees will feel that their opinions matter in building this plan, which will make them feel valued.

3. Employees will feel that they are an important part of the company, which could increase their feelings of loyalty and aid in your retention efforts.

4. Employees will feel that you are giving them new opportunities to learn and advance in their careers.

Empowerment Zone

Including employees in your planning process is another retention technique. Employees will feel that their opinions are valued. This is one of those ways they can make a lasting contribution to the company, and maybe they will last longer with the company because of it.

Wise Counsel

If you have not done the job for more than a year, check to see if there have been any significant changes. Machines, techniques, laws, and many other possible variables are routinely changing.

From the File Cabinet

Too many companies have made the mistake of thinking that only managers and above should be in on designing such systems. They probably ascribe to that "I'm the manager and you're not" school of thought. It threatens their sense of authority to include the rank and file employees in anything that is a management tool. So they put an elite group of managers on a committee. The product of such a committee often is a lengthy and difficult-to-use instrument that has little to do with the actual work of employees. Rather than becoming a document to motivate employees, it might instead confuse and frustrate the manager who has to perform the evaluations, and the workers who receive them.

In other words, we look at including employees in the process as a win-win situation. Both employer and employee will benefit by it. Such a deal!

Determining Who Should Be on Your Design Team

The number of employees in your company is an important factor in deciding the person or people to include in designing a performance appraisal process. This table illustrates some ways to look at this decision based on your company's size.

Who Should Be on the Design Team

No. of Employees	Who?	Rationale
10-15	CEO or owner	Might already be intimately acquainted with all jobs, or can take the time to talk to each employee about his or her tasks and responsibilities
15-40	CEO and at least one manager	Too much for one person to handle (and consider input from employees)
40 or more	committee that includes employees	Many and varied jobs require employee input

Revisiting Your Purpose

If you think that this project is already taking too much of your time, remember why you are considering performance appraisals in the first place. Let's review the reasons.

A Dedication to Motivation

The most important reason for doing appraisals is to motivate your employees positively. Recognizing accomplishments is a powerful way to motivate. Giving appraisals to your employees will show them that you and your company are interested in their work and their development.

Employees who feel that they are being taken for granted often are negatively motivated to behaviors such as absenteeism or looking for work elsewhere. Your system should be oriented toward motivation of all employees—motivating the strong performers to strive for more, and motivating the not-so-strong performers to want to improve. It also should point the way toward improving by including enough specific points to show how it can happen.

Wise Counsel

We sincerely hope that your major reason for designing a performance appraisal system is NOT because someone else—your boss, your attorney—told you to do it. Designing a system because you feel coerced into doing it sets you up for almost certain failure. Under that circumstance, it will feel like drudgery; something you want to do quickly and put behind you. Your chances of doing a quality job will be remote.

What motivates your employees? Put the following list of motivators in the order of their importance to your employees, with number one being most important.

Motivator	Rank
Money	___
Interesting job	___
Fear	___
Recognition	___
Advancement	___
Access to greater skills or knowledge	___
More autonomy	___
Flexible working conditions	___
Sociability	___
Security	___
Company loyalty	___
Being involved	___

If you chose money as the number-one motivator, you are typical of most managers taking this test. However, in a recent survey 90 percent of employees chose recognition as their number one motivator.

Communication Counts

Giving a performance appraisal is a great time to open those lines of communication with staff. As we have pointed out before, this kind of conversation will help both parties to learn. If your system is intimidating, it could squelch communication. You might not learn things you need to know to make your company a more efficient and cohesive place of work.

Just the Facts

Research has even shown that human beings prefer negative recognition rather than no recognition at all.

Appraisals Lead to Training and Development

Doing regular appraisals will help in determining if there are training needs for your staff. You can design action plans that address the weak spots as well as chart courses for individual personal development for achievers. Opportunity for development is one of the biggest factors mentioned in employee retention surveys. Twenty-first century employees want to work in places where they can grow and develop. These ambitious sorts will leave any place of business where they feel they are stagnating.

From the File Cabinet

Bill was a long-time employee at a shipping company. His department had had some serious management problems and high turnover. Bill took over much of the work for the employees who left and was an excellent worker. He requested a raise and perhaps an upgrade in his position. His boss told him no, so Bill updated his resume and started interviewing elsewhere. Then his boss asked Bill if he was committed to staying with the company. If so, they would consider a raise and upgrade. Bill felt insulted, having already been there ten years. "How much commitment do they want?" Bill wondered. Bill's company would have been well served by an effective evaluation process that would have shown Bill's successful performance.

Raises and Promotions

Your well-designed performance appraisal system can give you fair and legally defensible methods for giving raises and promotions—to the employees who deserve them most. Without performance appraisals, your decisions in this matter might be called into question—called favoritism or, even worse, discrimination.

The Least You Need to Know

➤ It's important to consider who is involved in designing a performance appraisal program.

➤ Very infrequently should the business owner or CEO be left out—it's your company, your philosophy, your plan.

➤ Committees including non-management employees are an effective method to plan your system.

➤ The major reason to develop a performance appraisal system is to improve employee motivation.

Chapter 6

First Things First

In This Chapter

➤ How to clarify your expectations

➤ The value of job descriptions

➤ Some sample job descriptions

➤ What happens if you don't have job descriptions

In the last chapter we asked you whether you knew what your people are doing. Well, it's time to ask yourself another question: Do your people know what your expectations are? In other words, have you articulated to them just what constitutes acceptable work? Some of us make the mistake of assuming that people will just know—intuitively—what managers are looking for in acceptable work. If you know, they should know too, right? Not necessarily.

Remember the differences between the various types of people. Have you ever had the experience of telling someone to do something and the person does something quite different from your request? You might have blamed the person for not listening to your instructions well enough, or you might have thought that you didn't express yourself very clearly. What probably happened is that the person you instructed filtered your instructions through his own personal filter. He listened well, but heard something different.

From the File Cabinet

Ensuring that employees understand your company's position is important—you cannot assume your view is the same as your employees'. For example, a manager tells a health care worker that patient care is the most important aspect of his work. The employee interprets this to mean ignoring paperwork is okay. In reality, the company can't stay in business without the proper documentation because the government will deny funding. Good patient care actually depends on proper and timely paperwork. As you can see, giving a good business reason for some of your requirements can often help employees understand the importance of what you are requesting.

So are you absolutely sure that your employees understand your expectations? It's a good idea to find out by asking them. You can't effectively appraise someone who doesn't understand what you consider good performance.

Close Up

A **job description** is a written document that usually includes a job summary as well as the essential duties and responsibilities, qualifications, and working conditions of a certain position. Job descriptions generally are used to select qualified employees in the hiring process and for performance appraisals.

The Beauty of a Well-Written Job Description

If your company has been in business for any length of time, you probably have documents called *job descriptions*. Or maybe you have something closer to task lists. If you don't have anything like job descriptions or task lists, we suggest that you write some as soon as possible.

Nothing Stays the Same

Job descriptions usually are dynamic. In today's fast-moving world, the way jobs are performed can change over time. Sometimes a job will take on a different identity depending on the person holding it. That's okay—and it allows employees to expand the skills they want to develop or delve into new areas of interest. It also allows you to meet the needs of an expanding business. Naturally, the job descriptions will have to be updated regularly to reflect the ongoing changes.

What's in a Job Description?

A complete job description should include most, if not all, of the following components:

- ➤ The full title of the position ("Director, Human Resources" or "Food Service Aide" or "Executive Assistant II")
- ➤ The department, if applicable
- ➤ Job codes or numbers, if applicable
- ➤ FLSA (Federal Labor Standards Act) Status: Is the position Exempt (salaried) or Non-Exempt (hourly)?
- ➤ The status of the job: full time, part time, or temporary
- ➤ The reporting relationship ("Reports to CEO")
- ➤ A job summary—an overview of the job's responsibilities
- ➤ Essential functions of the job—the duties that define the job
- ➤ Other duties or responsibilities
- ➤ Qualifications
- ➤ Physical requirements
- ➤ The date the job description became effective (which will change upon any revisions)

The format of job descriptions can vary widely; some examples are shown later in this chapter.

Essential Functions and ADA

The term *essential functions* came about as a result of the Americans with Disabilities Act (ADA). The ADA, enacted in 1990, is a federal antidiscrimination law written to protect the rights of qualified workers who are disabled. It assists qualified

Empowerment Zone

When firing someone for failing to do the job, a written job description shows the employee knew what was expected. Without a description, it's your word against the employee's—who can claim you had what constituted a verbal contract or agreement regarding what was expected.

Close Up

A job's **essential functions** are the fundamental duties that compose the job. Essential functions are those that are inherent in a particular job and that must be accomplished within the job.

63

Wise Counsel

The EEOC can impose very hefty fines on companies that violate the Americans with Disabilities Act (ADA). Each situation involving a disabled worker should be looked at carefully and reasonable accommodations considered fairly.

Just the Facts

During its ten-year history, The ADA has enabled thousands of physically or mentally challenged workers to obtain and sustain employment successfully. Additionally the ADA is responsible for requiring public accommodations such as wheelchair ramps and other building modifications to help disabled persons participate more fully in American life.

disabled workers in obtaining employment if they are able to perform the essential functions of a position, with or without accommodation. The ADA law applies to employers who have 15 or more employees and is enforced by the Equal Employment Opportunity Commission (EEOC).

How Can I Tell What's Essential?

To be essential, a duty must be inherent to the position. In other words, the job would not be the same job without that particular duty. It's perhaps easier to understand if we use an example.

In the job of an insurance claims examiner, essential functions are those directly related to reviewing and processing claims. Thus, an essential function would include careful identification of the physician's diagnosis on each claim examined. The claims examiner's desk might be in the same area as a clerical worker, and if the clerical worker is away from his or her desk, the claims examiner is expected to answer the phone. The responsibility of answering phones is not an essential function of the claims examiner's job. It's an additional duty, but if it was deleted from the claims examiner's responsibilities, it would not change the job of claims examiner.

You also can consider that a position should entail essential abilities. For example, a flight controller must be able to track multiple tasks at once. You really would not want someone doing this who could only focus on one thing at a time.

(Do) Sweat the Details: Defining the Job

Some people may wonder why you have to get so specific as to require the ability to speak on the job. It is done for a very good reason—so you can protect the rights of the disabled employee, should one exist. If the claims examiner could not speak, he or she would still be able to review claims. The disabled employee would be qualified to perform the essential functions of the claims examiner's job. And when getting a performance appraisal, such employee would be evaluated on how well he or she performed the essential functions of the job only.

The ADA makes the listing of physical requirements an important component of a job description. Some jobs might easily be done from a sitting position; thus a person in a wheelchair would be able to do the job if otherwise qualified. But if the position requires a substantial amount of standing and walking, it should state on the job description. Any requirements including the ability to speak, see, and hear should be spelled out.

Job Descriptions and the ADA

The ADA's intent is to ensure that qualified people with disabilities have an equal chance at a job. Also remember that *reasonable accommodation* is required if a qualified worker is able to do the essential tasks of a job, especially if it would require only minor modifications. (Making the answering of the phones optional to the claims examiner job if it was only five or ten percent of the job would probably qualify as a minor accommodation.) There are many physically or mentally challenged people who successfully hold prominent positions.

It is crucial to pay attention to these requirements to protect the rights of the disabled and to protect your company from potential violations of the ADA. Once again, it pays to be very clear in defining and describing what the job entails.

Get It in Writing

If your company does not currently use job descriptions, get busy writing! If you feel you are incapable of writing the details of the jobs in your company, ask your employees. Once again, your employees are in the best position to know what their jobs are all about. Also look at other similar businesses to see if you can get ideas. One manager we know took many job descriptions off the Internet to get the basic descriptions for his start up company.

Empowerment Zone

Be very specific in describing the physical requirements of the job. But also be realistic. Think about your own job and your ability to do it if you were to become disabled. Could you still function? Or more specifically, could you accomplish the essential functions of your job? Unless the disability is extensive, there are probably accommodations that could enable you to continue working.

Close Up

A **reasonable accommodation** is a modification made to a job in order to permit a disabled person to perform its essential functions. Although designed to require employers to be more flexible, the law does not consider reduced productivity to be a reasonable accommodation. Nor does it expect an accommodation that would create an undue financial hardship for the employer.

From the File Cabinet

There are many jobs that disabled workers can do and do well. Companies might find that if they extend themselves to accommodate disabled workers they can gain a lot of long-term loyalty. One company made a small accommodation for a maintenance worker with a mental disorder and found him to be one of their most productive and satisfied workers. A vocational rehabilitation program placed numerous disabled workers at a large fast food chain with excellent results. An international telecommunications company had a double amputee as a director of technology training who innovated many competitive programs for the company. Disability does not mean unable or unproductive.

But what if you need to give your workers some performance feedback, and it can't be postponed until job descriptions are written? This is one of those golden opportunities to communicate with your employees, if only to let them know that an appraisal is coming.

Here are some suggestions for doing a preappraisal meeting with an employee:

➤ Remember your purpose: to ensure that you and your employee are on the same wavelength when it comes to job performance.

➤ Ask the employee to tell you about the job and how they are feeling about it—this is a good way to become acquainted with the challenges that are encountered from day to day.

➤ During the conversation you can describe what your expectations are and exactly what you require as acceptable performance.

➤ Ask if he or she agrees or not—and listen to his or her point of view.

➤ Try to arrive at some mutual agreement regarding what a good job looks like.

➤ You might want to use this time for some goal-setting as well.

➤ Follow the conversation with a memo describing the things you agreed on. This will serve as a kind of informal job description until you get the real one done.

We recommend you wait several weeks after this conversation before conducting a performance appraisal. During that time you can observe the employee's current work habits and talk to others who are familiar with his or her performance.

JOB DESCRIPTION
Sales Support Specialist

Job Code:	1002	**Department:**	Sales
Reports To:	Sales Manager	**Status:**	Full Time
Date Effective:	5/30/00	**FLSA:**	Non-exempt

Job Summary

Assists sales staff in all support functions, including preparing sales materials and packets, assistance at presentations, providing correspondence and phone follow-up, serving as a resource for problem resolution.

Essential Functions:

• Provides administrative and clerical support to sales executives in the Large Sales Group.

• Serves as liaison between clients and sales executives during and following sales transactions.

• Researches and resolves problems and concerns of clients regarding product order and delivery.

• Ensures appropriate sales materials are available for current products by regular inventory and ordering.

• Assists sales executives at sales presentations in the field as necessary.

Other Responsibilities:

• Stays current on new product information by attending regular sales conferences.

• Provides back-up assistance to department receptionist with answering phones and other clerical responsibilities.

• Attends all staff meetings.

• Follows all departmental and company policies and procedures.

Minimum Qualifications:

• High School graduate

• At least two years clerical experience working in a sales environment

• Familiarity with PCs and business software.

• At least one year of experience in a public contact position.

Skills & Abilities:

Excellent communication skills – verbal and written.
Ability to multi-task in a stressful environment.
Ability to use multiple line phone system.
Bi-lingual English/Spanish is preferred.

Physical Requirements:

Ability to speak and hear by phone and in person up to 8 hours a day.
Ability to lift and carry boxes up to 50 pounds on a regular basis.

This is one example of a typical job description format.

JOB DESCRIPTION
HOUSEKEEPER

Department:	Janitorial	**Date Effective:**	June 15, 1995
Area:	2 South	**Date Reviewed & Updated:**	August 12, 2000
Supervisor:	Amanda Dolittle	**Reviewed by:**	Sally Semple, HR Anayst
Status:	Part time		
Shift:	Evenings		

Position Description

Essential Duties:

1. Maintains cleanliness of assigned department according to Janitorial Standards, including:

    a. Damp mops all floors on a daily basis.
    b. Strip and wax all floors weekly.
    c. High and low dust all offices in assigned department on daily basis.
    d. Clean and disinfect all restrooms on daily basis, including sinks and commodes.
    e. Vacuum carpeted areas daily.
    f. Wash interior of windows in all offices monthly according to posted schedule.

2. Responds to emergency calls for housekeeper in a timely manner by:

    a. Logging call in department emergency log.
    b. Notifying supervisor of emergency situation.
    c. Perform necessary clean up as required.
    d. Obtain signature on housekeeping incident report.

3. Maintains adequate supply of cleaning supplies by:

    a. Review product inventory at beginning of each shift.
    b. Note on Supply Log those products that are low.
    c. Complete Product Order Form for products that need replenishing.
    d. Place Order form in Supervisor's in-box before end of shift.

4. Other duties as assigned.

Other Duties:

1. Follow all departmental procedures and policies.
2. Ensure familiarity with and practice of all safety precautions.
3. Attend at least one staff meeting monthly.
4. Be courteous to all staff.

Physical Requirements:

Must be able to stand, walk, crouch and stoop for several hours per day as required for cleaning duties.
Must be able to push and pull a cart of supplies that weighs 100 pounds.
Must be able to lift and carry objects up to 75 pounds.

This is an example of another format commonly used with job descriptions.

The Least You Should Know

➤ Employees should be familiar with the company standards and your expectations of good work.

➤ A well-written and up-to-date job description is an invaluable tool.

➤ If you don't have job descriptions, take the time to write them.

➤ If it's too late to write job descriptions, clarify expectations in a conversation before conducting a performance appraisal.

Chapter 7

Everything You Need to Know You Learned in Grade School

In This Chapter

➤ Not everyone takes criticism well

➤ How to focus on improvement

➤ Performance appraisals are not a test

➤ Steps to take to ensure employee buy-in

Before you take pen in hand to actually write a performance appraisal, take a few minutes and review the most important reason you are undertaking this task. Money or legal considerations aside, we passionately believe the most important reason to do a performance appraisal is to motivate someone to want to improve. Also to give your employees credit and feedback on what they are already doing right.

Often people think that in order to motivate someone to improve, you need to point out something they are doing poorly or wrong. Motivating for improvement does not mean you have to find fault with a fantastic employee. But even the best person can continue to innovate and evolve. Ultimately, improving the person is improving the company. With a fantastic employee you can encourage them to stretch further in their goals. And if they are already stretching you want to reinforce and acknowledge them. If their performance is less than adequate then you don't want this to be punishment, but rather informative and helpful in motivating this type of employee to improve.

How you word your comments has an enormous impact on whether you will motivate a worker—or possibly squash him or her. In the spirit of win-win, this chapter will offer some preliminary suggestions on how to say what you need to say and reach a motivational result.

Lessons from the Classroom

Many of us received our first formal appraisals from our teachers at school; some of those lessons stay with us for a lifetime. Even though we are no longer in elementary school, feedback from a supervisor can have the same long-term effect on an employee. Some people hold memories—and grudges—for a long, long time, if not forever. Other workers might not react emotionally but might feel angry enough to reduce, rather than increase, their performance. And others might just use this type of experience to begin exploring their option to move elsewhere.

From the File Cabinet

At an elementary school, the second grade teacher was a stern and serious young woman who could be intimidating. In an attempt to motivate a shy pupil, Miss Cratched called on her to answer a question. The teacher referred to her as the "quiet one," and insisted the girl stand. The girl didn't know the answer and struggled to respond. Miss Cratched scolded her in front of the class. She called on another student and had him answer the question correctly. Then Miss Cratched chastised the girl again, this time for not paying strict attention to her. Perhaps Miss Cratched didn't intentionally humiliate the girl, but she also didn't motivate her to ever want to contribute again.

Words Can Hurt

The childhood chant "sticks and stones can break my bones, but words can never hurt me" just isn't true with many people. Words can hurt like swords to someone's self-esteem. Maybe you were treated harshly as a kid, in the military, or on a sports team. Maybe you feel that the only way to get respect is to show your authority. It is possible that you don't feel this way at all but have been supervised by someone who acted this way. But if you are a manager of people, it is *your job* to respect your workers' feelings and to understand how feelings can impact their job performance. Not paying attention to that detail will lose you many good workers over the years.

Understanding Cultural Differences

A manager at a high tech company was frustrated by what seemed like his employees' indifference to his directions. The manager had been born and raised in Spain and New York, while his four employees were all from Southeast Asia. His direct style of communication, including open frustration, was always met with polite agreement. Unfortunately, his employees did not understand what he really wanted from them—they thought he just was exerting his position.

When the manager took the time to hear the employees' point of view, he was really surprised. They did not understand the business reason for doing the task that was being asked of them. His open frustration only served to silence them into a polite acknowledgement of him being in charge. They were able to explain that engineers in their country were never expected to do the tasks he'd been assuming they would do. With a little counseling and feedback the manager was able to communicate more clearly, without using assumptions, and to not be as openly exasperated when he was not sure people were following his directions. He was also encouraged to ask his employees what they thought he expected of them, and what their understanding of his directions were. For the first time in their eyes, the employees were able to be more direct in responding to him because he actually seemed to want them to give him feedback.

Empowerment Zone

As a manager, it is your job to think of the people you manage as individuals and vary your way of communicating, appropriately and as necessary. This includes understanding personal, gender, and cultural differences and how these might influence the reception of your communication style.

Focus on Motivation and Improvement

Before you deliver performance feedback, tell yourself that your objective is to build confidence in the employees and loyalty to the company. The outcome of this conversation is to send the worker off with renewed enthusiasm to do excellent work, and that they will know what excellent work looks like. If you sound judgmental you will have the opposite effect. If you come off as indifferent, bored, or bothered with the task, this also won't make for great results. Consider the person's individual personality. If you don't know the person well, it's best to err on the side of cautiousness. Even better, try to spend time in the beginning of the interview asking them questions about themselves and how they are feeling about their work, if you don't already have a good idea. For example, "Bill, I really have never had a chance to get to know much about you as a person and what you're thinking about your job and the company. Do you want to spend a few minutes filling me in? In the future, I plan to try and do this with all of my direct reports."

Nervous Is Normal

People who have been in the working world for any length of time might have had negative experiences in meetings with their superiors. They might very well come into this meeting nervously anticipating criticism. Others might come in eager for enthusiastic recognition. Whatever the anticipation, you want to be the one to start off setting the right tone.

Accentuate the Positive

Start off by mentioning a strength the worker has exhibited. Everyone has some strengths. Try to find one or more areas or behaviors you have seen that show strength or promise.

Sample language to compliment behavior includes statements such as

➤ "I appreciate your punctuality. You are usually the first person to arrive each day."

➤ "People always comment to me about your upbeat personality. You are a positive influence on the department."

➤ "You haven't missed a day of work in three years. I really value that kind of work ethic."

Try not to evaluate how important you find that strength or skill. At this point, it doesn't matter if the strength is or is not the most valuable to your company or you. Your intention here is to let the worker know you have observed behavior worthy of praise.

"What Do You Think?"

Another effective approach is to give some positive observations first, and then ask the employee to tell you how he or she feels things have been going before you continue the evaluation. You are not trying to trick the employee into admitting weakness or to get him or her to convince you of greatness. The point is to be involved in understanding how your employees see themselves, you, and the workplace. This will improve your overall abilities to give good feedback that people will find useful.

Techniques in Action

Here is an example of one of these techniques at work. Melanie started as a new HR director in a department that had employed several different HR directors in the last few years. No director seemed to stay very long. There were a lot of complicated, intense, internal politics. The company was located in an ethnically mixed, low-income neighborhood, and the makeup of the company's workforce reflected this community.

Sandy was a long-term employee in the department. She had lasted through the previous four directors and was confident she could handle, and live through, the next. As support staff, Sandy was not respected by the elitist management staff. Sandy was, however, a mover and shaker among the line staff, who looked to her as an ally and an informant. She was blunt and to-the-point. Her style of interaction definitely was different from Melanie's. Sandy looked at Melanie as another manager who would be out of touch with the workers, and believed that she could outlast her, too.

Melanie sized Sandy up immediately. She could see that Sandy was smart, involved and, well, a bit hidden and evasive. But Melanie also could respect the power Sandy had among the staff. As a new employee at the company, she valued Sandy's knowledge of the company's history and asked a lot of questions to learn more.

After several months supervising Sandy, Melanie sat down to evaluate Sandy's performance. "What I like about your performance is the forthrightness of your communication," said Melanie. "You don't play around, you just put your opinion right out there. People respect your honesty and listen to you. That is very good for our department." Using sincerity and humor, Melanie went on to recommend times such behavior is appropriate and other times it is not so appropriate.

Sandy was surprised, but flattered, if not flabbergasted. None of her previous supervisors had ever considered her boldness an attribute. They had assumed that her directness was due to her background, being from an ethnically diverse, low-income neighborhood, rather than being an assertiveness skill that can be learned. The previous supervisors had attached negative views to this kind of behavior. Sandy actually enjoyed this performance appraisal. She relaxed and the conversation continued comfortably.

Over time, Melanie was able to mold Sandy's sometimes abrasive directness into a real asset. Their working relationship and mutual respect grew stronger. Melanie had taken a quality that other managers had found undesirable and shaped it into a strength. Sandy continued to grow in her job and ultimately went back to school to get a degree in Human Resources.

This Is Not a Test

A lot of managers have a habit of relating the function of completing performance appraisals to that of grading exams in school. They tend to select ratings that range between Excellent and Poor, much the same way a teacher will grade a student an A or F—and those other letters in between. Perhaps they think they must grade on the "curve," allotting so many As or Excellents, so many Bs or Goods, and so on. The misguided rationale this type of manager uses is "Not everybody can be at the head of the class—that's just the way it is."

From the File Cabinet

As an undergraduate at the University of California at Santa Cruz, Robert did his thesis on whether students could reliably convert the evaluations they were given to letter grades. There was a controversy over whether graduate schools already did this when evaluating the applying Santa Cruz students, and how this was affecting students' chances of getting into the schools of their choice. Robert was able to prove in his small sample of 30 students that people could convert them in a consistent and reliable way. The subjects tended to key in on words like good, excellent, poor, very good, and average, which most of the professors had resorted to using. (He's waited 24 years to have some use for that study!)

A job is not like school and a performance appraisal is not a test! Contrary to what some people in management think, employees should be evaluated individually, not collectively. Individual appraisals should not be regarded as being in competition with others in the department. This is not a test or a game or a competition. We cannot emphasize this concept enough.

Wise Counsel

If you have managers that tenaciously cling to the old school method of appraisals that are punishing, they will need to be coached and mentored to change their ways. Their failure to abide by the new practices can appear in their own performance appraisals.

Don't Make Your System Competitive

If you administer your performance appraisal system as a competition, you ultimately will kill the motivation of the workers who are not in first place. And if you only reward those who you regard as first-place winners, you probably will never have a full staff. The turnover from the disappointed "second-rates" is going to be high.

A competitive program might emphasize the importance of a ratings system, allowing only a few "excellents," and encouraging a contest-like environment to see who would get the highest ratings. Whereas a noncompetitive program would be designed to treat people as individuals, not comparing scores, but using the appraisal to motivate people at different places in their careers.

Once again, this doesn't seem like rocket science, yet it sometimes is a very difficult concept to grasp, especially when you have been treated in this type of competitive manner by other managers (or parents) and then find yourself promoted to managing others. So our advice bears repeating. We've said it before, and we'll say it again: The main purposes of performance appraisals are improvement, feedback, and communication—for your staff and your company.

Drum Roll, Please!

Okay, now you've got the message. You've decided to do performance appraisals for your staff. You have grasped the concept that their purpose is to improve staff and company. You've learned what your people are doing and have observed them doing it. You've set your goal on motivation for all. Now it's just time to go for it, right?

Well, almost right. First you have to let your employees know that you're going to appraise them. There should be no surprises, remember? Now if performance appraisals have been part of your company's culture, and your staff has already grown to anticipate them, you might not have to do a formal program *roll out*.

But if you have changed your program substantially or are doing performance appraisals for the first time, you've got to let your workers know in advance what is going to happen and why. You need to get your employees' *buy-in* of the program—or it will have little, if any, motivational effect.

Close Up

A **roll out** is the formal presentation of a new program or product. Usually a roll out has been designed to have a live presentation with overheads, handouts, full explanations of the product and procedure, and an opportunity to ask questions.

Training for Managers

If you are the CEO or a senior executive of a larger organization, you first will want to train your managers in the new program. This is important stuff—don't shortchange the training on this program. If you believe in the concept of motivation and improvement, you have to make sure that your management team—those who represent you in the field—are clear on your beliefs. If you have a human resources department, it can certainly help with training managers. But your sanction and championship of the program must be stressed.

Close Up

Buy-in is the process of ensuring understanding and acceptance of a new idea or program. Either your employees "buy it" or they don't.

Wise Counsel

A CEO or other senior member of management who thinks he should be protected from his staff will never be a well-respected leader. Those who make the effort to communicate and be involved have a much better chance of building a loyal and devoted staff.

Just the Facts

Holding meetings and having every manager and employee sign in on a sign-in sheet documents their attendance and being informed about the program. This kind of documentation might prove very useful in the future, should someone challenge the consistency of your program.

A Memo Doesn't Count as Training

Sure, you could announce the program in a memo or a newsletter. But if you want it to mean something, to be something memorable, schedule meetings—on all shifts so that all staff can attend. It's important that as many employees as possible hear your message and your support of a program that is designed for their betterment and the betterment of the company. This is your opportunity to get staff to link their personal goals with the goals and objectives of the company.

Think Win-Win

You actually can encourage people to make the connection that their own success is the company's success. It's your best opportunity to sell that connection—don't blow it! It makes perfect sense that if all employees are doing outstanding work the company should benefit. However some people can lose track of this fact. What's good for the company should be good for the employees as well. Employees are the company after all and the connection should be made continuously. When your staff is truly clear about that concept, you have strong and loyal employees willing to go the extra mile to be sure the company succeeds. It's powerful!

Don't Shortchange the Roll Out

Assuming you have already adopted a format for your performance appraisals, this is a good time to introduce it. If not you might want to delay the roll out program, say if you do not have enough employee feedback on the format to feel confident in its' success. If you do have your format down have samples and overheads so that everyone can understand the program. Be willing to spend time to respond to their concerns and questions. If you give the impression that this is not that important to you, your employees will get that message loud and clear, and your chances of having a successful roll out will be significantly lessened.

The Bottom Line

This isn't fluff or one of those idealistic human resources concepts that you have to tolerate. Your performance appraisal system concerns the ability of your company to accomplish its goals, to make improvements, increase growth, and retain talented staff members. If you don't believe that passionately, then you'd better go back to chapter one and start over.

Here is a sample agenda for a roll out of a new program. It can be adapted for large or small companies. You can get others involved but if you are the top boss, you better be there. If you have a small organization (fewer than half a dozen employees) a less formal approach might be better but the essentials remain the same.

Empowerment Zone

A roll out is not a time to delegate the responsibility to some underling. If you are too busy to show your personal commitment, you cannot possibly hope your employees will buy in. This is a top priority, one that directly affects your company's bottom line.

➤ Welcome to attendees by CEO: Thank the employees for attending. Encourage questions and participation.

➤ Background: State your intentions for the program. Share your passionate beliefs about the program.

➤ Introduction to the program: Use overheads and handouts. If you've included employee participation in the program design, be sure to acknowledge that now.

➤ Stress employee involvement in program: This also is an opportunity for them to give feedback to their supervisors.

➤ Implementation: Discuss timing, logistics, and how everyone will be appraised.

➤ Encourage questions and feedback, now or later. If you sense negativity, suggest meeting outside the meeting at a later time.

➤ Share your enthusiasm and support of the program.

Do I Have to Do a Dog and Pony Show?

A live, company-wide meeting with the CEO will get the best attention. It shows this is important—so important that the CEO and other bigwigs are making the presentation. You are giving the new program the same kind of time and attention that you would a new product or service that you were introducing to the public.

So yes, we advocate the dog and pony show approach. If everyone hears the same message at the same time, there will be less opportunity for misunderstanding.

Formal or Informal—Where Do We Go Next?

The next two chapters, Chapter 8, "The Casual Approach: Can We Talk?" and Chapter 9, "Formalities: My Form or Yours?" take you into the appraisal meeting with an employee. Whether you have an informal meeting or a more formalized procedure really depends on where your company is in terms of having a company-wide performance appraisal program. If you've got one, you probably have been supplied with a form and hopefully some instruction as to how to complete it. But even if you have no form, you can and should still give your employees feedback.

The Least You Need to Know

➤ A performance appraisal is meant to motivate, not to punish.

➤ Look for the positive qualities of performance behavior.

➤ Don't "grade" your department's appraisals on the "curve"—this is not a test.

➤ Roll out the new performance appraisal with a mandatory, company-wide presentation given by the CEO.

Chapter 8

The Casual Approach: Can We Talk?

In This Chapter

➤ The simplest form of performance appraisal

➤ The do's and don'ts of a performance feedback conversation

➤ Making an informal appraisal a formal part of a personnel file

➤ How to document performance appraisal conversations

What if your company is small enough or new enough that a formal roll out would seem a bit pretentious—but you still want to do performance appraisals? Although we don't advise that you ignore all the foregoing chapters, you still have an opportunity to use performance feedback in its simplest and most basic form.

If you are a small company (fewer than 20 employees) you might not want to design a formal system—at least not until the company has grown. Small companies have the advantage over larger corporations in that people find it easier to establish working relationships. If a company has 20 employees, most of those people will get to know each other—no matter how busy each individual is. When a company has 2,000 people, you probably will know only a small percentage of them. Being familiar with the people you appraise, can make the process easier.

Square One—The Basics

This chapter shows you how to do a performance appraisal in its simplest form: a conversation in which a supervisor or manager discusses with an employee his or her assessment of the employee's job performance. But you don't need a form to give honest, thoughtful feedback. Take out a blank sheet of paper—or turn to your word processor—and make some notes.

Close Up

The word **behavior** refers to an individual's demeanor or mode of conduct. This includes the actions or reactions of a person under specified circumstances.

Empowerment Zone

If, while preparing for a performance appraisal discussion, you realize that your expectations have not been explicit, it's not too late to meet with employees to give them the specific expectations you have for their various positions. Then postpone the appraisal meeting until everyone is adequately prepared.

Just Start at the Very Beginning ...

Try to answer questions such as

➤ Have you directly observed this person's work?

➤ If you have observed this person's work, what sort of *behavior* have you observed?

➤ If you haven't directly observed, who have you spoken to or could you speak to who has directly observed?

➤ How have you measured productivity for this person's specific job?

➤ Were specific goals established and has this person met them, exceeded them?

➤ Has the employee met your expectations—either implied or explicit?

➤ What are some specific examples of behaviors—actual accomplishments or incidents?

➤ Were there any important company initiatives that this person contributed to?

➤ Did this person receive any additional training? Have you seen improvement?

➤ Was the person counseled for any reason? Have you seen improvement?

➤ Are you aware of any personal or company-wide goals that the person has expressed an interest in?

These kinds of questions should help to trigger your memory to recall the past year. Again, if you have not worked closely enough with this person, get feedback from others who have more direct knowledge—but make sure you consider any personality conflicts or whether the person giving information has an axe to grind for any reason. Try to confirm reports from more than one source if at all possible.

Being Prepared Makes a Positive Impression

The more information you gather before the actual meeting, the more prepared and relaxed you will feel. If you decide to wing it and enter the conversation like you don't have a clue what this person did all year, this will not be a motivating meeting—for either one of you.

A One-on-One Conversation

Let the worker know you would like to meet with him or her to discuss the past year's job performance. Schedule a time when you can meet with no interruptions, and allow enough time to have a real conversation. If you schedule another appointment too tightly after this one, the employee might feel rushed. Keep in mind that this is a very important meeting. Your employee's feedback really matters and he/she should not be rushed.

Empowerment Zone

Some companies ask employees to submit a list of accomplishments for the year, as a kind of self-evaluation. Make sure you have more than this to base your comments on or employees feel they are doing your job as well as their own.

From the File Cabinet

Amanda had the responsibility of appraising six direct reports with whom she had worked for only four months. She obtained information from others that had worked with her staff members. And she also talked to the entire team to find out about their working relationships with their new team members. She had individual meetings with all her direct reports and shared the feedback she had gathered. Following each meeting, for each of her newer employees she wrote a brief but cordial memo citing the short appraisal period and observations she had gathered. Her appraisals were handled quite quickly and efficiently. No one felt slighted since everyone had time to discuss performance, whether or not they had a formal appraisal form completed.

Keep Things Informal

If you are doing this kind of informal appraisal, don't have a written document waiting for your employee. Topics might be brought up in this conversation that should be added to your documentation. You can use your notes during the conversation, and it would be courteous to let the person know in advance that you will be referring to notes you have made.

However, do let the employee know that you'll be generating a written statement following the conversation that summarizes the agreements you have reached during your discussion. This statement will become a part of the employee's personnel file.

Start with Some Small Talk

Start the meeting off with some conversation that is friendly and not performance-related. Talk about the weather (if you must) or some other topic that is of mutual interest. This is where having a sense of the person and what he or she is about comes in. People like it when you show a real interest in who they are. (Hopefully you do this all the time, not just at evaluation time.) The purpose of this "small talk" is to relax both of you.

Put Yourself in Your Employee's Place

It's natural that you might feel nervous. Almost anyone who has ever given a performance appraisal also has received one, and knows that there typically is some anxiety on both sides. This kind of meeting might feel somewhat confrontational and most of us don't like confrontation. Even when it is not confrontational, employees still may feel nervous about your opinion of them and may just want to know that you do approve of them. Believe it or not, many people actually give their bosses a lot of credit and importance, and really do want to please them and be seen as valuable by them. So use appropriate small talk to relax yourself as well as your employee. If you can find something to laugh about, it reduces tension quite well.

Wise Counsel

Even though you might have been treated inappropriately by your own supervisors during performance appraisals, this is not a time to be haughty and superior. Your employees already know you're the boss. You don't have to give them "attitude" to prove it.

Components of a Performance Appraisal Conversation

Although we call this an informal process, you are still doing an appraisal of someone's performance. So this is informal but not entirely casual. You may not have a previously completed document in front of you, but all the requirements of respectful communication apply here. The following suggestions can help you keep the conversation on track:

➤ Explain your beliefs about performance feedback.

➤ Stress that this is a two-way conversation; the employee is welcome to give feedback as well.

➤ Reinforce that the overall intent is for the feedback to be motivational—the purpose of the meeting is to find ways to help both the employee and the company achieve goals and make improvements.

➤ Explain that you might be referring to some notes, and that you probably will make notes during the conversation.

➤ Tell the person that following the conversation, you will put something in writing that ultimately will become part of the employee's personnel file.

➤ Let the employee know that he or she will have an opportunity to review your written statement, sign it, and receive a copy of it before it is placed in the file.

➤ Assure the employee that they will have an opportunity to add their own statements to the document if he or she chooses to do so.

Remember Those Positives

Once you're relaxed and you've gone over the logistics of your format, it's time to focus on the actual performance appraisal. As we said in Chapter 7, "Everything You Need to Know You Learned in Grade School," you should start with something positive. People love to get compliments. Hopefully, there will be a lot of positives to mention. And if there are not a lot of positives, find something. It's possible to make lemonade from almost any lemon.

Empowerment Zone

When giving performance appraisals, it's okay to admit that this is an experience that makes you nervous. Find a way to acknowledge your own nervousness. It will help establish rapport and break the ice.

Just the Facts

It's important, even in an informal appraisal, that you let the employee know that they are free to add written comments to your documentation. Many times employees won't add a thing, but since the document goes into their personnel file, it needs to be handled in the same way a more formal appraisal form would be handled.

Try to get the employee to tell you what he or she thinks about the job. If the employee is hesitant to get started, refer to your notes to mention specific incidents.

Make This a Motivational Conversation

You should not be the hard-nosed coach of a professional sports team who is going to bully a good performance out of your players. As we suggested before some of the most successful coaches have been very open and supportive of their players. Be honest and supportive. If aspects of performance are not entirely acceptable, try to suggest ways of making improvements—and encourage the employee to do so as well.

Do You Hear What I Hear?

Listen—*really* listen to what the employee says. Maintain eye contact. Be open to different ideas or concerns that might come up. If a topic surfaces that needs more research on your part, say so. This is not the time to wing it if you don't have all the facts.

Document the Goals

Set goals for the coming year. Encourage the employee to come up with his or her own list of goals, and come to some agreement about goals that are mutual. It's important to work with the employee to come up with goals that not only motivate the employee but are also related to company goals as well. To simply assign a goal may not be motivational. Your intention is to come to agreement on what the goals might be. You may have to coach some employees to find those relationships between personal goals and company objectives. You may also have to help them specify the behaviors that they need to increase or decrease to meet these goals.

When the conversation has concluded, thank the employee for taking the time to meet with you. Reiterate the fact that you will put the highlights of this conversation in writing. If the conversation has remained warm and sincere, you both should be smiling at this point. Shake hands and estimate a time you will have the document for review and signature.

If you suspect an employee might turn this meeting into something unpleasant, you should refer to Chapter 13, "Potential Problems and Difficult Situations."

Informal Appraisal Do's and Don'ts

Although this is a more informal method of giving a performance appraisal, it is still an important meeting that requires professional behavior. Just because you don't have a form to complete, doesn't mean that you don't have to do your homework and treat your employee with the same respect that you would expect from your own supervisor.

➤ **Do** prepare before the meeting.

➤ **Do** schedule enough time to have a relaxed conversation.

➤ **Do** expect that there may be disagreement on some points.

➤ **Do** discuss the intent of the meeting and its documentation.

➤ **Do** be sincere and supportive.

➤ **Do** maintain eye contact.

➤ **Do** encourage participation.

➤ **Do** listen and be open.

➤ **Do** thank the employee for his or her time and participation.

Here are some **Don'ts** to help keep your conversation from derailing:

➤ **Don't** try to wing it.

➤ **Don't** take phone calls during the meeting.

➤ **Don't** be overly critical.

➤ **Don't** patronize.

➤ **Don't** interrupt.

➤ **Don't** try to rush through.

➤ **Don't** be sarcastic.

Put It in Writing

It's important to get your thoughts down on paper while they're still fresh in your mind. Try to leave some time before your next appointment so you can put your comments in writing as soon as possible. Although you might be certain that you'll remember everything, the longer you put it off, the more you will forget. The agreements that you made should be documented immediately after the meeting.

Wise Counsel

Trusting your memory can sometimes lead to embarrassing situations. If you are doing a number of consecutive appraisals, it's very easy to confuse who agreed to which goal; your credibility will be forever damaged if that happens.

The document should be in letter or memo form. It should cite the date of the meeting, the agreements made, and any other pertinent details that should be part of the employee's record. When you have finished completing the document, give a copy to the employee to review and sign.

This example shows documentation following an informal performance appraisal. Since there is no form, the important points and agreements are written in memo form and signed by both the giver and the receiver.

MEMORANDUM

TO: Emily Employee

FROM: Brenda Boss

DATE: January 10, 2001

RE: Performance Appraisal

We met on January 5, 2001, to discuss your performance with ABC Company for the past year. This memo is written to memorialize the agreements reached at that meeting.

You began your employment with ABC in December, 1999, as a clerk typist in the Marketing Department. Your supervisor at the time, Martha Manager, has described your performance in her department as exceeding her expectations. Upon her recommendation, I promoted you to my executive secretary on May 29, 2000.

In the administration department, you had the responsibility of coordinating our move to new offices in June. You did a fine job organizing the new office and setting up a workable filing system. I also commend you for patiently working through the computer problems that followed the move. Your expertise with the computer hardware and software is appreciated. The spread sheets you have completed for the Board meetings are very good.

Feedback I have received from clients regarding your performance in dealing with them is quite positive. We did agree that if you have a problem with any one as you did with a client from XYZ in November, that you will come to me rather than try to deal with it yourself.

We also agreed that in the coming year you will continue to increase your business knowledge by taking an evening class. You expressed a desire to learn the budgeting process and I agreed to let you work as part of the budget team when we begin the process in June.

It has been a pleasure working with you for the past 6 month and I look forward to a productive coming year. You will be eligible for a salary increase in June, 2001.

Signed_____
          Brenda Boss

Signed_____
          Emily Employee

The Least You Need to Know

➤ Even if you don't have formal appraisal systems and forms in place, it is still possible to do an informal—yet effective—appraisal.

➤ The simplest form of a performance appraisal is a one-on-one conversation.

➤ Start an appraisal conversation by mentioning the positives.

➤ Let the employee know that you will document the appraisal.

➤ Document the appraisal soon after the meeting, and let the employee review and sign it.

Check all
that apply:
My job rating
is...
☐ bad
☐ poor
☐ unmentionable
Thank you.

Chapter 9

Formalities: My Form or Yours?

In This Chapter

➤ How to know whether you need to use a form to do performance appraisals

➤ What do you mean, I have to appraise myself?

➤ Different strokes for different folks

➤ How to prepare for more difficult appraisals

We show several examples of performance appraisal forms in the chapters of Part 6. But that barely scratches the surface of the number of possible forms out there in the business world. Is there a perfect form? We seriously doubt it. But is there a form that might work better for your company? There is a good chance that you can find or design a form that meets your needs.

This chapter explores the notion of using a form, and what to do if you don't like the form your company wants you to use.

Do I Need to Use Yet Another Form?

There are some companies that can be described as forms-happy. Usually in such companies there is an abundance of forms for any occasion, including the form required to order more forms. Kind of reminds you of your Uncle Sam ....

Some human resources departments also can be described as forms-happy; those who work there will not complete any transaction without having the appropriate form submitted. And the appropriate form had better have the appropriate signatures on it—or it will be summarily returned to you—probably with another form attached that points out what aspects are incomplete.

Empowerment Zone

If you are the head of the company, ask for feedback from other managers and employees regarding whether the appraisal forms are meeting the needs of everyone. Check to see that your managers read and understand it in the same way, and ask if the form is easy and efficient to use.

Close Up

Competency is the state of having the correct or needed skills for a certain purpose, function, or position. In a competency-based performance appraisal, each required competency would be evaluated in some quantitative format, for example "scores 98 percent or better on all reorientation exams."

If you work for a company such as this, we understand why you might be reluctant to add yet another form to your repertoire. And as we pointed out in the previous chapter, using a memo or letter format instead of a form certainly is an acceptable method of doing a performance appraisal.

The Advantages of Using the Company Form

If your company uses a certain form, there probably are good reasons for it. Here are some of the common reasons companies use standardized forms to document employee job performance:

➤ If everyone in the company is reviewed on the same form, it sends the message that there is a program that is consistent for all levels of employees.

➤ If the form has been prepared with the company's philosophy in mind, there might be elements of the form that reflect company goals. Thus, it can be a guide to align the individual's accomplishments with those company goals.

➤ The form might have been designed with certain regulatory requirements that are called for depending on the industry in which you work. For example in the health care industry you often see the requirement for *competency*-based performance appraisals that must show observance and measurement for position-specific competencies.

➤ If it is a well-designed form, it should have space not only to review past performance, but also to set goals for the coming year.

➤ The form can walk you through the proper steps to make sure you don't forget anything.

There are probably many other good reasons to use a specific form to do performance appraisals. And if your company has given you forms to use for this purpose—and they are conducive to your needs—by all means use them.

How to Complete a Formal Performance Appraisal Form

Some performance appraisal forms are pretty self-explanatory. You basically fill in the blanks, all of which should be plainly labeled. If the form is more complex, very often the instructions to complete the performance appraisal are printed right on the form itself. If the form uses a *ratings system*, you simply need to choose the rating that best fits your judgment of the performance.

Although some forms lean toward eliciting a subjective opinion, the better ones require written detail if you score anyone above or below what is considered the minimally acceptable score. For example, if you rate someone's performance as unacceptable, you have to provide a behavioral reason for choosing that rating. Conversely if you rate a performance as exceeding expectations, you also have to detail the reason using behavioral examples.

Appraisal forms that use a ratings system generally are fairly easy to complete. The major advantage is that if the form is easy to complete, managers will, in fact, actually complete them. Requiring behavioral examples might take a bit more time. But a prepared manager should be able to complete a ratings-based form quite efficiently in a minimum amount of time.

The disadvantage of forms that use a ratings system is that they frequently call for the manager to rate not behaviors but character traits—which tempt one to use subjective opinions. Trying to rate character traits leaves a company much more open to a claim of discrimination than a system that rates actual behaviors using behavioral examples.

Close Up

A **ratings system** is a method of appraisal that uses a structured scale which gives employee traits or behaviors a score or rating; the ratings usually range from "poor" or "unacceptable" to "excellent" or "exceeding expectations."

Wise Counsel

Ratings tend to set up more of a competitive feeling among employees. You might think that a performance appraisal is a confidential document. Guess again. More often than not, employees share their scores with each other. And you'd be amazed how much hurt can result from one worker being rated "Good" while a co-worker is rated "Exceeds Expectations." That's one of the reasons that being able to qualify a rating with behavioral examples is crucial.

Behaviors are actual observable actions, such as "accurately proofreading reports before submitting." A character trait is usually a descriptor of a quality, such as "reliable." Without giving an example of why a person is reliable, it smacks of someone's subjective or personal feeling as opposed to a more objective observation.

We'll talk more about the rating systems and other form types in later chapters.

From the File Cabinet

It is not surprising that a ratings system evokes a competitive response reminiscent of the competitiveness and emotions of families. Many people can remember being compared to brothers, sisters, cousins, or even friends. One woman said her mom would always compare her to her friends when looking at everything from grades to boyfriends. Being a sensitive person, she also was very sensitive to any kind of professional comparison; work evaluations felt like her worst nightmares. It didn't help that her boss would point to her "pet" employee, as the worker phrased it, and chide other workers for not "working more like him."

Just the Facts

One of the most important points of the appraisal form is to document feedback and improvement. It's not going to be graded on how aesthetically pleasing it appears. So do what you must to make the form succeed functionally for you and your employees.

When the Form Doesn't Fit

If you feel unduly limited in your ability to do a proper performance appraisal with the form you've been given, there are ways around this problem. Our advice is to use the form, but add to it whatever you feel is lacking. It is a very common practice to attach another sheet of paper (or more) to add more text to an appraisal form.

Some supervisors feel free to write in the margins or on the backs of the forms. Actually this technique is great if you truly consider the appraisal a two-way conversation. The person being appraised might prompt you to change or add something that you hadn't previously thought of. Changing it on the spot or crossing things off will show your employee that you are really valuing his or her input.

Appraise Thyself

Self-appraisal is a technique that seems to be growing in popularity. In this approach, you give your employees a form and they appraise themselves. Ideally you will use the information they give you to complete another performance appraisal for each employee. The self-appraisal is not meant to take the place of the appraisal that a supervisor gives to his direct reports. By evaluating themselves, employees are able to give their manager a different perspective of their performance and hopefully a better understanding of the potential obstacles that may impede performance.

From the File Cabinet

A CEO had all of his direct reports complete self-appraisals. He then would simply sign his name on the self-appraisal, and the document would become the formal performance appraisal. His direct reports soon learned they could write almost anything, and it would become their documented performance appraisals. However, it did nothing in terms of giving them any real feedback or a different perspective. It also didn't give a positive message. Instead, it said, "I am too busy and important to bother to write anything myself."

The easiest way to do self-appraisals is to give an employee the same blank form that the supervisor will complete for the employee. That way the employee will use the same criteria to evaluate his or her own performance. Then comments, ratings, and scores can easily be compared.

There are many good reasons to use the self-appraisal:

➤ It makes employees active participants in the appraisal process.

➤ Employees rate themselves using the same criteria that you will use to rate them.

➤ It makes each employee reflect on his or her own performance and achievement of goals.

Just the Facts

Surveys about self-appraisal have shown that the vast majority of employees who self-appraise rate themselves at the same point or lower than their supervisors would. Employees actually tend to be harder, not easier, on themselves!

➤ An employee might bring up accomplishments or challenges that you might have forgotten to include in your appraisal.

➤ It helps to promote the two-way conversation that should occur during a performance appraisal.

➤ It helps to identify training and development needs.

Self-appraisals are an opportunity for the supervisor to do some performance coaching. The conversation can proceed to setting goals to further develop the employee's skills and confidence in his or her performance. Supervisor and employee collaborate on the plan for the future, which should help to build or strengthen the working relationship between them.

In talking to colleagues it was interesting that there was a wide range in how people reacted to self-appraisal. Responses ran from, "Great, now they are making me do their job!" to "I really like detailing my accomplishments because I know them the best." But frequently there was some hurt; some people felt their managers did not take the time to really see the good or bad work that went on in the department. As we have said before, this is your chance to connect with your employees in a meaningful way; they want it, expect it, and usually are disappointed with the results if it is not done with enough effort or thoughtfulness.

Different Strokes for Different Folks

We've already discussed the fact that people are different—and sometimes you have to use a different approach when conducting performance appraisals. It just would be too easy if everyone reacted the same. And no one is ever going to say that a manager's job is an easy one.

Any department probably will have those employees who will willingly embrace the concept of performance appraisals, approach the process maturely, and work with you to make the experience a success for each of you.

Some departments also might have more challenging employees when it comes to appraisals; these employees might be negative, argumentative, or silent and non-participatory. Your approach to appraising employees will have to be modified for whatever different type you are dealing with.

Avoid Bias Based on Personal Feelings

It's natural that you might like some people better than others. But try to keep clear that a performance appraisal is not meant to be a personality contest. Taking your personal feelings out of the process sometimes is difficult, but not impossible. Your task is to look at performance, not personality.

People whose personalities are distinctly different from yours might be harder for you to relate to. But you should be able to evaluate whether they have performed up to expectations. Rating someone's personality can stray too far into that subjective area that can be considered discriminatory. Remember to mention behavioral examples if you feel some trait has affected performance.

Advance Preparation

All of your employees deserve your advance preparation to a certain extent. As we have stated before, your opinion as the supervisor carries a lot of weight, so thinking and planning in advance is important to anyone for whom you do a performance appraisal.

However, there might be some employees who have presented some performance problems and who might require additional preparation time on your part. If you feel that some changes must take place in an employee's behavior to enable him or her to perform adequately, you will need to carefully plan how you will communicate that message.

You might need to do some research and reflection to determine what motivates these individuals. It might be something quite different from that which motivates your star performers. It is worth the extra time it takes to determine the motivators. It can make the difference between maintaining marginal performance and inspiring major improvement.

Empowerment Zone

Personality only comes into play when you can see it influencing a work-related behavior. An example of this is when you feel an employee is abrasive. If this abrasive behavior makes other co-workers afraid to approach the employee, personality can interfere with important work functions.

Just the Facts

Your intent should not be to squash your employees with criticism, but rather to motivate them to improve. To merely point out deficiencies without a plan for improvement is akin to shooting yourself in the foot. All you will do is get the person upset or confused, without providing the knowledge to change the situation.

Common Types

We want to share some tips with you about some of the types of employees you might encounter and how they might react to a performance appraisal meeting. As a manager, your job is made more difficult because you need to understand the various types of personalities—but in evaluating performance, you have to resist evaluating personality (unless it impacts performance). This can be a challenge.

It Won't Work: The Pessimist

The pessimist tends to look at the dark side of everything. He has a negative, sometimes sarcastic, comment to make about nearly everything. He puts down any new initiative introduced by management as yet another hopeless failure.

In dealing with a pessimist, as with any personality type, you should observe the impact, if any, his pessimism has on actual performance. These types very often tend to share their negative comments with the staff and can cause morale problems. In that case you might tell him that his behavior has a negative impact on his co-workers.

If his attitude toward new initiatives causes him to not comply with company changes or policies, you should counsel him on his failure to follow procedures.

That's a Great Idea (Can You Believe How Stupid It Is): The Passive-Aggressive

The passive-aggressive employee does most of her dirty work behind your back. She might pretend to accept your direction, but when you are out of range she will publicly complain and criticize. Beneath the surface of her behavior, this employee might feel that she is trapped and has no other option or choice in being able to express herself.

One way to respond to passive-aggressive behavior is to be direct. You might say to this employee:

➤ "Please come to me directly with your concerns. I promise to listen carefully to them and to let you know what I will or will not do about them. If you don't like my response you can bring it up again in a staff meeting to see how others might feel about it, and so I also can hear their views."

➤ "I want you to know that airing your complaints to others who can't do anything about them hurts productivity and morale."

If other employees have complained to you about this employee's passive-aggressive behavior, you can bring this out, saying you also have instructed people to be direct about not wanting to be burdened with this kind of negative talk.

If you have been overly defensive or punishing when workers bring up problems, you also need to look at your part in this cycle and do something about it. This could include listening carefully to worker complaints and attempting to see their perspective; helping them to be more direct with their co-workers; not glossing over their concerns; be willing to confront this type of recurrent problem with the employee who continues to engage in it after other workers have been direct about it.

Please Don't Notice Me: The Introvert

The introvert says very little to you or anyone else. He lives in his own world where few others are admitted. It is difficult to get him to participate in his own appraisal or any other communication plan.

> **Empowerment Zone**
>
> When dealing with passive-aggressive behavior, be aware that co-workers are not always honest about their feelings regarding the complaining employee. They might even seem to be going along—or worse, joining in somewhat—and then complaining to you about it later.

This person might need practice, help, and shaping to become a more involved employee. You don't necessarily have to push too hard with this type of person. Do encourage this employee to work on being more interactive in expressing his likes, needs, and expectations—of the company, of you, and of himself. This will be your way to make sure he can get what he needs from his work, and that you also can get the kind of work you need from him for your business needs.

We have lots of suggestions for encouraging silent employees to open up in Chapter 12, "Dialogue is a Two-Way Street."

Hidden Agenda: The Self-Righteous

The self-righteous employee usually carries a social, political, or personal agenda into the workplace. She often makes interpretations about the institutions or managers decisions that may or may not be related to her agendas. She often is so focused on making management the "bad guy" that she can't recognize enlightened managers from any others. In fact, sometimes the self-righteous employee has a valuable perspective but feels the need to polarize everyone else on the issues. In other words, she might see things only in black or white, good or bad terms.

You might want to help the self-righteous employee to consider the conflict she causes within the workplace by looking at things in an all-or-nothing fashion. It is important that she understand how this behavior can negatively affect morale and productivity; worse yet, it probably turns other people off to her social, personal, religious or political message, which might be important and valid in many aspects, just not carried into the workplace.

No Energy: Burned Out

The burned-out employee has been at the same job in the same place too long. Feeling trapped by economic necessity or just force of habit, he can't see any light at the end of the tunnel. He might passively accept any appraisal and consider it the same thing he's been receiving forever.

You might need to confront the burned-out employee with your observations of his lack of enthusiasm, even if his performance is competent. You might ask him what would help to make him more invested in his job, such as a change in responsibilities or the possibility of a promotion or transfer; or perhaps some sort of training to bring new skills to his work.

This is one of those areas where you must focus on your intention to motivate an employee to improved performance. If his performance is competent but lackluster, you may need to probe to find out what might make him more growth-oriented. In doing this you may also help to retain this employee who otherwise may leave the job. Even if they don't leave, you want to have people who feel good about their work, because they will transmit that energy to customers and co-workers.

The Least You Need to Know

➤ If your company has provided you with a certain performance appraisal form, there are probably good reasons to use it.

➤ If the form doesn't fit your needs, add to it or modify it to fit better.

➤ Self–appraisal can be a good technique if your employees are ready for it.

➤ Performance appraisals for certain types of employees will require more than the ordinary amount of preparation.

Part 3

What's My Line: What to Say and How to Say It

A performance appraisal meeting should be an open, dynamic conversation that encourages an exchange of ideas and feedback. It might not have felt like that in the past, however. The chapters in Part 3 are designed to arm you with the techniques necessary to reach a successful outcome.

This is an important discussion and one that will be most satisfying if both you (the manager) and the employee being appraised feel relaxed rather than uptight. There are lots of tips you can use to encourage a shy employee to participate more fully in the conversation. You'll also want the employee to collaborate with you in establishing goals for the coming year.

You also should be prepared if the appraisal does not go as planned. There are signals to watch for and methods to deal safely with even the most difficult employee.

Chapter 10

Prepare and Practice

In This Chapter

➤ How to prepare yourself physically and mentally

➤ The right way to prepare for an appraisal meeting

➤ Where to have the meeting

➤ Avoiding the five most common mistakes

➤ How to set the stage for your meeting

This chapter takes you right into the performance appraisal interview. Hopefully by now you have done your research, determined whether or not you are using a form, and put your thoughts down on paper. Now you might be feeling it's time to just get this meeting over with.

But not so fast! As we have pointed out, this meeting is important—as important to the employee as it should be to you and the company. It deserves special preparation. This is not a meeting to rush through. You need to feel ready for the conversation, and to make the environment as comfortable as possible for both you and the employee.

Taking Care of Yourself

Employees might think that all the stress is on them when it comes to performance appraisals. But the supervisor or manager also can feel stress—perhaps to a greater degree because of the number of appraisal interviews he or she might have to deliver.

If you are a supervisor with many employees to appraise in a short amount of time, don't underestimate the need to take good care of your physical and mental well-being. You want to feel strong and clearheaded for these meetings. You owe it to employees to be alert and rested rather than burned out.

Taking good care of yourself means

Empowerment Zone

At a minimum, take a few minutes between each review to sit in a chair and do some focused breathing. This can be as simple as closing your eyes and taking a deep breath in, then exhaling slowly while counting to ten. With each subsequent breath picture yourself sending oxygen and blood flow out to your hands and feet.

➤ Getting enough sleep at night. Being sleepy or cranky won't make this job any easier.

➤ Eating a well-balanced meal—not just a donut and coffee—prior to your appraisals.

➤ Getting regular exercise; doing so helps to calm your nerves and refresh your mind. You might take a walk around the block before each appraisal to get the blood circulating and to feel more relaxed.

➤ Try to put aside other demands and projects when doing these. Negative stress is cumulative; the last straw breaks the camel's back.

If you are feeling ill or out of sorts, it's probably best to postpone doing an appraisal. When you are tired and headachy, it's harder to choose the right words to say—and your words bear a lot of weight with your employees. If you do have to postpone an appraisal, reschedule it as soon as possible.

Always Be Prepared—Professionally Speaking

Taking good care of yourself is only part of the preparation process prior to doing a performance appraisal. There are a number of points to go over mentally to make sure you handle this meeting as professionally, thoughtfully and efficiently as possible. You owe this kind of mental preparation to yourself as well as to the employees who will be appraised. Keeping these tips in mind will help to make the experience more pleasant for both of you. Of course, there are no guarantees about the results since people can throw you a curve ball from time to time. But our experience has shown us that remembering these details can only help, rather than hurt.

This Meeting Matters

The appraisal appointment means a lot to your employee's self-esteem and makes a big difference in his or her loyalty to your company. Make sure you give the appointment the appropriate time and attention. To treat it as something you can slip in quickly between other responsibilities will trivialize it, and your employee surely will sense that.

From the File Cabinet

One director had to ask his boss four or five times when they were going to meet for his appraisal. Appraisals were tied to salary increases, and the director was trying to buy a home, so he was very motivated to know how he was doing at the company. His boss kept setting a date to do it, and then without any explanation, the day would come and go with no appraisal. The director felt angry and embarrassed that he had to bring it up again and again. This treatment gave him the message that he should start looking for work elsewhere.

The appointment to meet for an appraisal should be made in advance. You should have taken time to prepare for the meeting and the employee also should be given a chance to prepare. Try not to spring it on someone at the last minute; a week's notice is appropriate.

If you have a company policy stating that performance appraisals are to be scheduled on the anniversary of a hire date, pay attention to that date. Give yourself a week or more in advance to prepare.

An appraisal that appears as if it has been done carelessly or at the last minute can send the message that the employee's performance has little value in your eyes.

Wise Counsel

Don't be late to your appraisal meetings. Being late sends the message that an employee's work is unimportant to you. This might not be your intention, but it's what employees believe. Make the appraisal a priority.

Allow Enough Time

When making the appointment to give an appraisal, reserve an appropriate and a respectful amount of time on your calendar. You want to have a real conversation, taking time to exchange ideas and plan future goals. You should plan on at least an hour for most employees. If a meeting takes less than the hour you have reserved, you can use the rest of the time to make notes or document the agreements arrived at. You may need to plan some time at the end of the day or the beginning of the next day, before starting new evaluations, to make notes you did not have time for during the last round of appraisals.

105

Empowerment Zone

Don't rush through an appraisal. No matter what the level of employee, everyone deserves to take pride in their accomplishments. If you hurry through the meeting, you're telling the employee that you have more important things to do than to share the pride of achievement. You will hardly inspire loyalty.

Wise Counsel

Sitting behind a desk sometimes is looked upon as a barrier to conversation. It magnifies the distance between you and the employee you are appraising. If possible, try to sit at a table next to each other, or in chairs that are side by side. It might take some getting used to but it encourages more equal and open conversation.

Don't Procrastinate

When you see those appraisal due dates coming up on your calendar, make completing them a priority. You probably have many other important appointments on your calendar, but these meetings with employees should take precedence. If you give your employees the impression that you are too busy to complete their appraisals, they might use their waiting time to look for work elsewhere.

Hold the Discipline

Sometimes it's difficult to look forward to an appraisal because you have some bad news to deliver. If an employee is not meeting expectations, hopefully you will have had meetings before this one to counsel him or her. A performance appraisal is a poor time to punish an employee for past behavior—punishing and disciplining have very little motivational effect.

Instead, bring up areas that need improvement and discuss possible development strategies. Try to get the employee to suggest ways to improve performance. This is an opportunity to explore potential roadblocks and training needs. Mutually agree on goals aimed at increasing the quality of the work.

If an employee has been a performance problem—either not working as required or some behavioral problem such as poor attendance—schedule a separate meeting to discipline or counsel him or her. Don't wait until an annual appraisal to give that kind of corrective feedback.

Pull Up an Easy Chair

Where do you plan to conduct the appraisal conversation? If you have an office—one with a ceiling and a door, not one that is a less-than-private cubicle—that would be the obvious choice. If you decide to use your office, make sure it is the proper atmosphere for this kind of conversation.

You've heard the advice that "location is everything" and it's no different when planning for a performance appraisal. For example if your office is cramped and uncomfortable, you might want to consider an alternative location. Likewise if your office traditionally has been known as the place where disciplinary meetings are held, you might want to find a more *neutral space*.

Sometimes a conference room can feel like a more neutral space. If there is an available space that you can reserve that doesn't carry any baggage with it, that might be a suitable alternative location. However, wherever you meet, make sure that that the room is private. A performance appraisal should be done in a confidential manner.

The Five Fatal Mistakes

Once the appraisal meeting has started, there are certain protocols that are expected. Now that you have prepared for the meeting with such care, don't blow it by committing errors that might seem minor to you but that could make a devastating impression on your employees. The following sections describe what we find to be the five most common and fatal mistakes managers can make during a performance appraisal.

No-No Number One: Taking Phone Calls During the Appraisal Meeting

If anyone has ever interrupted an important meeting with you to take a phone call, you probably know how inappropriate and downright rude it seems. It certainly gives the impression that a phone call is considered more important than you and what you are talking about.

Managers who take phone calls during appraisals are showing no respect for the person they are meeting with. Nearly everyone has voice mail nowadays—and some of you might even be fortunate enough to have support staff who can answer the phone for you and take a message. We really mean this—no phone calls—even from your own boss!

Close Up

A **neutral space** is an area that is considered safe, or a location that has no connections to previous emotionally charged or stressful events. If your office is known as the place where people are disciplined (or even terminated), it won't seem like a neutral space.

Empowerment Zone

We feel pretty passionate about this no phone calls rule. But if there really is some overriding emergency—such as a birth or death—and you are anticipating such a call, tell the employee in advance that you might have to take an emergency call—and ask for his or her understanding and patience.

No-No Number Two: Being Disorganized

Remember how important this meeting is to your employee. If you are not adequately prepared or are looking for files or notes during the meeting, it will give a negative impression. Your preparation, research, and note making should have occurred before the actual meeting with the employee. If you are unprepared and try to wing it anyway, the employee will know that and feel that they are not worth your advance preparation.

Wise Counsel

One of the most common mistakes managers make in any situation is to underestimate the intelligence of their employees.

Wise Counsel

Being Timid Tim can cause you—and those who follow you—serious problems (and possibly cost you and your company a lot of money) well into the future. Employees who receive less-than-honest performance appraisal are potential time bombs. If anyone in the future tries to give them a more truthful appraisal, some of these employees could create legal dilemmas (see Chapter 13).

No-No Number Three: Appearing Disinterested or Distracted

If some life event has occurred that leaves you unable to give the employee your full attention, you are better off postponing the appraisal meeting. It is very easy to read someone's face and see whether he or she really is paying attention or not. Don't think you can fool your employees into thinking you actually are listening when you're not.

Glancing at your watch, computer screen, the lights on your phone, or any other distraction is pretty apparent to the employee who is focused on you and this conversation. Once again, it's a matter of respect. If you are not fully tuned in, your employees will sense that (and probably tune you out!).

No-No Number Four: Being a Timid Tim

The appraisal conversation is a significant event that should be open and honest as well as motivational. There will be times when you will have to deal with difficult topics. As a manager, it is your responsibility to diplomatically cover all the necessary topics with the employee. If you are too timid to share information that needs to be shared, you are not doing your employee, yourself, or your company any favors.

Managers often will skirt issues that have a potential to cause disagreement. It is much easier to focus on safe areas with positive feedback. Areas needing development frequently are skipped over by Timid Tim—and those are the areas most in need of exploration. If you don't cover them until you are totally fed up, the employee will feel tricked and betrayed. "If I was so bad, why didn't you say something earlier?" is a common feeling that comes up when employees have had inadequate communication regarding performance. So even though the purpose here is not to discipline, a performance appraisal is the time to focus on general directions for improvement and to encourage the employee to help you plan for that.

No-No Number Five: Being a Rigid Rochelle

Conversely, some managers feel they are not doing an adequate job as a boss if they do not find something to criticize in every aspect of someone's performance. They can compliment only to a certain point, but then they usually will add some criticism lest their employees feel overly confident. Their aim might be to motivate, but often this rigid approach will have the opposite effect and will make employees feel there is no use in trying because nothing is good enough.

From the File Cabinet

A 30-year-old "wunderkind" just out of a Ph.D. program was made acting CEO of a well-established team of executives. Because he was much younger than his direct reports, he felt the need to prove his superiority when giving performance appraisals. He went out of his way to be critical of each person's performance even though he had worked with them only two months. One of the best and brightest on the team, the CFO who had led a dramatic improvement in the company's financial condition, also received a lukewarm appraisal and was given the impression that his praiseworthy accomplishment was merely an average expectation of the job. The CFO and others on the team soon found jobs elsewhere.

Opening Remarks

Okay, you've done your homework. You've made careful preparations. You have sworn to not make any of the five big mistakes. And the employee has arrived for an appraisal. What do you say now?

How About Those Red Sox?

As we've said before, breaking the ice with some small talk can relax both of you. It is important to choose the topic carefully, otherwise the small talk could backfire. Specifically, steer clear of controversial topics such as politics or religion. Try to find a safe topic that most people will have an opinion on—be it the weather, a sporting event, a television show. If you can open with some casual conversation, it will make the rest of your conversation easier. As we mentioned earlier in Chapter 8, "The Casual Approach: Can We Talk?" opening with a bit of small talk typically makes the conversation flow more readily. If you are the type who thinks that small talk has no place in a serious conversation, you might find it more difficult to get some people talking at all.

Just the Facts

It is good practice to start many kinds of conversations with ice-breaking "small talk." It is recommended for situations other than performance appraisals, such as interviewing applicants. It is considered a relationship-building technique and as such should be something you are interested in as an employee's manager.

Empowerment Zone

When you speak from the heart without trying to be superior or patronizing, the words will sound real and sincere. That kind of honesty can be disarming. And if you show your willingness to be that open and honest, it should open the door to an open and honest conversation.

The Preamble

After the small talk, you should make some opening remarks to address the reason for the meeting. Yes, of course, your employee already knows this, but this is the time to share your philosophy about performance appraisals. It's a good idea to have some opening remarks rehearsed. Explain your purpose: to reflect on past accomplishments, share feedback, and agree upon goals for the future. Your opening remarks will lay the groundwork for the actual performance feedback. Don't shortchange this opportunity to set a positive tone.

Talk about the company's goals and vision. If personal goals have been established already, link the employee's goals with the company's goals. If goals have not been established, here's your opportunity to identify goals that can be blended into the company's. Motivate the employee to see that his or her success is connected to the success of the company—and vice versa.

Sincerity Counts

Even though you might be addressing such lofty topics as company goals and vision, try to remain conversational and sincere. To speak to an employee as if you are making a speech to a crowd will not encourage a down-to-earth conversation.

If you truly believe the philosophy you are sharing, your comments should come out with truth and conviction. Employees will know if you are faking it, so don't share what you think is a company line if you don't believe it.

Conversational Rather than Adversarial

Using this sincerity, it's a good time to explain your method of reviewing performance. You could say, "My intention is to share my perceptions of your performance over the past year, not to criticize. We want to focus on accomplishment of goals and agree upon goals for the coming year."

Encourage a two-way conversation. The employee might remember things that you have forgotten. Acknowledge that and invite the employee to talk about such things and anything else he or she feels is pertinent.

The Least You Need to Know

➤ You need to feel good, physically and mentally, to deliver successful performance appraisals, so take care of yourself.

➤ Spend time to carefully prepare and practice each appraisal.

➤ Respect your employee's time by preparing adequately and allowing enough time for the meeting.

➤ Provide a comfortable, confidential location in which to meet.

➤ Schedule meetings for discipline or counsel separately from the appraisal.

➤ Avoid making the five most common mistakes during a performance appraisal.

➤ Open the meeting with sincere and honest conversation.

Chapter 11

Script or Ad-Lib?

In this Chapter

➤ How to deliver performance feedback

➤ Finding the positives in anyone's performance

➤ Tips on style

➤ Think behavior, not personality

If you've done a good job with your opening remarks, you and your employee should be relaxed enough to begin the actual performance review. You've set the stage—you are not going to focus on criticism, but rather on motivation.

This chapter will help you navigate successfully through performance feedback—and assess whether you are complimenting your employees or finding ways to help them to improve their job performance.

Handling the Form

If you have completed the company appraisal form, in your own manner or following convention, you now are faced with a decision. The employee has not yet seen the completed form. Should you read through it aloud, or should you let the employee read through it while you sit there in silence?

How you proceed is a matter of personal style. It also depends on the type of the form you are using. If the form has a list of traits or behaviors with a ratings scale, you could simply read down your list of ratings. You might want to highlight those items that have an unusually high or low rating. Those items call for more explanation; the employee deserves to know, and in fact might ask, why they have received the score they have.

Performance Review

Employee Name: _____   Date of Appraisal:_____

Reviewed by:_____   Department:_____

Period of Appraisal: _____   Division:_____

Ratings Scale:	Unacceptable	Needs Improvement	Meets Expectations	Outstanding
Score:	1	2	3	4

(Directions: Evaluate performance in each of the categories by placing score in far right column.)

Category	Explanation	Employee Score
1. Attendance	_____	
2. Punctuality	_____	
3. Initiative	_____	
4. Cooperation	_____	
5. Work Habits	_____	
6. Safety Habits	_____	
7. Accuracy	_____	
8. Productivity	_____	

This form illustrates a performance appraisal with a ratings system. Notice how the form calls for a "check the box" approach without requiring any behavioral description or reason for selecting the rating. Forms such as these often elicit subjective or personal responses.

Another approach is to take more of a "big picture" look at the appraisal. You could start by asking how the employee feels he or she has done over the past year (or whatever period you're talking about). Naturally, if the employee has completed a self-appraisal, you will know this already and can use that as a starting point of conversation.

Describe your interpretation of how successfully he or she has accomplished goals or expectations. Some people are very free about giving comments. Others might need prodding with questions such as, "Do you agree with my last statement?"

If the employee disagrees with your interpretations, give him or her your time and attention to explain his or her point of view. The employee might have ideas that you have not thought of. If after hearing the explanation you still are in disagreement, say something such as, "I understand your feelings about this. Let's try looking at it from another perspective."

Start with Positives

Regardless of whether you choose to read over the entire form or take a "big-picture" look, it's always best to start with positive feedback. Typically, it's not difficult to find a few or more areas of good performance. Opening a feedback session with positive examples sets an upbeat tone. We also stressed this technique in Chapter 8, "The Casual Approach: Can We Talk?" Whether the performance appraisal is formal or informal, many of the techniques remain the same.

In a best-case scenario, things will go well, and it won't be difficult to keep the mood upbeat. If the performance clearly is outstanding, this is a good time to encourage the employee to suggest ways for continued growth and success. If the performance is less than outstanding, you should sensitively plan how you will deliver the message and still be motivational. We describe how to do that in Chapter 12, "Dialogue is a Two-Way Street," and 13, "Potential Problems and Difficult Situations."

It's What You Do

When commenting on performance, focus on actual behaviors that you have observed. It's all too easy to fall back on complimenting subjective traits; for example, "You're really dependable—I like that about you."

Empowerment Zone

We recommend that you make the appraisal more conversational, which could mean not going over the form point by point. You're going to give the employee a copy of the form; he or she can read it later. Now is your time to ask for and give feedback.

Empowerment Zone

Don't underestimate the power of a sincere smile. It can help break the ice if need be, and it certainly sets a warm tone. Don't think employees can't spot a phony smile! They know if it's real—it's also obvious in your tone of voice.

It's much more effective to describe the behaviors that led you to make this judgment. For example, "You have never missed a deadline. I have consistently received the monthly reports by the fifteenth of the month." Another example on teamwork might be, "You routinely, sometimes as often as twice a week, offer to take work from your coworkers when you finish your billing and they are getting behind."

Commenting on actual behaviors shows that you have observed their performance and documenting actual behaviors can help to validate ratings if they ever are called into question.

Feedback DON'Ts

You want your meeting to continue in a positive and productive spirit, so it's important to keep in mind some of the things that can end or destroy the conversation rather quickly.

DON'T Patronize

There's nothing that turns an employee off faster than you coming on like a parent or the Supreme Being. Managers who talk like know-it-alls, always one-upping comments made by employees, don't encourage two-way conversation. Yes, you might be the boss, but the appraisal is supposed to encourage and clarify, not be an opportunity for you to show off your exalted position or knowledge.

From the File Cabinet

A new supervisor, fresh from his postgraduate program, was so determined to show off his higher education that he couldn't resist talking to his direct reports using an intellectual but obscure vocabulary. He seemed to enjoy the possibility that his employees might not know the meaning of the words he used. The fact was that all of his direct reports knew exactly what he was saying and bitterly resented his inability to speak to them as equal human beings using normal conversational language. Being pretentious rarely is impressive or effective.

DON'T Do All the Talking

There are times when managers have so much to say that they don't let the employee get a word in edgewise. Especially if the employee tends to be rather quiet, these managers can really take over and never look back. It might be attributed to nervousness, or the inability to allow silence in any conversation. Regardless, it is not an effective approach to appraisals. Feedback should be mutual in an appraisal. (We'll talk about techniques to encourage reticent employees to open up in Chapter 12.)

This is an opportunity for the employee to give you feedback on your management or leadership style. Other topics to explore could be the kinds of equipment, training, or support that would help the employee improve job performance. If you talk nonstop and never invite participation, your staff will get the impression that you are not interested in anyone's opinion but your own.

Empowerment Zone

Employees who feel disrespected and unappreciated might start looking for a job where they will get respect and where their opinions will be welcomed.

DON'T Answer Your Own Questions

This one is related to talking too much and is just as big a turnoff as doing all the talking. If employees take too long to answer questions, some managers just blurt out the answers for them.

For example, the manager says, "Your accuracy rate is 85 percent. Now don't you think you could bring that up to 95 percent by next month?"

After a split second, the manager continues, "Of course you could. That's your goal and I'll be looking for your improvement."

Allow the employee a reasonable amount of time to reflect on what you have said and to respond. In this scenario, you might not hear that there are legitimate roadblocks to improved performance, and you are not really getting employee buy-in on an agreed-upon goal. This "agreement" feels more like an ultimatum to the employee.

DON'T Dwell On the Negative

We've already recommended that you start with positives. However, suppose an employee has not met expectations in several areas of performance. If you simply review the list of failures and express your disappointment, it won't be a very motivating conversation.

We're not suggesting that you blow off talking about the unacceptable performance. This is your chance to find out why the employee is having a hard time meeting expectations. Ask the employee to explain the difficulties by asking questions such as

➤ Are you unclear on performance expectations?

➤ Are you having conflicts at work (or home) that are interfering with your ability to do the job?

➤ Do you feel qualified to do the job?

➤ Do you need more training?

➤ Is there some sort of support that could be provided?

Wise Counsel

If you are coming on gruffly to an employee, describing failed performance in great detail, you run the risk of an unhappy employee becoming a potentially disgruntled employee. He or she could call in sick for the next week or more—or worse—to achieve whatever might make him or her feel avenged.

Close Up

The **halo effect** is the technique of rating all employees as "good" or "acceptable" in all areas regardless of actual performance.

It's also important to find out if the employee is just in the wrong job. The situation could be a bad fit for the employee's skills or your company's culture.

This is not a time to beat up your employees (figuratively speaking, of course), but to coach them to find out what about the job is working for them—and what isn't, and what could make them happier. You might be in a position to coach them right out of your department and into something that is a better fit and where they will do better—for the improvement of your company as well as the employee.

Being supportive and encouraging, you can have a very motivational effect on your employees' performance and morale. It also might motivate them to move on, but you will help them to make the decision on their own, rather than your having to fire them.

Having said this, there is no guarantee that even the most adept and sincere delivery will always have a positive effect, or that you won't have an angry employee on your hands if things don't work out. (We detail ways of handling potentially violent situations in Chapter 13.)

The Halo Effect

The opposite of being overly negative is known as the *halo effect*. This all-too-common method of giving consistently—but undeservedly—positive performance appraisals is the bane of new managers everywhere. (We give you specific techniques of dealing with the aftermath of the halo effect in Chapter 13.)

The halo effect amounts to taking the easy way out in a number of ways. First, if you are using a ratings system form, it's very easy to place an "X" or checkmark in the same box all the way down the form.

	Poor	Needs Improvement	Good	Outstanding
1. Follows Directions	____	____	x	____
2. Punctuality	____	____	x	____
3. Cooperation	____	____	x	____
4. Writing Skills	____	____	x	____
5. Accuracy	____	____	x	____
6. Attendance	____	____	x	____
7. Courtesy	____	____	x	____
8. Customer Service	____	____	x	____

This is a sample performance appraisal that uses a ratings system. Managers who are prone to the "halo effect" typically rate all employees as good or acceptable whether they deserve it or not. Also typically, there would be no further explanation to justify the ratings.

It's also easier to give an entirely good performance appraisal with no feedback for improvement—it's a no-brainer. It might be easy, but it does absolutely no good for the company or the employee. The employee will get a false sense of security, or will get the impression that the manager has no interest in his or her performance.

The opposite of the halo effect is—what else?—the horns effect in which a manager will rate an employee as "needing improvement" in everything. It's unlikely that every facet of someone's performance is at the same level. And if you document it as such, you had better have some behavioral examples to justify all those ratings. Without them, you could be accused of discrimination.

Empowerment Zone

It's distressing for an employee to work somewhere for years, getting excellent reviews, only to be given a review by a new manager who rips him or her apart. The employee feels it is a total betrayal—and in a way, it is. Either the employee thinks the new supervisor is unfair in the appraisal, or that the old supervisor was untruthful. Either way, it feels like a trick to the employee.

From the File Cabinet

The halo effect is one of the most frequent and potentially damaging problems in corporate performance appraisals. Nearly every company has a situation in which a manager wants to terminate an employee, but finds after a review of the personnel folder that all of the performance appraisals are good ones. It's painful to review a personnel folder and find that although there are several disciplinary write-ups for excessive absence, all the performance appraisals rate the employee with excellent attendance! This kind of inconsistent documentation either handcuffs companies from taking any action or leaves them wide open for wrongful discharge lawsuits.

Is It Behavior, Personality, or Work Skills?

Trying to focus solely on work skills when someone's personality is extremely different from your own can be very hard to do. There are many people in today's world whose lifestyles might be radically different from yours, and it's hard to not be conscious of those differences on a daily basis when you work closely together.

Just the Facts

The difference between a behavior and a personality trait is that a behavior is an observable action or way of conducting oneself, whereas a trait is a distinguishing characteristic or quality. An example of a behavior is "arriving to work on time;" an example of a trait is "punctual."

Your job as a manager requires that you look beyond what might seem like peculiar behavior and evaluate how well the job is being accomplished. For example, Howard's personality might rub you the wrong way—he might be quiet and reserved, whereas you are outgoing and talkative. It might frustrate you that Howard ignores your overtures to engage in conversation. But unless that conversation is essential to the work being done, you cannot be critical of his performance just because he is quiet.

In another example, if Sarah never accompanies the staff when they socialize after work, should she be criticized for not being a team player? How she conducts herself after work should not be evaluated in an appraisal. It's how she works with her co-workers during the course of the workday that matters. She might be quite effective working with others on the job.

From the File Cabinet

Some American companies have criticized workers for speaking in a native language other than English. Their argument was that speaking together in a language other than English seemed exclusionary to other workers. The other side of the argument was that not allowing workers to communicate in their native tongue was discriminatory, especially when it was not with customers or other co-workers with whom they needed to interface on a business basis. The courts decided that you cannot enforce an English-only rule if it does not relate to the work being done. Conclusion: Respect differences that do not interfere with business.

Remember to look for observable behaviors that have some effect on performing the actual work or have some impact on the job being done. Try to express the behavior in an active sentence. You might want to praise an employee for displaying a trait—you can still do this in a behavioral context by putting it in a sentence that includes an action verb. Here are some examples:

➤ Sam shows he is a good team player by consistently contributing in team meetings and giving constructive feedback to his co-workers about their ideas.

➤ Mindy displays great pride in her work by consistently submitting reports that are not only accurate, but also extremely organized and easy to follow.

➤ George shows initiative by regularly asking to be included in new projects and trying new skills that he would like to master.

➤ Marjorie's leadership is apparent in the way she listens to employee suggestions and follows up on them.

Using this technique shows that you have taken the time to observe the behavior you are describing. If you haven't actually observed someone's performance, talk to someone who has.

Take some time to practice making statements that describe a quality, and then justify it with a behavioral example. There are a number of books on the market that give you endless examples of this technique. But with a little practice, you probably will become a master in a short time.

The Least You Need to Know

➤ Using the performance appraisal form and following its format while giving feedback is a matter of personal preference.

➤ When giving feedback, start with the positives.

➤ Don't patronize, monopolize the conversation, or stress the negative.

➤ Avoid using the halo (or horns) effect when rating performance.

➤ Evaluate actual work performance, not personality or behavioral traits.

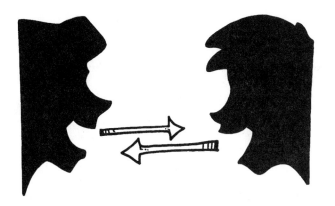

Dialogue Is a Two-Way Street

Employees who truly feel empowered usually have no problem holding their own during a performance appraisal. And some managers know how to share the conversation. But sometimes a two-way conversation is difficult to create.

Feedback should go both ways during a performance appraisal. As thorough as your observations might be, it's possible that you might learn new facts at this meeting. Hopefully you will gain a greater understanding of your employees' views of the workplace. And if you want to truly agree upon future goals, you need open, honest communication.

This chapter will show you ways to ensure that the performance appraisal is an even conversation shared between two people. We'll share tips on how to encourage employees to take part in the process—even the ones who are determined to not participate.

Encouraging Participation

Let's face it: Some people need very little encouragement to participate. These are the folks who will offer their opinions at the slightest opportunity, even when it's not asked for. But there are others who don't respond as readily. How can you ensure that your employees feel comfortable and welcome to share their thoughts during a performance appraisal?

Start with a Question

A common technique to get people talking is to ask an *open-ended question*. This technique is used frequently when interviewing someone for a job. It will help you to gain more information than if you were to use a *closed question* such as, "Do you think XYZ was a successful project?" It's quite easy for the employee to answer "yes" and leave it at that.

Close Up

An **open-ended question** is a question that is designed and worded to elicit more than just a "yes" or "no" answer. A **closed question** is one that can be answered with a one-word answer, such as "yes" or "no."

Empowerment Zone

Not only will using open-ended questions help you with performance appraisals, they also should make your next blind date or evening with the in-laws a lot more interesting.

Instead ask, "Could you describe what made XYZ project a successful project for you?" Or if that is not the case, "What made this project frustrating or impossible to do the way you thought it should be done?" or "How could it be done differently next time?"

Open-ended questions often start with phrases such as

- ➤ "How would you describe ..."
- ➤ "Tell me about ..."
- ➤ "Could you give me some details on ..."
- ➤ "In your opinion what is the best way ..."

Such beginnings invite a response that is longer than just a single word.

One way of getting around very brief responses is to ask, "Can you elaborate on that further?" Even if the employee says "No, I can't," keep going with "It might be difficult for you to be more specific, but if I don't hear more from you about what does or doesn't work for you, it makes it harder to fairly evaluate you, or to plan for your future needs. Can you please try to help me with this?"

If you know a certain employee tends to be rather quiet, you could plan some open-ended questions prior to the meeting. Include them in your notes and use them if necessary to get the employee talking. Remember, part of this process is to try to understand an employee's world of work and their experiences of triumph and frustration.

Do You Want to Know a Secret?

Probably the best advice we can share about getting people to participate fully is simply to listen—really listen—to their responses. By listening thoughtfully you let employees know that their comments matter—that they are important and worthy of your attention. How often does this happen to you: Someone asks you a question, then doesn't listen and almost answers the question for you! It's pretty irritating.

Those of us who are more extroverted and who like talking fall into this trap. We ask a question and don't listen to the answer while we formulate our next question or comment in our minds. Our attention—or lack of it—shows on our faces. Effective listening, often called *active listening*, is a skill worth practicing and developing.

Good listeners are highly valued as communicators because people enjoy talking to them. By listening and responding appropriately to what you are hearing, the conversation is dynamic and real—it's in the moment. And it builds rapport like nothing else during a performance appraisal.

Close Up

Active listening means listening in an attentive and thoughtful manner, and showing obvious interest in what is being said. It often is accompanied by body posture, eye contact, head nodding, and short words indicating your understanding, such as "I see," and asking appropriate questions that indicate that you have heard and understood what the speaker has said.

I Say Again ...

Another suggestion that is part of active listening is learning to summarize or to paraphrase. This basically means letting the employee talk for a while and then, when he or she seems to be done and waiting for you to respond, you recap by bringing out the main points of what you just heard.

For example, "So John, let me see if I get this right. During the last quarter you have been unable to make your numbers because engineering was late in coming out with their updated version of MXVPZ. Customers are unwilling to buy the system until it includes that upgrade. You are asking for firm release dates so that you can make the customers more comfortable with committing to the product."

If John was unsure whether you were paying attention before, your accurate reflections of the main points he made will at the very least show him you were actively listening. Summarizing and paraphrasing are skills that, if practiced effectively, help to prevent misunderstandings as well as promote an atmosphere of mutual respect.

Hold the Interruptions, Please

Being a good listener means that you should not interrupt someone in the middle of a thought or sentence. There are times you might feel you know what the other

person is saying and don't need any further explanation. However, interrupting is almost always looked upon as disrespectful. While the employee is telling his or her side of the story, it's possible that something might come up that will change your opinion about or rating of his or her performance. So listen—without interruption.

Eye-to-Eye

Good, steady eye contact also encourages open, honest conversation. By looking into another person's eyes, you signal your complete attention. If you look away from the employee—at the floor or at your notes or documents, the employee might not be able to tell whether or not you are actively listening.

From the File Cabinet

Here's a rather extreme example of poor eye contact: In the CEO's office at a large corporation, a candidate for corporate director of HR was being interviewed. The CEO was very prominent in his industry, but he was very uncomfortable maintaining eye contact for longer than a second or two. During the interview he continually glanced at the floor, until at one point he leaned completely sideways in his chair and began pulling lint off his socks. He never skipped a beat in the conversation, but his behavior made the candidate more than uncomfortable. And it gave a very odd (and unflattering) impression of the company!

You can take eye contact too far and actually stare at someone, which is almost worse than no eye contact at all! It's a matter of intensity—our advice is to keep it comfortable and warm. Be observant of the person you are meeting with. This will help to guide you on what is comfortable for them.

Take a Few Notes

It's appropriate to take notes during an appraisal meeting. You don't want to forget any new information heard during the appraisal. It's advisable to tell the employee what you are doing by saying, "I'm going to write this down while we are discussing it. Please continue. I am listening." And if you do take notes, make sure you are doing it with an open mind and not doing this just for show. Again, sincerity is the key here—otherwise you will breed resentment, not respect.

You shouldn't be writing for the entire conversation. That will make eye contact nonexistent. If there is a point at which you feel you should take down notes in detail, ask to pause for a moment while you write.

Wise Counsel

Keep in mind that people from other cultures have different norms about eye contact. However, just because someone is from a different culture or country does not mean they actually practice different norms. If in doubt observe their behavior to learn what is their practice.

Respect Opinions

In a real two-way conversation, you should hear different points of view. Although you don't have to agree with different opinions, it's important to respect the employee's right to have that opinion. There is nothing wrong with saying, "I understand your point of view, although I don't share it." And a follow-up could be, "How can we move our two views of success closer to each other?"

Give the employee an opportunity to share openly. If you were to loudly disagree, laugh, or deride opposing views, the employee might decide not to trust you with any more information. In summary, here are six tips to a successful two-way conversation:

➤ Ask open-ended questions.

➤ Listen actively.

➤ Summarize to ensure understanding.

➤ Don't interrupt.

➤ Tell the employee you'll be taking notes; then take them.

➤ Respect differences of opinion.

Focus on Performance, Not Money

Very frequently, performance appraisals are directly tied to salary increases. It's natural to assume that good performance should result in an increase in salary—or a *merit increase*. Unfortunately, when this direct link is stressed, employees might tend to focus only on the increase rather than on the appraisal itself.

Close Up

Merit increases usually are the end product of a formal performance appraisal program that connects certain levels of performance with varying levels of salary increase.

Empowerment Zone

If you don't separate the performance appraisal and the merit increase into two meetings you run the risk of feeling pressured to start the conversation by announcing the increase, if any. The rest of the meeting then might be spent trying to justify the decision. You will never have a productive two-way conversation if you open with the money part.

Keeping the two concepts separate is not the easiest thing to do. It's true that things other than money motivate people, but almost everyone is interested in getting a raise. Perhaps the simplest way to keep the concepts separate for the employee is to physically separate the discussions. Explain that there will be two meetings—one to review performance and the second to discuss the salary issues.

Your reason for separating the two concepts also can be related to having a two-way conversation. During the first meeting, the employee might bring things up that can change the appraisal result. To remain open to potential changes, you will not confirm any salary increase until the appraisal is completed.

The announcement regarding the two meetings should be made when you roll out the appraisal program, or at least in advance of the appraisal meeting. Give the employees a chance to understand the concept and the reasoning behind it. If they know the arrangement in advance, they will be better prepared to have that two-way conversation during the appraisal meeting.

Looking Ahead

Another important aspect of the performance appraisal is setting goals for the coming year. By identifying and agreeing upon goals, you lay the groundwork for the future and make next year's appraisal process more clear-cut. Goals that are measurable and observable are easier to evaluate—try to keep that in mind. If an employee suggests a goal that sounds vague, ask, "How would we know if you were successful at this?" or "How could we measure that?"

Tie In Corporate Goals

If your company has made available a list of corporate goals, bring out the list so you can review them with the employee. No matter what level the staff member, employee contributions should be tied in to some—if not all—of the corporate goals. Some employees might see connections easily. Others might need your coaching to see the relationship between what they do day to day and the company's goals.

Tie into Personal Values

As a manager, you might already be familiar with an employee's values or motivating forces. Using that knowledge will help you craft goal statements that will meet the employee's needs as well as relating to company goals.

When working toward goals that have mutual value to the employee and the company, industry-related educational goals can be identified. The need or desire for inside training, or outside higher learning, can easily be seen to meet both employee and company requirements for quality and excellence.

Buy-in usually happens when the employees choose or agree on the goals. People work harder on goals they believe in; they shouldn't be forced to accept objectives they don't believe in. Find ways to make the goals your employees' choice as well as yours.

Make 'Em Stretch

As in any goal-setting process, don't be afraid to raise the bar. Try to ensure that goals are achievable but somewhat of a stretch. For employees whose performance is marginal, setting the goal to meet the job's basic expectations might be enough of a stretch.

Empowerment Zone

In some economic environments, raises are small enough that to some employees the feedback and recognition are more important than the raise. If you value an employee, let him or her know that with specific and insightful feedback. Formulated or unfocused feedback has poor impact.

Wise Counsel

If management and staff have been left out of the corporate goal formulating process, the goals might not be realistic. If meeting goals isn't practiced at the top, your job is tougher. Show your people that you practice what you preach—even if your superiors don't.

From the File Cabinet

At a large company kickoff for a Total Quality Management (TQM) program, some people believed the program would lead to more accountability and better employee relations and performance. Others thought it was the "consulting flavor of the month." With over 100 managers and supervisors present, it was ironic that the CEO began to publicly humiliate one of his directors because some piece of equipment was not present. What do you think this did for company-wide respect and dignity, two of the newly stated goals of the company?

Empowerment Zone

The number of goals is variable depending on your philosophy, business, and personal preferences. We suggest that you have at least four major goals identified for each employee, although the number may vary depending on the level of the employee. For example, higher-level staff may have a greater number of goals than more entry-level staff.

When you come to agreement on the goal, use your summarizing technique to make sure you both agree on the words and their meaning. Write it down, right then and there, to be sure you each are clear about the goal. Continue this process with each goal until you have a sufficient number to work toward.

Reaching Closure

Once you have had your two-way conversation about performance, made appropriate notes, and agreed upon goals, you're almost done. Before you close the meeting, ask the employee for any additional comments.

Give the employee a copy of the completed appraisal form. If you have made substantial changes on the form, make sure you give the employee a copy with all the changes. The employee should have a chance to write any additional comments on the form if desired. Some employees might not be ready to do this on the spot. Let them take a copy with them, think about it, and if they choose to, add their comments to the form.

If the employee chooses to take the form and write comments later, ask that he or she return it at your next meeting. At that meeting, give the employee the opportunity to add comments directly on the original appraisal. Be sure that both of you sign the completed original performance appraisal. Also be sure to give the employee a copy of the signed original. The completed original should be placed in the employee's personnel file.

Always make sure to have the appropriate signatures on the performance appraisal. The appraisal could be needed to support a decision for promotion, demotion, or termination. The form also could be discovered during a legal proceeding. Signatures show agreement of both parties (and could help to protect you and your company in the event of a lawsuit).

At this point the process is complete and you are done. Congratulations!

Empowerment Zone

If you have not reached agreement on every point, an employee might refuse to sign the appraisal form. Should this occur, find someone (perhaps another manager) to serve as a witness, then write on the form, "Employee refuses to sign." Then you and the witness to the refusal also should sign.

The Least You Need to Know

➤ Be sure each appraisal is a two-way conversation between supervisor and employee.

➤ Use the six tips to encourage participation.

➤ Separate the appraisal meeting from the meeting to announce a salary increase.

➤ Mutually agree on goals for the future.

➤ Don't forget to sign the appraisal form when it is completed, and give a copy to the employee.

Chapter 13

Potential Problems and Difficult Situations

In This Chapter

➤ How to deal with difficult appraisal meetings

➤ How to deal with emotional employees

➤ How to recognize and deal with a potentially violent employee

➤ Handling the "halo effect" from previous appraisals

➤ Dealing with negativity

Our sincerest hope is that if you have followed our advice on honest, sincere, and timely feedback, you won't run into any serious problems. However, there is a chance that you are a new manager having to clean up from the sins of managers past.

There also are some situations in which you might have to tread carefully. We want to share our tips on how to deal sensitively but effectively with some of these potential problems.

If You Anticipate Disagreement

Despite our best intentions, most of us occasionally come into contact with someone whom we cannot get along with. In addition, some workers might have a style that

Empowerment Zone

Remember to take good care of yourself before a difficult appraisal (see Chapter 10, "Prepare and Practice"). Try to anticipate where the disagreements might occur and write out possible responses. Stick to performance facts and arm yourself against being drawn into an emotional response.

affects you in an emotional and negative way. When such people report to you, they challenge your management capabilities. Before giving performance appraisals to these people, you will need to do some serious preparation.

What is it about this person that you have trouble with? We've previously discussed the problem of personality conflict. Only if it in some way impairs their own or others' performance should you critique someone's personality in a performance review.

But what if the problem is more serious than a personality conflict? What if you've had issues with this person that resulted in emotional outbursts? You might have appraised this employee in the past and had an unfortunate outcome. How do you handle people's displays of emotion?

From the File Cabinet

At a big-city police department, Officer Friendly, who takes reports from the previous shift, typically blasts, lectures, and puts down the officer giving the report, especially if that officer is relatively new on the force. Officer Friendly is otherwise highly skilled and experienced with excellent work habits. His sergeant and captain are aware of how harsh and punishing he can be to new recruits, but they just attribute it to his personality style because "it doesn't affect his work."

In reality, such behavior affects everyone's work. New officers tend to avoid Officer Friendly and are reluctant to tell him important information that could prove to be critical to the department. Turnover is high and morale is low.

Emotional Outbursts

Emotional outbursts typically occur if the evaluation is not a good one. However, it could happen that an employee will burst into tears if the appraisal is good—but just not good enough. For example, the rating was "good" when the employee expected "outstanding." Tears or other displays of emotion can be rather disconcerting.

In the presence of tears, it's important that you maintain your own calm. Give the person room to show this kind of emotion, and don't assume you need to do something to change the response. Often, this behavior is involuntary and can be a sign of hurt, surprise, fear, or feelings of rejection.

If you are the type that can't stand such behavior—maybe you think tears are a foolish waste of time—try to reframe how you are looking at it. You might not deal with your emotions this way, but it is one way that some people cope—by showing open emotion. You could busy yourself finding a box of tissues, but it's best to not show any emotion yourself, other than some true empathy.

You could try saying something along the lines of, "I know this can be a hard process. I'm just trying to give you feedback on your work performance."

Allow some time for the employee to regain composure. It is all right to ask the person if he or she is okay or needs some time before going on.

If the employee is unable to stop crying after a few minutes, you might suggest that the person leave the room for a little while to get some fresh air. If there is not a private place for the employee to regroup, offer to leave them in your office for a few minutes, and tell them you will return to continue. Don't try to continue the conversation until the tears are in check. Rescheduling the appointment for a later time might be your last resort.

When Anger Bursts Out

Should an employee shout at you in anger during the course of the appraisal, it is especially important for you to remain nonemotional. Shouting back, even if you think that that's the only way you will be heard, will serve only to escalate the shouting match.

Sometimes an effective way of reducing someone's volume is to start talking very quietly in return. The shouter might have to lower his or her voice

Wise Counsel

Although you might find it difficult to remain silent, it is oftentimes a reasonable response during an emotional outburst, at least at first. Many people have an *irresistible* urge to keep talking just to break the silence. This is one of those situations where the less said the better.

Just the Facts

Meeting conflict with the same level of intensity only serves to bump it up a notch. Research on sibling behavior in families shows that if there are three rounds of "You did it"—"No, You did it!" there is a very high likelihood that there will be physical escalation (such as to hitting).

to hear what you are saying, and maintaining a calm demeanor might help to reduce the emotion. However, if the shouting continues you should quietly tell the person to take a break until he or she has regained control. If you feel threatened in any way, don't hesitate to ask for assistance.

The Threat of Aggression

Maintaining a safe workplace is an ethical and legal requirement. And certainly you want to keep yourself safe from any workplace violence. If you believe there is a potential for violence from any employee, you must take measures to protect yourself and your place of work. In fact, if you are thinking along these lines you owe it to yourself to get consultation from others including those outside your workplace. It is important to be balanced in your approach and to make sure you have the facts to support your concerns. On the one hand you don't want to jump to conclusions, yet you don't want to ignore your intuition. Reasons to believe there may be a potential for violence are not always easy to assess. Certainly a report of an employee threatening violence would give you reason to investigate the threat and take precautions if you can establish that the threat did indeed occur.

Empowerment Zone

An excellent resource for in-depth information on potential violence is Gavin de Beker's book *The Gift of Fear, Survival Signals That Protect Us From Violence* (Little Brown and Company, 1997).

Other warning signs of unstable behavior will follow, but there is no sure way to absolutely predict future violence. Unfortunately the best predictor of a person's potential for violence is a past history of violence, something most employers are not always aware of. We have uncovered situations and there are some pretty famous cases where in fact employers were aware of but ignored violent or very disturbing behavior, only to have a much more serious incident follow later in time.

Most people do not become violent, yet there are many instances of violence each year in the workplace. It is also important to review your company's policies on violence.

A potentially dangerous employee often exhibits warning signs and signals. These include

➤ Unusual or erratic behavior.

➤ Making threats of any kind directed at employees or supervisors.

➤ Paranoia, in which the employee thinks everyone is against him or her, or sees signs of things being connected that are not.

➤ Prior encounters with law enforcement or a history of assaultive behavior.

➤ Obsession with, access to, or bragging about weapons.

➤ Abuse of drugs or alcohol.

➤ Frequent job changes.

➤ Marginal performance.

➤ Frequent anger or frustration.

➤ Inability to deal with criticism.

➤ Frequently holding grudges for a long time.

➤ Possible low self-esteem.

➤ Inability to accept responsibility; blames others.

➤ Difficulty concentrating.

➤ Rigidity in approach to people and problems.

➤ Making statements that reflect feelings of hopelessness.

➤ Other co-workers expressing fear of this person.

Close Up

The **Employee Assistance Program (EAP)** is an employee benefit frequently provided by employers. The EAP should be staffed by licensed mental health providers who can do psychological assessments and provide brief treatment for employees.

The preceding behaviors are warning signs of a potentially high-risk employee. Employees who exhibit these signs should be handled with extreme care. If you have an *Employee Assistance Program (EAP)*, this is the time to strongly encourage the employee to make an immediate appointment. Before proceeding with a performance appraisal, especially if performance is substandard, consider whether this person should continue working for your company. Even if you decide to terminate an employee, you still want to offer them some help with their problems. Your EAP is one resource. If you don't have an EAP, then it is a good idea to locate a local mental health professional and refer your employee there with an offer to assist with payment for a specific number of visits.

If an employee has previously been identified as potentially dangerous, you must plan in advance before holding a meeting with this individual for any reason. In all honesty, if this person has exhibited a number of the symptoms of a dangerous person, a performance appraisal probably is not what is required. If the employee actually has committed violence or already has been counseled and failed to improve significant work deficits, then terminating the person's employment with your company might be the best solution. If the situation is not that far along, or the person has been a good and stable employee in the past, maybe a fitness for duty evaluation is called for before going into performance issues.

From the File Cabinet

One employee we worked with was referred to the EAP because she was saying things to her co-workers that were scaring them. The EAP had originally consulted with the manager and HR about how to approach the employee and help her accept an immediate referral for professional assessment and possible treatment. A psychiatric evaluation determined that the employee was suffering from psychosis, including paranoia and delusions. With some time off and the appropriate help, this valued and long-term employee eventually was able to return to work without future problems.

Wise Counsel

Don't let your independent spirit or machismo get in the way of your judgment. In the face of potential danger, it's better to have help with you or nearby. Even Batman had Robin as a backup.

To prepare for a meeting with a potentially violent employee:

1. Don't plan to meet with the person by yourself. Have your superior present or ask another manager whom this employee likes or respects to be present.

2. If you have a violence response team or a security department, appoint a security guard (or member of the violence response team) to be in the immediate area, near your office—not necessarily by your office door as this might be shaming or humiliating, but somewhere where they will be seen by the employee as they come toward your office.

3. Review your company emergency plan, if one exists.

4. Carefully plan your comments. You must not use words that could humiliate the employee or make him or her feel ashamed.

5. Be prepared to refer the person to the EAP or some other form of counseling, if needed.

6. Have a plan for summoning appropriate help in place before the meeting.

7. Do not have the employee sit between you and the door, possibly blocking your quick escape.

Unexpected Violence

It's possible that someone you might never suspect to be potentially violent might erupt uncontrollably during an appraisal meeting. What should you do then?

This is the time to activate your company's emergency response plan if one exists, and to alert someone from your violence response team or security department. If this is not an option, or while you are waiting for help to arrive, these tips can help you keep the situation from escalating.

➤ Do not respond emotionally, if at all possible.

➤ Don't avoid eye contact—but don't stare, as this could be interpreted as a threat.

➤ Speak in a slow, matter-of-fact manner, using a low tone and a calm voice.

➤ Allow some silence rather than responding emotionally.

➤ Try not to show fear, even if you feel it.

➤ Don't engage in counter-threats.

➤ Focus on the future rather than the past.

➤ Try and speak in a firm but soothing voice, trying to calm things down.

➤ Don't crowd the employee; give him or her physical and emotional space.

➤ Never block a doorway—that can make a paranoid person more nervous (and it's a good idea to not have the employee between you and the doorway in case you need to leave).

➤ Really listen to what the person is saying and use the summarizing technique to repeat what you've heard.

➤ Don't criticize the behavior the employee is exhibiting.

➤ Try to be empathetic while remaining cautious.

Just the Facts

It is the law in several states that companies have a company-wide emergency plan in place for responding to a potentially violent employee (or customer). If you do not have such a plan, consider crafting one, and see if you can get input from specialists such as mental health professionals, law enforcement, and/or security specialists.

You must always take threats seriously, even if you don't really believe the employee plans to carry them out. Clearly not all threats are the same, but depending on your policies, even the threat of violence may be grounds for immediate termination. It never hurts to get consultation from different sources when you are in this type of situation.

What to Say When

No matter what the employee's behavior, it's important that you continue to treat him or her with respect and dignity. Sometimes this isn't easy, but research has shown that humiliating someone who is out of control will only escalate the unwanted behavior.

Just the Facts

A threat is an expression of an intent to do harm. One threat expert points out that people who make threats usually are desperate and feel they have very little power. The value of a threat is that it is meant to cause fear and uncertainty.

Here are a couple of sample lines to use during difficult situations:

➤ Should the employee make threats to you, try to downplay it by saying something like "I can tell you are upset now, and anyone might be in your situation. I know after you've had time to think about it, you'll realize that you don't mean what you just said."

➤ Should the decision be to terminate the employment of the individual, say something like "We do care about you as a person and will try to give you the assistance we can in helping you make a transition to a new job." A referral to an EAP at this point would be appropriate.

Countering the Halo Effect

It's all too common for a new manager to discover that for years his or her predecessor has given remarkably similar and positive appraisals to everyone in the department—even the poorest of performers. Giving good appraisals is easy and usually it will not cause any conflict or argument during an appraisal. However, taking this easy way out can leave new managers with situations that are stressful, if not potentially volatile and expensive.

Typically a new manager can size up the strong from the weak performers by spending some time getting to know the people in the human resources department. It might seem quite simple at first—make an action plan for the weaker performers, give them an opportunity to improve, and replace them if they don't. However, in reviewing the personnel files of the weaker performers, what happens when all of their previous performance appraisals are good?

Terminate 'Em

Some of the more aggressive managers have proceeded with terminations despite the past positive appraisals. And some of the more litigious employees have easily found attorneys willing to defend them in wrongful termination cases. Sure, you probably can maintain such a termination, but usually at a very big cost—we're talking VERY BIG cost—like several years' worth of compensation. Is terminating a weak employee worth the expense?

What You Can Do About Substandard Performance

Do you want to accept substandard performance rather than risk a lawsuit? No, you don't. What you can do is start telling the employee the truth—tactfully. Find out why this employee's performance is less than acceptable. Is it from a false sense of security or are there other issues affecting his or her ability to perform? It might be a training issue or some other correctable problem.

When you give feedback to a "haloed" employee,

➤ Be encouraging and optimistic—your new enthusiasm could inject energy into a burned-out staff.

➤ Focus on goal-setting.

➤ Clarify your expectations.

➤ Explore reasons that the employee has not met expectations.

➤ Probe to discover what motivates the employee.

➤ Treat the employee as an individual with individual needs and goals.

➤ Be honest about what you feel are the employee's shortcomings.

➤ Don't criticize your predecessor, but encourage the employee to look at things differently.

Wise Counsel

Unless your company has money to burn, you don't want to risk a wrongful discharge case. Even if you win, which seldom is certain, your legal fees and lost productivity costs are going to be sizeable. This is definitely a time to look before you leap.

Just the Facts

One recurring reason for performance failure is that an employee was promised an orientation that either didn't occur or was much shorter than planned or promised.

Sure, this is going to take some time—if you are expecting an instant solution, you'd better have the financial backing to afford a potential lawsuit.

By taking the time to learn their feelings and behaviors, you might be successful in winning over these employees. Give them the opportunity to adapt to the changes that you bring to the company or department. Some, if not all, might adapt quickly and well to the changes you introduce.

141

The Negative Employee

We've previously mentioned the employees who find the dark side of everything. No matter what the topic, these individuals will find something negative to focus on. They are the pessimists who seem to have been born under a dark cloud. Very often these people have fallen under the influence of some negative mentor—someone who has made the dark side appear glamorous.

No matter the source of their negativity, these people are very challenging to deal with in the workplace. Some of them are quite verbal and perhaps even charismatic.

Wise Counsel

If you are a new manager evaluating challenging employees, be sure to assess whether they pose real problems to productivity or morale. Also take a look at whether any safety issues have been ignored in the department as problem employees may often, intentionally or unintentionally, ignore them.

Wise Counsel

It's important that you distinguish whether an employee just says negative things or actually is threatening the safety of others or the organization. In most cases, these individuals are full of words but very little action.

Their constant chatter can influence those who work around them. They are capable of doing a lot of damage to a department or even to a company unless they are dealt with properly.

These tips can help you to be more successful in giving feedback to the negative employee:

➤ Meet with the employee individually to say that you have observed his or her dissatisfaction with the job and the company.

➤ Ask if there is anything you can do to help change the negative perceptions.

➤ Probe to find out what exactly it is that makes the employee so unhappy. "Everything" is not an acceptable answer—you want specifics.

➤ Stress that if there are actual problems, you are ready and willing to deal with them.

➤ Be sympathetic and don't judge the employee— you sincerely want to find out what is the source of the dissatisfaction.

➤ Share with the employee how his or her behavior has negatively affected co-workers. Make it clear that as a concerned manager, it is your place to ensure that negative comments and behavior don't continue.

➤ Let the employee know that any kind of intimidating behavior is unacceptable coming from any employee, and warn them that behavior that borders on threatening, or actual threats, might be grounds for termination, and you don't want that to happen. (This is when an employee has exhibited this kind of behavior or you have reports of employees acting in this way.)

From the File Cabinet

Kate met with her manager and described how she was overworked and completely stressed out. The manager was empathetic and asked Kate to be more specific. She said that her co-worker Janet was always dumping on her and on the other staff. The department was always short-staffed, had difficulty hiring replacements, and was using temps who kept quitting. Janet also apparently was giving the others the hardest work to do. The manager told Kate she would talk to Janet, and gave her permission to turn down Janet's work requests. Kate went to the EAP to get help in being more assertive.

Sometimes when you let the negative person know you are on to his or her behaviors, the employee will clean up the act. If the employee is in denial, this is a time to draw a connection between the negativity and how this is making it difficult for the employee to meet the goals and visions of the company. You've got to be sure of your facts during such a meeting. If the behavior is contrary to what your company stands for, you must make that point in the performance appraisal. It is one of those times you can confidently issue an ultimatum—either cheer up or ship out.

The Least You Need to Know

➤ Spend extra time preparing for appraisal meetings that you anticipate will be difficult.

➤ Don't let yourself be drawn into an emotional response.

➤ Pay attention to the warning signs of a potentially violent employee.

➤ Become familiar with techniques to deal with an out-of-control employee.

➤ Coach "haloed" employees to better performance or another job.

➤ Don't let negative employees bring down department morale.

Aftershocks

Once you have finished delivering all the performance appraisals you are responsible for, you probably will heave a giant sigh of relief. You've met your goal of giving all your direct reports a performance appraisal. Congratulations!

But your job is not finished. In fact, it has only just begun. Managing performance is a job that doesn't end with a completed performance appraisal. Ideally it's a continuous process. The time right after an annual appraisal is the perfect time to make a commitment to continue managing the performance of your direct reports. In front of you is the document reflecting the goals you set and the agreements you made. How are you going to measure whether and how these goals and agreements are accomplished?

This chapter is dedicated to your activities after the (in most cases annual) performance appraisal. We sincerely hope that the majority of your employees will be energized following an appraisal and will go off to do great things for you and the company. However, we also will cover how to handle potential problems that might arise.

Follow Up

Very soon after completing a performance appraisal, you need to review, document and date agreements that were reached during the appraisal meeting. If certain targets were agreed upon, put them on your day planner or whatever method you use to track your responsibilities. If you have agreed to meet again after a certain length of time, you want to make sure that you honor that commitment. Should you forget that first appointment, all bets (and agreements in this case) might be off. Your integrity is at stake here, at least in the eyes of the employee with whom you've made the agreement.

Empowerment Zone

Probably the biggest complaint that bosses and employees have of one another is "lack of follow-through." If you say you're going to do something, do it! You can't build trust without remembering (and honoring) your commitments.

Honor Your Agreements

Even if you are not entirely ready to give the feedback you have promised, acknowledge that you know it is due and make an agreement on when it actually will be delivered. If you say nothing and assume the employee will wait until you are ready, you could be making a big mistake.

The dates you agree upon might be indelibly impressed on your employee's memory. Should you forget, no matter how unintentionally, you will send a negative message that might never be retracted. This is one of those times to put yourself in the employee's position and think about how you would feel if the situation were reversed. You probably would accept an acknowledged delay—but if nothing is said, it's hard to not believe that a commitment was forgotten. And that conveys the message that the commitment did not mean very much.

Ways to Ensure that Commitments Are Kept

A commitment is a powerful word that connotes something pretty important. When you commit to something, you are making a promise to follow through. Do whatever is necessary to be sure that you are able to keep your promises:

➤ Ask your employee to bring a planner or calendar to the appraisal meeting so both of you agree upon and note follow-up dates at the same time.

➤ Put reminder notices in your planner or in your computer's reminder system.

➤ Let your staff know that follow-up meetings are priorities and are not to be canceled for other meetings.

➤ Talk about follow-up schedules at staff meetings or in staff memos to remind you as well as the staff that they are coming.

➤ Maintain a staff calendar online or on a wall that displays dates for follow-up meetings.

➤ If you are prone to forgetfulness, acknowledge that and ask your staff to remind you when follow-up times are scheduled.

➤ Consistently put performance follow-up first on your to-do list.

How Often Must I Follow Up?

To answer this question, you have to refer to the agreements you made with your employees. Some managers put everyone on the same schedule; for example, they follow up monthly or quarterly.

Depending upon levels of performance, you might want to have individual follow-up schedules. If productivity goals are set according to a certain schedule, you might want to use that schedule to give feedback to your staff.

There is no perfect plan that works for everyone. The point is to make an agreement to give feedback and then to follow through by giving it. It doesn't have to take a lot of time. But you want to make sure your employees know you are paying attention and that you care about their abilities to achieve goals.

How to Tell If Someone Has Disengaged

With some people, it's pretty obvious that they are in disagreement or upset about something. Some people are very direct and express their concerns. Others might look sad or dejected and say little. Still others might show signs of anger. All of these emotional signals can be read quite easily by a manager or supervisor who is paying attention. Using understanding and some of the techniques we mentioned in Chapter 13, "Potential Problems and Difficult Situations," you might be able to address emotional issues with your employees.

Close Up

To **disengage** is to release your-self or withdraw from a previous involvement or position, or to detach.

But what about those people who traditionally show little emotion? Are you sure you can tell when they are distressed? Or do they act stoic and put up a front? All too often an employee might be so disappointed by the feedback given in an appraisal, he or she might consciously or even unconsciously start to pull back or *disengage* from their work and probably the company. If a formerly productive employee disengages, it might take some time for the manager to realize the person has slowed down. The person might influence co-workers and cause others to be less productive.

Sometimes, you unintentionally might have hurt a strong yet sensitive employee enough to cause him or her to look for work elsewhere while continuing to go through the motions with you and your company. If the employee doesn't come forward and show you his or her concerns, how will you be able to dissuade that person from leaving?

Here are 12 signs that an employee has disengaged:

➤ Taking more than the usual sick days or absences from work.

➤ Coming in late and leaving early.

➤ Lack of contribution at meetings.

➤ Flat demeanor—no animation or emotion.

➤ Sarcasm and put-downs of the company and/or its policies.

➤ Reduction in output and quality of output.

➤ Little or no interest in new projects.

➤ Marked change in attitude or personality.

➤ Inappropriate laughter.

➤ Increase in personal phone calls.

➤ Change in style of dress—either more casual or more formal.

➤ Lack of interaction with co-workers (when previously there had been interaction).

If an employee exhibits two or three of these signs, this is probably an indication that there is a problem of some sort. If four or more are present, it is a pretty sure sign that this person has disengaged.

Not Ready to Say Goodbye?

Can this situation be saved? Well, that depends on how much damage has been done. If a number of the preceding warning signals begin to occur shortly after a performance appraisal, there is a better-than-average chance that your feedback has rattled this person's morale.

Although the employee has decided to no longer communicate with you, it definitely is time for you to initiate communication. If you really want this person to

Wise Counsel

There might be problem employees that you would like to encourage to disengage and resign. Saying nothing, and simply hoping that they will do so following a poor performance appraisal is too indirect—and ineffective. The only appropriate way of dealing with employees is directly. It is more respectful to tell someone honestly that you feel they are not doing the job well enough to continue.

Empowerment Zone

The only way to determine if someone is showing disengagement signals is to actually observe the employee's behavior. Don't accept second- or third-hand information. The observer might have an axe to grind and may not be telling the whole truth.

continue working with you, you will need to conduct an *intervention*—the sooner the better.

Call the employee to your office, or some neutral location where you can have a confidential conversation. Your purpose is to get him or her to open up and admit whatever is the problem that is altering behavior. You might try one or a variation of the following opening remarks:

Close Up

An **intervention** is the act of coming between people and situations as an influencing force to modify or hinder some action.

➤ "It seems to me that you are distant and withdrawn at our staff meetings. I am concerned and would like to help. Is something bothering you?"

➤ "Your attendance has been very erratic lately. Would you like to talk about it?"

➤ "Since we had our performance appraisal meeting, it seems to me that your attitude has changed. What can you tell me about this?"

Some people might open up immediately and if so, let them talk. Let them vent, if necessary, and get everything out on the table so you can deal with it. Even if you thought you had covered all this during the performance appraisal, don't interrupt.

Just the Facts

Employees can disengage for reasons that have nothing to do with a performance appraisal. It's always best to try to learn whether there are other possible causes—such as a traumatic personal event such as divorce or the death of a loved one.

If the Silence Persists

It's possible that the employee might need a bit more effort to get him or her to open up. Gentle probing at this point is advisable. If the employee is not willing to talk about it easily, the hurt feelings might run deep. And if you are overly aggressive in your approach, it is unlikely you will persuade the employee to level with you.

Some probing questions you might try are

➤ "I care about your feelings. Can you help me to help you?"

➤ "I feel that I have done or said something to hurt you. It is important to me that I try to resolve this with you. Can you help me by giving me more explanation?"

➤ "I want to try to make things better if I can. I cannot help you unless you talk to me. Can you try to explain what's bothering you?"

Empowerment Zone

Try to evaluate the depth of the problem while listening carefully to the employee. Sometimes the person has been hurt so deeply and is so vindictive that the situation might not be worth salvaging. Letting the employee resign as a personal decision might be the better choice.

Wise Counsel

Make sure that you evaluate fairly, according to known performance expectations. Inventing new expectations at performance appraisal time can cause legal problems and cause strong performers to seek employment elsewhere.

➤ "I can see that you are angry. Can we work together to try to resolve this?"

➤ "I can see you are upset. Is there anything I can do to make you feel better?"

➤ "I think that you had strong feelings about your performance appraisal. We have not had an opportunity to cover everything that's important to you. Can we do that now?"

If, after all your efforts, the employee still will not talk to you, you might have to let it go at this time. Ask the employee to come and talk to you when he or she feels ready—and realize that time might never come.

Restoring the Faith

So now let's say you saw the warning signs, you intervened in time, and the employee has agreed to share his or her feelings. That's only half the battle. What you do next might help to determine whether this person stays with your company or moves on. You will have to revisit the performance appraisal process to find out what went wrong or where the major disagreement lies.

You might already be aware of the points of disagreement in the performance appraisal. It's possible the source of disagreement was not fully explored earlier because of the employee's reticence. Look at it now and determine whether something can or should be changed or modified. Sometimes if it is something very small—such as changing a descriptive word or two—you might be able to satisfy a concerned employee.

Words that describe someone's performance can be loaded words. You might unknowingly have chosen words that made a lot of sense to you but which offended your employee.

From the File Cabinet

In a performance appraisal, a manager described an employee's report writing as "dense." The manager meant the word "dense" to mean rich and full of detail. However, the employee heard the word "dense" and immediately assumed her manager was accusing her of being thick-headed and slow. The employee was so hurt that it was weeks before she was able to talk civilly to her manager. And it was only through another employee's intervention that the manager became aware of her *faux pas*. Many words have more than one meaning—so choose your words carefully!

Compromising Positions

Once you have identified the cause of an employee's problem, you will have to evaluate whether you can, or are willing to, make changes to make the employee feel better. If it's simply a matter of semantics, it might be quick and easy to change the language. However, if it is a bigger modification that will change the evaluation, you must consider how willing you are to compromise.

This might be one of those times when negotiating skills come in handy. Try different approaches and language to come to a mutually agreeable compromise. If you are completely unable or unwilling to compromise, realize that the outcome might be that the employee will quit. Be very sure that your reasons for noncompromise are valid ones, and it's not just your pride getting in the way. It's very difficult to recruit a replacement for a strong performer. Be very sure you are ready to risk losing the employee.

Just the Facts

A survey done in 1997 by Lee Hecht Harrison, a professional outplacement agency, cited the following costs of replacing staff:

➤ Very Hot, Desirable Skills: Replacement cost is four times the annual salary

➤ Senior Management: Replacement cost is three times annual salary

➤ Managers: Replacement cost is two times annual salary

151

Don't Forget the Follow-Up

Hopefully, you will be able to come to a compromise or mutually satisfactory agreement with a disheartened employee. It's now perhaps even more important that you pay attention to meeting your commitments. Remember what the sensitive points are with this employee. Just making some changes on the performance appraisal might not be enough to keep someone who has already threatened to leave. If the employee is worth keeping, your relationship with that employee is worth nurturing.

The Least You Need to Know

➤ Pay attention to and honor any agreements made during a performance appraisal.

➤ Remember that managing performance does not happen just once a year.

➤ Become familiar with the behavioral signals that someone has disengaged.

➤ If the disengaged employee is worth keeping, use effective communication techniques to win him or her back.

➤ Remember to follow up with all of your employees.

Part 4

When It's Your Turn to Receive

Until now we have focused predominantly on giving an appraisal to another individual, which typically is the supervisor's or manager's role in the appraisal process. The chapters in Part 4 will look at the process from the other side of the equation—those of you who are on the receiving end of an appraisal. And let's face it: Most of us—even if we're titled executives—still have to receive appraisals from somebody, be it the boss or the board, or sometimes even the public.

As the person being appraised, you shouldn't have to feel like a powerless victim. If you have spent any time at all reading the previous chapters you can see that we believe in making the appraisal an even, two-way conversation. We'll share some tips with you that will make your next performance appraisal a more pleasant and satisfying experience for all involved.

Chapter 15

The Importance of Being Prepared

In This Chapter

➤ What are your goals in this job?

➤ How to make sure your boss is familiar with your goals

➤ How to think in terms of accomplishments

➤ How to prepare yourself—mentally and physically

Whether or not they are in a position to give appraisals to others, most people approach receiving a performance appraisal with some trepidation. There's something about being judged that can put us on edge and make our palms sweat. Unfortunately there probably is no way we can make that nervous feeling go away for you completely. But we can share some experiences that might make you feel more prepared for that inevitable meeting.

We all wish we had the perfect boss who would prepare so correctly and sensitively for our appraisals that all we had to do was to show up. However, in the real world there are few, if any, perfect bosses. There are many who strive toward perfection, but even they can forget or overlook things that you think they should remember. It's awfully stressful at the top—and it's not at all uncommon for even the best boss to short-circuit on occasion.

So this chapter is written to help you fill in the gaps that might have been left by your supervisor, so you will feel like an empowered participant during your performance appraisal.

Establishing Your Goals

Everyone has goals, whether they know it or not. Some folks are exquisitely goal-oriented and chart goals on practically a daily basis. Indeed, it's proven that people who are religious about setting goals, and taking tangible steps to accomplish those goals, tend to be more successful than those who cast their fates to the wind.

Empowerment Zone

Ben Stein, a man whose career has carried him from the White House to network television, offers this simple advice for how to succeed: "The indispensable first step to getting the things you want out of life is this: Decide on what you want."

Just the Facts

There are a lot of day planners on the market that help you organize your entire life in terms of goals. They work on the idea that if an appointment isn't directly connected to one of your life's goals, you should take it off your calendar. This could become a little excessive, but some people find it helpful.

Many people are very clear about their job goals. But probably just as many are not so clear. They take a job because they need a job—not exactly a clear goal there. For those of you who need a little help articulating goals for your current job, try this little exercise.

Goal Identification Exercise: Why Do I Work at My Job?

Ask yourself why you are working at your current job. Write down everything you can think of. Even if you feel you are only working for a paycheck—why do you need the paycheck?

I work at my job because …

1.

2.

3.

4.

5.

6.

Having trouble coming up with reasons? Well, let's start with the paycheck situation. If you work for a paycheck, what do you need the paycheck for? To pay your rent or mortgage—that's a pretty good reason. Do you need to support your family? Or to pay for your education? To get health benefits or to build a retirement account? Or to take a vacation? Or what else?

What we're getting at here is that working for a paycheck is a means to an end or goal. How important is it that you meet that goal?

Some people choose to work at a relatively boring and repetitive job so that they conserve their energy for their avocations— such as hang-gliding, mountain-climbing, or playwriting.

From the File Cabinet

A working woman had a relatively sizeable inheritance and her house was paid for. She worked in a mid-level job with lots of frustrations attached to it. When asked why she continued to work, she explained that her parents would never approve of someone who just kicked back and lived off their savings. She had inherited their values as well as their money. She also worked because she liked solving problems and interacting with people.

Your goals should represent things that are really important to you. Even if the goal is to get out of your current job and get a better one, that's a great goal—career advancement! Lots of people take jobs that might lead to something bigger and better someday.

Here are some common reasons people take jobs:

➤ To learn a new industry.

➤ To gain more computer skills.

➤ To learn to work with the public.

➤ To finance a college degree.

➤ To make money during the day so they can do theater at night.

➤ To make a difference at the company.

➤ To get a different perspective of a chosen industry.

➤ To get skilled and experienced enough to be promoted.

➤ To learn enough to become a business owner someday.

➤ To support a spouse's career goals.

➤ To ensure that the kids stay at a good school.

➤ For love of the work.

➤ To be around other people.

➤ To get away from the house and kids.

➤ To get a feeling of accomplishment.

Wise Counsel

If you cannot think of any good reason to be at your current job, you probably are in the wrong job. Perhaps you have a serious philosophical conflict with the company or with the people there. With a serious conflict of values or philosophy, you might be unable to align your goals with company—and you probably are setting yourself up for failure or at least unhappiness.

Empowerment Zone

Scott Reed, a public relations and business consultant, as well as former Executive Director of the Republican National Committee, is responsible for the following memorable statement: "This one step—choosing a goal and sticking to it—changes everything."

All of these are positive reasons that someone would work at a certain job. Maybe doing this exercise will help you realize why you stay where you are currently working—or need to find somewhere else to work.

Make Sure Your Boss Knows Your Goals

Bosses with enlightenment and wisdom buy books such as this one and make goal-setting with their employees a priority. These managers would be very familiar with your individual goals. Unfortunately there are still many bosses who don't consider goal-setting with their employees an important responsibility or are just plain too busy to get around to it. (Obviously they haven't read this book!)

If your boss hasn't taken the time to establish goals with you, you must proactively ensure that he or she is aware of the goals you have set for yourself.

Semantics Are Everything

Keep in mind that your boss might not be entirely interested in your supporting your avocation, or even supporting your children or aging parents. He or she is going to focus more on goals that support corporate agendas. There are ways to blend these goals so that they work together toward a common end. It is your job to word them in such a way that they cover both bases. If the company does not succeed, you will be unable to meet your financial or other goals—so your effort to make sure the company stays in business actually is helping you to meet your ultimate goal.

How do you do this? Think about how your job fits into the bigger picture of the corporation. If you are an executive, it might be easy to see where and how you fit in. But even if you are in a support position, there probably are obvious links between you and the success of the company. You just have to be creative enough to find them.

For example, let's take an entry-level position that most people are familiar with. Let's say your job is to take the drive-through orders at a fast-food restaurant. How does your job affect the bottom line of the company?

If you give excellent customer service, are polite and cheerful as well as efficient, and make very few errors, your performance might ensure many repeat customers at your restaurant. And if there is increased business, your job is secure. So your goal could be exactly that: increase repeat visits to the drive-through window because of efficient service. It's important that you word your goal correctly—your goal is not just efficient service, but rather increased business through efficient service. This is how to tie your goal in to the company's goals.

Productive Repetition

If your boss is not into goal identification, you have to coach him or her into it. Depending upon your individual situation, this can be quite challenging. The direct approach is the most obvious and should be the best way to go about it. You simply make an appointment with the boss, discuss your goals, document them, and it's done.

But if that isn't possible or feasible, here are a few more suggestions:

Empowerment Zone

Remember your boss might be as nervous—or more so—than you are. Think of ways to help put him or her at ease. Small talk, commenting on your own nervousness in a light way, or sharing a light observation or joke might help the whole process.

Empowerment Zone

Remember bosses are only human—at least we assume they are. If by chance they forget they are human, maybe there are some ways to remind them in an effective and nonthreatening way. Humor might help.

➤ Write a memo listing your goals for the year, send it to your boss and request that it be placed in your personnel file.

➤ Write or print your goals on a large piece of paper and post them at your work station.

➤ Talk at staff meetings about goals in general as well as your individual goals, and suggest having a *standing agenda item* to discuss goal accomplishment.

➤ At this year's performance appraisal, come prepared with goals for the coming year, whether your boss brings them up or not.

➤ Talk goals with the boss every chance you get; don't let him or her forget them.

How to Think in Terms of Accomplishments

Some people have no problem bragging about themselves, and yet others who have reason to brag are often are reluctant to talk about the good things they have done. More often than not in the business world, he who blows his own horn is more successful than he who does not. People are busy and moving at the speed of light—or so it often seems. Some things stand out and are remembered, whereas others are noteworthy but forgotten in a whirlwind of other projects. You can't let your accomplishments go unnoticed and forgotten.

Close Up

A **standing agenda item** is a topic that is placed on every meeting schedule; a permanent fixture, as it were.

Who? Me?

"What accomplishments?" the more modest might ask. "I was just doing my job." Don't think that way. Just as your goals are linked to the company goals, your success at your job is linked to the company's success. You have to think of it that way. In general, men actually seem more comfortable talking about accomplishments than women do. This is one area in which it pays to play the same game.

From the File Cabinet

An article in a well-known business journal discussed a study that found that Asian Americans were not moving into management as fast as their numbers, qualifications, and education would suggest they might. One reason given for this (aside from possible race bias) was that most Asian cultures value a modest approach to work accomplishments. It would be considered rude in Japan, for example, to talk about your successes to your boss or ask for a promotion. But in corporate America, if you don't ask for promotions and toot your own horn, it is taken as a sign that you are not ready to move up.

If you do "your job" as a claims examiner, for example, you ultimately are saving your company thousands of dollars in claims errors. Think in terms of those savings—that's what the company is interested in, and that's what your doing your job has made possible.

If you work for a profit-making company, your accomplishments should impact the bottom line. Just like the fast-food worker, everyone who works for a company has some relationship to the bottom line—or they wouldn't be employed. Don't expect your boss to explain that relationship—create the relationship yourself.

Your efficient work has positively impacted other processes in your company—and that in itself is an accomplishment worth bragging about. It's not difficult to find those connections if you really think about it.

If your job involves working with the public, customer service resulting in satisfied customers can be seen as an accomplishment. If you are a line worker whose product is relatively free of bugs or flaws—that is an accomplishment that affects the bottom line.

Even nonprofit corporations need to have a positive income position. So the job you do also affects the bottom line. Nonprofits can't afford to be in a negative income position.

Ask for Help

If you find it hard to think in terms of accomplishment, ask a friend or advisor for help. It's sometimes much easier for another person to see the wonderful things you do. Someone else might be able to describe a part of your job in terms of how it affects others in a positive way. So if you can't find a way to say it yourself, by all means ask for and make sure that you get help.

Here are some tips for how to turn a job task into an accomplishment:

➤ Relate your job to the bottom line, financially speaking.

➤ Think of how your performance has positively impacted customers or co-workers.

Just the Facts

Some work areas seem to have a harder time relating their function to profitability. Human resources often is looked upon as an expense with no revenue. But HR can save substantial costs by protecting against legal fees and helping to reduce turnover.

Wise Counsel

It's not the company's responsibility to find ways to make you happy. Happiness, including finding personal fulfillment in a job, comes from inside you. If you find yourself unable to care about whether your company succeeds or not—you might want to look for more meaningful work, or at least a company where you can care about the co-workers, workplace, or customers.

➤ Describe how your actions save the company money, such as by preventing lost revenue or business.

➤ Connect your actions with increased sales and business.

➤ Show how your performance has resulted in more positive outcomes for people or products.

➤ Prove how you were responsible for repeat business or more satisfied customers.

Mental and Physical Preparation

This chapter has addressed how to get you prepared to meet with your boss about your performance appraisal. If you read the preceding paragraphs, you now have an idea about setting goals, connecting them to the company, ensuring your boss is aware of your goals, and how to describe your job performance in terms of accomplishments. You are ready for that appraisal. Or are you?

Just as we advised the person who is the appraiser, the appraisee needs to be just as prepared mentally and physically for what could be a stressful meeting. It's important for you to get sufficient rest and exercise as well as healthy nutrition to feel well and strong. Here are some suggestions for staying as relaxed as possible prior to the actual meeting:

➤ Take a walk or exercise the day of or the day before the evaluation.

➤ Mentally rehearse going through the review and being relaxed and confident and able to respond as needed.

➤ Remember that your boss is human and find ways to relate to him or her.

➤ Prepare for the worst-case scenario, even though it rarely happens.

➤ Assume the best will happen, because if you do a good job, hopefully it has been noticed. In many cases reviews are not all that bad and can be enlightening.

➤ If you know your boss is way off, prepare to not take personally his or her off-putting behavior such as arrogance, not listening, disinterest, rudeness, interruptions, sarcasm, belittling comments, subtle put-downs, unfair comparisons, and disinterest. Realize he or she has the problem, not you.

➤ Spend time preparing, with a friend, spouse, or co-worker, to let go of anxiety, anger, doubt, and other emotions.

➤ Visualize a relaxing scene or a safe place.

➤ Have faith in yourself—you can do this.

➤ Eat a balanced, healthy meal before going to work in the morning.

➤ If your anxiety is just too high for comfort, you might think about getting professional counseling with a licensed mental health therapist.

From the File Cabinet

An employee was so intimidated by her supervisor that she was having panic attacks and waking up at night for weeks before her evaluation. With the help of an EAP counselor, she reviewed her qualifications, co-workers' opinions of her work, and feedback from physicians and her past bosses. After doing all of this she was able to see that even if things went as she feared, she could choose to use the positive feedback she had gathered to counter her boss's put-downs, or she could get another job. She practiced assertive responses to her boss's abrasive behavior. The evaluation went okay, and she was able to use the assertive skills in future conflict situations.

Even the worst review can be helpful. You will learn about yourself or your workplace and the information then can be used to decide on whatever change might be needed.

The Least You Need to Know

➤ It's crucial that you identify your goals at your present job, whether your boss has requested it or not.

➤ Connect your goals to the company's goals.

➤ Let your boss know that you have established goals.

➤ Practice talking about your job in terms of your accomplishments.

➤ Use mental and physical relaxation exercises to be prepared for your appraisal meeting.

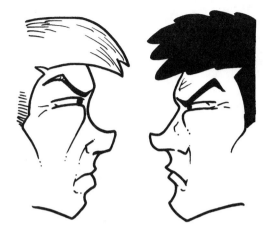

Chapter 16

Keeping a Face-to-Face from Becoming a Face-Off

In This Chapter

➤ The do's and don'ts of communication during an appraisal

➤ Everybody's nervous—how to deal with it

➤ How to ask for specifics

➤ Challenge yourself with goals for the future

The day has come when you sit down with your manager to talk about your performance appraisal. By now you have done your preparation—you know why you have this job, you are able to tie your goals to the corporate goals, you have listed or memorized your accomplishments. As prepared as you are, there is no way of knowing exactly how this conversation will play out until it actually does.

Hopefully you know your manager at least somewhat and have identified him or her as a certain management type (see Chapter 4, "What's Your Style?"). You might be able to anticipate things that could come up if you are familiar with your boss's style. But even if you are not exactly sure, this chapter will give you some tips on how to communicate in most situations.

The Do's of Communication

We've already discussed what works from the supervisor's point of view (see Chapter 8, "The Casual Approach: Can We Talk?"); because this process is a two-way street, the same advice holds true for you now. You will get things off to a good start if you come in smiling and shake your boss's hand. This will signal that you are starting off in a positive frame of mind. If your boss also is open and informed, the conversation should proceed in a positive way. It's best to let the boss take the lead, at least in the beginning. The following steps can encourage a positive conversation between you and your manager.

Do:

➤ Start with a smile and a handshake.

➤ Engage in relaxing small talk. Let your manager take the lead—but if he or she doesn't, it's okay to break the ice with some noncontroversial topic such as the weather or a sporting event.

➤ Make good eye contact; concentrate on not staring or squinting.

➤ Sit comfortably with your hands in your lap or on the desk or table.

➤ Listen carefully and actively.

➤ Follow any instructions you are given; for example, to hold your questions until the end.

➤ Respond when spoken to in a calm, nondefensive, and even tone of voice.

➤ Use the summarization technique to make sure you are on the same wavelength.

➤ Be open to the opinions expressed.

The Don'ts of Communication

Now let's look at some things that might make the conversation less successful. When it's time for your performance appraisal, the following are some communication don'ts.

Don't:

➤ Come in with a negative attitude—it shows on your face and will guarantee a less-than-successful outcome.

➤ Frown or grimace—try to keep your face relaxed.

➤ Fold your arms across your chest—it's a closed stance and is not compatible with an open conversation.

➤ Interrupt—your turn to talk will come.

➤ Look away for long periods (out the window, at the floor).

➤ Drum your fingers on the table or fidget, it will increase your nervousness as well as your boss's.

➤ Speak in a hostile manner—even disagreements can be handled politely.

➤ Get up and walk around the room.

➤ Be sarcastic or insulting.

Does it seem like a lot to remember? Well, that might be true, but if you utilize positive communication techniques you will be more in control, making any conversation easier and more productive. It's definitely worth practicing.

A good way to practice these techniques is to roleplay with a friend before you have an important meeting such as an appraisal. Give your friend the preceding list of do's and don'ts, and let him or her give you feedback following the conversation.

Very often, we are not even aware of how our faces look when we're speaking. And unless someone points it out to us, we might not realize that our body language is inappropriate.

Just the Facts

For those of you who follow politics, remember when George Bush, Sr. looked at his watch a few times during a televised debate, it gave people the impression he was bored or nervous and wanted to get out of there. Many analysts felt this was a crucial mistake.

Is it worth the trouble to rehearse before an appraisal meeting? You bet it is. Practicing with someone else is extremely helpful. The other person—if he or she can be honest with you—will be able to tell you things about your tone and maybe even your expectations. Make sure the person you practice with is someone you trust in both intentions and judgment.

If you need more preparation, you also can try to relax with your eyes shut and practice deep breathing while you imagine yourself going through the evaluation process in a relaxed, good-humored way. This kind of imaginary rehearsal paired with a relaxation exercise is a good way to decrease your anxiety about the meeting.

Your Manager Is as Nervous as You Are

Although they might not want to admit it, and might be unhappy that we're letting the cat out of the bag, managers really are as nervous—sometimes even more nervous—than you are when appraisal time rolls around. It's a lot of work preparing for and delivering an appraisal. It took us 14 chapters to describe the process, after all! And without preparation it could be a very unpleasant, if not downright embarrassing, event.

Delivering an appraisal can be or seem like a pretty confrontational situation. And the point is worth repeating that lots of people have a very hard time dealing with confrontation—so your supervisor might be sweating this meeting more than you realize.

Just the Facts

Every company we have worked with has cited managers' procrastination in completing performance appraisals as a major problem. And a major reason for their procrastination is their fear of confrontation—whether or not they will admit it.

Even when the manager thinks you are great and plans to recognize and praise you, you still might be disappointed. Anyone who has done reviews knows that it's possible to pick the wrong things to praise. And you might not get what you want in terms of compensation—even if you are an outstanding employee.

Sometimes when they are nervous, some people might appear extra serious, formal, or rigid. It's a way of controlling their emotions, but it comes across in a somewhat threatening manner. If your manager seems overly uptight, try to remember that it might just be an act to cover his true feelings. And try not to take it too personally.

A lot depends on the kind of relationship that has been established between manager and staff. If there is a trusting relationship, the nervousness factor should be substantially reduced.

When Conditions Are Less than Perfect

Okay, if you have a great manager and there is a lot of trust, you might not need this book. Chances are good, however, that you might have some less-than-perfect circumstances to deal with. You can still handle the appraisal interview in a professional manner.

Participate

We have given managers ideas on how to get employees to participate, so let us reiterate that the experience will be more satisfying if you engage in a conversation. Passive-aggressive behavior is not going to work in your favor here. Become fully involved in the conversation.

Respond to questions appropriately and ask questions if there are things you don't understand. If you are asked a question that you can't answer immediately, it's okay to ask for some time to think before you respond. Short periods of silence are to be expected.

Some people get caught up in the belief that they have to keep some conversation going every second. The need to talk continuously emphasizes your nervousness, and can be pretty irritating. Suppress the urge to fill the air with idle talk just for the sake of talking.

Don't Argue

There are ways to get your ideas heard without becoming argumentative. If something sounds wrong to you, try sentences such as

➤ I understand what you are saying, but I don't agree.

➤ May I explain my point of view on that subject?

➤ I interpreted that situation in a different way.

➤ I appreciate your point of view, although mine is somewhat different.

Then explain your side of the story calmly, professionally, and unemotionally. If you get your hackles up, so to speak, you invite more argument in return. For example, an "I'm the manager and you're not" type might be compelled to get louder or more aggressive if you were to exhibit argumentative behavior. If you get quieter, it actually will make their behavior more exaggerated, and you will seem more professional.

We'll go into dealing with unusual aggression in Chapter 17, "When Your Boss Makes Dilbert Look Good," and the flip side—from the manager's perspective in Chapter 13, "Potential Problems and Difficult Situations."

Ask for Specifics and Clarification

If your manager makes a comment about your performance or behavior that you believe is not true, ask for specific instances in which the behavior was witnessed. Be calm but firm in asking for specific occasions. If your manager can't provide any details, you might be able to change the appraisal. Unfortunately, the more insecure managers probably won't let you change their comments. So when you are given the opportunity to write your own comments, you should write about your specific disagreements.

Empowerment Zone

If you can counter with your own specifics that refute your boss's comments, that will strengthen your ability to have the appraisal changed. This is another good reason to do your homework before the appraisal meeting.

Wise Counsel

No matter what your manager says, this person is your superior. Things said during this meeting can and will be held against you. If you want to have a future with this company, use great tact and diplomacy. Be more professional than your manager, if possible. If this is about personality and not performance, let your positive, professional personality be the one that stands out.

169

If your manager is being hard-nosed and inflexible, you might have to rise above it, maintain a professional demeanor, and rely on your ability to write your own comments which will become part of your personnel file. Some managers cannot deal with anyone who challenges their authority. No matter how right you think you are, such a manager is not going to budge.

Close Up

To be **proactive** is to take the first step first, to show the initiative to start something (perhaps a new project or program) before being asked.

Establishing Your Goals for the Future

Here we go again with the goals. Now we're focusing on what you plan to accomplish in the future. Ideally you will work through these with your manager. But it would be *proactive* to come in with a list or at least some thoughts about where you want to be by next year.

Once again, you want your goals to be related to company goals—so the more you know about those goals the better. If your manager has not shared the company goals with you, ask to see them. You also might be able to find out what they are in a company annual report, if your company publishes one.

From the File Cabinet

A shipping and receiving department was asked to cut the order and shipping turnaround times by 10 percent or more for the coming year. Both the lead clerk and his supervisor were asked to make this a goal, as the customers internally and externally were concerned about the long waits for products. The two employees said they needed an updated computer system with new tracking software that would help them to decrease wait times by 15 percent or more. They were able to make the argument for getting equipment they had previously been denied, because they tied it into their individual departments' and the companies' goals.

You might have very specific things in mind, and your manager might want to change them somewhat to fit his or her own vision. Try to be collaborative about this process. Your purpose is to agree upon goals and come up with a list that you both can live with.

Challenge Yourself

If goals are too easily achievable, they lose their power as goals. A goal is meant to make you stretch for something. Maybe you're not there now, but next year you will have acquired the experience to reach for something new. Try raising the bar, and work on achieving your personal best.

With each challenge there is that fear of the unknown—"what if I can't make it?" That fear will make you work harder, which is what a goal should make you do. Use goal-setting as a method to extend yourself; to increase your education and experience to new levels of accomplishment.

To settle for something easy diminishes you. Set a goal that will stretch your limits. That kind of goal setting requires commitment. Are you truly committed to this company—to helping the company as well as yourself—succeed?

Empowerment Zone

If you are aware of obstacles that might prevent you from being able to accomplish a goal, bring them up. But be prepared to suggest a solution to the problem. You will score major points if you show that you have thought the problem through and can recommend how to fix it.

From the File Cabinet

After 15 years, a data entry clerk felt unchallenged and unmotivated. Whenever she had mentioned the possibility of training for a higher level job, her supervisors tended to either ignore it or discourage it. Over the years she'd had supervisors who were threatened by her goals, and others who underestimated her abilities. After some counseling, which helped her see that she needed to take charge of her own goals, she began taking courses outside of work. Eventually she moved up into a higher-level programming job outside her unit, within the information services division of her company. It took about 1 $\frac{1}{2}$ years, but she never has felt better about herself and her work life.

If you are already goal-oriented, good for you! If you are not, give goals a shot. They have a way of propelling you in the right direction. The clearer your goals and the clearer your vision of the future, the better chance you have of getting there.

Take a chance and set a higher goal than you have previously. It's the risk takers in this world that are the highest achievers. There is a time and place for playing it safe. But if you really want to accomplish more in the working world, aim high. It might be scary at first, but soon you will feel your confidence grow as you take real steps toward accomplishing your goals.

The Least You Need to Know

➤ Utilize techniques for positive communication during a performance appraisal.

➤ Resist the temptation to be passive-aggressive or noncommunicative.

➤ If you disagree with your manager's evaluation of your performance, probe for specific behavioral examples of things mentioned in your appraisal.

➤ Prepare your goals for the future in advance.

➤ Establish goals that will stretch your capabilities.

Chapter 17

When Your Boss Makes Dilbert Look Good

In This Chapter

➤ How to handle a negative or hostile boss

➤ Techniques to try to make the situation better

➤ How to tell when it's better to retreat

➤ What is your recourse if things go really bad?

It would be nice if all bosses could be at least somewhat reasonable. And the same should be said for employees. But in the real world—where we all reside—we know that there are some people who are beyond difficult. Chapter 16, "Keeping a Face-to-Face from Becoming a Face-Off," gave you some suggestions to help you handle various appraisal situations. This chapter takes you beyond the difficult situation, and addresses a more potentially dangerous situation.

Just as managers have to learn to recognize and deal with potentially violent or abusive employees, employees also might have to learn to recognize and deal with unreasonable and possibly abusive supervisors or bosses. These bosses spring from the same kinds of backgrounds as the more extreme employees—they might have had an abusive family background, or have been abused by a former boss and are emulating that behavior, or they might just be burned out in their jobs. Because they are unhappy or unfulfilled, they seem to need to make others unhappy as well. It is also possible they may be clinically depressed and their depression is characterized by anger, impatience, and perfectionism with others and very possibly themselves as well.

Just the Facts

Not all people who are clinically depressed are abusive or outwardly angry. Many people with depression appear happy and are very accommodating and pleasant towards others. Depression, whether it is visible to others or not, is treatable and unfortunately most of the time goes untreated. This is another time when a referral to an Employee Assistance Program would be very useful.

Empowerment Zone

Hostile bosses frequently are hiding their insecurities behind a mask of anger. If people are too intimidated to confront them, these angry bosses think their lack of knowledge or skill will never be found out.

It's important for you to recognize when you are dealing with such a supervisor and how far you can go to defend yourself before backing off. With truly unstable people, no matter how reasonable you are, you won't be able to succeed at getting them to see it your way. There are other options open to you.

Techniques To Diffuse Anger

Some bosses use negativity and anger as control mechanisms. Many people are put off or intimidated by such behavior and will not dare to confront the angry boss. And because the behavior is so effective in keeping employees in line, the boss continues to use it.

Such bosses can be very belittling to employees. If you ask a question for clarification, he or she might bark an answer and perhaps berate you for asking. Establishing a trusting relationship with this kind of supervisor might be almost impossible—at least in terms of getting the kind of treatment you would like from them on a consistent basis. Employees end up afraid to say anything to him or her, even to communicate information that is critical to the business. Ultimately it is just plain bad business, not motivating, and unprofessional behavior for a supervisor or manager to treat people this way, or for senior level management to allow other levels of management to continue to treat employees this way.

To anticipate a performance appraisal with this kind of person is potentially very unsettling. Often this kind of boss will put off appraisals indefinitely. And because the employees are not looking forward to the meeting, they say nothing, thinking it's better to not be appraised than hear what the boss has to say.

So if Mr. or Ms. Hostile is your boss, is there anything you can do? If you anticipate the worst at your performance appraisal, these tips might help you maintain control:

➤ Be on time for the appointment so you don't give your boss any additional reasons to criticize you.

➤ Speak clearly in a modulated tone of voice, no matter what tone the boss uses.

➤ Be polite and professional, even if you think your boss is not.

➤ Listen carefully and think before you speak.

➤ Try to maintain composure no matter what is said. Fighting fire with fire is not recommended when your boss is a blowtorch.

➤ Try not to take the comments personally. Filter the anger out and focus on any useful feedback.

➤ If you disagree with the comments, state your disagreement and ask for clarification or specific examples.

➤ Be reasonable—even if your boss is not—and state your own specific examples.

➤ As tempting as it might be to tell your boss off, don't. Your boss has a lot of control over your career, but so do you. There are more tactful ways you can attempt to deal with the problem—outside of the performance appraisal.

➤ You could try a very assertive tactic and address the style of delivery, for example, "I want to hear your feedback, but I would appreciate it if you would not use that angry (or sarcastic, or belittling) tone with me."

➤ Take pride in looking cool and calm, letting your behavior be the professional model to follow.

➤ Keep positive affirmations playing inside your head to ward off any put-downs.

Dealing with anyone who has a problem with anger is not fun. When it's your boss and the anger is frequent, it can make for a very unsatisfying work experience. Avoidance might be the best strategy under such circumstances.

Anger often is caused by the following things:

➤ Chronic stress.

➤ Depression.

➤ Low self esteem.

➤ Fear of shame (I don't want to look bad).

➤ The need to control and the fear of losing control.

➤ A martyr syndrome: The manager doesn't take care of his or her needs, so why should they treat their employees well or take their needs into account?

➤ Fear of embarrassment, loss of position in the world, loss of love or affection, or physical harm.

Any of the preceding causes of anger can make people feel bad about themselves. Often the only way they can deal with it, as they see it, is to make others around them feel as bad or worse. Sometimes they are just plain unaware of their behavior and the way it affects other people.

Just the Facts

In some of the couples research on responding to an angry spouse, John Gottman, Ph.D. found that if the non-angry spouse could respond in a neutral way for five seconds, it had a very settling response on the angry person.

Try to keep that in mind when the anger seems to turn on you, it may have more to do with your boss than with you. Even if you have done something that needs correcting, you don't deserve this kind of treatment, but you cannot control their behavior, only your own. Take a deep breath and silently remind yourself that you are okay; it's the angry person who has the problem. You might even be able to move beyond feeling uncomfortable and just coping to actually probe your angry boss's behavior. "Why do you seem so upset with me, I'm confused by your tone here?" Whether you try to control your own internal response and try to settle your own feelings while being quiet, or being more active and assertive, it is important not to get angry in return. It's not easy and like anything else worth doing, it takes practice.

Some people are very good at this technique. Perhaps it comes from a very strong self-esteem, but they can deflect someone else's anger quite successfully. Observe others who handle angry people well. You can learn a lot from their actions and behavior.

We know that it is not easy to do, and your boss is not your spouse, but the principals of nonescalating behavior apply. Don't meet one level of aggression with the same level or higher aggression, or you will bump it up to the next level of conflict.

When To Shut Up

With an overly arrogant or hostile boss, there might come a time when no matter what your good intentions are and what technique you practice, it is ineffective. If you have very strong beliefs that your boss is way off base in his or her evaluation of your work performance, you might not want to give up your case at this point. But defending your position at this particular meeting probably will lead to more hostility or a stonewalling approach, and might add fuel to the criticism of your performance; it could also cost you your job, so weigh your options carefully. It's time to thank your boss (although you might find that hard to say) for his or her time and ask to leave the office.

If there is any discussion about signing the performance appraisal, defer that activity until you have an opportunity to write your own rebuttal comments. It is your right to add commentary on your performance appraisal and good forms provide space for that. If your boss withholds that right from you, you can write a separate document refuting whatever you feel is unjust and have it placed in your personnel folder.

From the File Cabinet

It is common when you are hit with something unwanted that you keep saying to yourself, "I can't believe this." This stance creates a kind of psychological conflict; it is like a denial of the facts. It keeps you from trying to influence or deflect the other person's behavior or opinion, which might just deepen the conflict or keep it going. One way to get some internal resolution and to lessen immediate conflict is to say to yourself, "This really is how he or she thinks. This is happening, and I might have to wait until later to plan my response to this because opposing him or her now will get me nowhere."

You will be in a much stronger position if you politely end the meeting rather than staying to argue. As your own anger or frustration builds, you might say things that you will regret later. You will be much more prepared to make a counter-argument when you have had time to reflect on the meeting.

Arguing with an angry person usually has a negative outcome. If you become more belligerent or burst into tears, such behavior will be used against you. Getting emotional will hurt you in this situation. It might be just what your boss wants you to do, so don't extend that favor. If you feel negative emotion overtaking you, heed that signal and attempt to make a polite exit and ask to be excused.

What To Do Afterward

After a painful appraisal, one that you feel misrepresents your performance, undoubtedly you will feel some angry, depressed, or, at the least, some disappointed feelings. When you are in such an emotional state, don't expect to come up with a way of resolving this immediately. Take some time to regain your cool—take a walk to clear your head, talk to a respected co-worker or friend, or call the EAP for advice or counseling.

Blow Off Some Steam

A technique that really helps to release some of the anger and emotion is to go home and write down all of your feelings, holding back nothing, saying everything you wanted to say to your boss but couldn't. Get it all out. You may feel a great sense of relief to let go of all those repressed emotions. But as powerful and compelling as this document might seem to you, don't send it! Before you send anything, have a trusted friend review it with you.

Other things you can do to reduce your own feelings of distress are to

➤ Sit quietly and do some deep breathing exercises.

➤ Talk to a friend or spouse, but pick carefully—you don't need a lecture at this point.

➤ Watch a comedy—something like the Marx Brothers, which often depicts some rude bad guy getting his just desserts.

➤ Go out and do some vigorous exercise, but pace yourself, especially if you don't exercise regularly.

➤ Plan a few days off if you can get them without getting into more conflict at work.

➤ Participate in shopping therapy?

Yes, you do eventually want to write a rebuttal, but telling your boss off in an angry way will not have a positive outcome.

Wise Counsel

Whatever strategy you decide on is dependent on several variables, including your comfort level and how powerful your boss is at the company. If your boss owns the company or has a similar level of long-standing tenure, your chances of prevailing carry a lot of risk to your continued employment, and even if you stay there the atmosphere might be quite difficult.

Strategize Your Next Move

Remember that you want to remain reasonable. Reacting in anger would reduce you to your boss's level—and you already are in a subordinate position, which is more vulnerable. However, you still have options open to you. Let's explore some of them:

➤ Do nothing. Consider the source of the criticism and let it roll off your back.

➤ Write a professional rebuttal that will become part of your appraisal and will be placed in your personnel folder (if your boss objects to this, seek counsel from human resources).

➤ Write a rebuttal and make an appointment to discuss it with your boss, after which your document will be added to your appraisal and placed in your personnel folder.

➤ Seek support from another manager who, in a separate meeting, can act as a mediator between you and your boss—sometimes a third party can help promote understanding.

➤ Write a professional rebuttal and send it to your boss's boss requesting an opportunity to discuss your concerns.

➤ If your company has a *grievance procedure policy*, use it to file a formal grievance against your boss—the issue then will be reviewed by other parties and probably will be seen by your boss's boss.

➤ Start looking for another job—your relationship with your boss might never get to a level you are comfortable with.

➤ If your performance appraisal has been used to limit your salary increase, your employment, or your ability to seek promotional opportunities, you might want to consult one of the regulatory agencies listed in the telephone book or an attorney.

➤ Wait it out. Many bosses like this ultimately either leave or are fired.

If you have limited options or many years and seniority at your company with many weeks of vacation, you might decide to work on not letting this person get to you. You might draw your satisfaction from the job and not from your relationship with your boss. You might develop a philosophy, which allows you to accept your boss as limited and realize that you can succeed despite him or her.

Empowerment Zone

If your company has a human resources department, that might be where you want to go first before taking any other action. A good HR department will not take sides in these kinds of issues and can advise you on what rights and options you have according to your company's policies.

Close Up

A **grievance procedure policy** is a program designed for internal review of problems between management and staff and typically is composed of objective, in-house reviewers.

From the File Cabinet

Sometimes it is more than the current situation that makes this feel so awful. Check to see if there is some historical relationship or event that mirrors your current relationship with your boss. A woman we worked with was able to see how her cold boss mirrored the memory of the behavior of her cold mother. The kind of invalidating feedback she got in interactions with her boss were almost the same in tone of voice as much of the indifference and rejection she felt from her mother growing up. Just making this connection helped to take some of the sting out of her current situation.

Legal Recourse

This is a very big, and possibly very expensive, step. You must be very certain of your facts before you consider legal recourse. Prior to going to an attorney, we recommend that you talk about this case in great detail with a trusted friend or two—someone you can count on to be completely honest with you. Be sure to disclose everything—both sides of the story as you understand it. Let this objective person or persons give you their unbiased opinion of the strength of your position. If your friend strongly believes your case has merit, then it might be time to seek legal assistance.

Just the Facts

If you believe that your job performance appraisal has been impacted by discrimination because of your race, age, national origin, sex, or other factors, you first should contact the Equal Employment Opportunity Commission (EEOC) to file a claim. The EEOC will evaluate your claim, and if it is a strong case, will defend you at no charge.

How to Choose an Attorney

You should look for an attorney who specializes in employment law. Before representing you, the attorney will want to know what has been lost as a result of the appraisal. Unless there has been some loss of income, it is doubtful the attorney will take your case. Your pain and suffering might be very real to you, but without a financial loss, what are you suing to recover?

If you are not sure where to start looking for an attorney, check with the local bar association. These organizations often run a low-fee consultation service, for about 30-45 minutes with an attorney. Only attorneys in good standing with the bar association and experts in your area of concern are available to do this consultation. The fees are used to run the service and the attorneys volunteer their time. This enables you to get good, unbiased information. And you can check out a lawyer with no future obligation to continue with them.

Check with your EAP as it might offer a consultation with a lawyer for free if it is one of the covered services.

Things to Consider Before Filing a Lawsuit

It is not easy to file a lawsuit against an employer. It can be frustrating and time-consuming. If you stay employed while the lawsuit is pending, things might be very uncomfortable for you on the job; however, the law does protect you from retaliation for filing suit, so you can't be fired or have some other disciplinary action solely because of the lawsuit.

If you choose to get an attorney and fight your situation in the courts, it could be very expensive. You might find attorneys willing to take your case on *contingency*. But many attorneys will expect some payment up front, or after the case if you don't win in court.

Think about whether you have the strength, time, support in your personal life, and fortitude to fight the legal battle for your rights. At least every week in the newspaper you can read of examples of an employee or group of employees who have prevailed in a lawsuit against an employer and ended up with large financial settlements. In most of those cases, the incident with the employer occurred several years prior to the settlement. It typically takes several years for these kinds of cases to be fully investigated and then scheduled in busy courts or the EEOC.

Ask yourself if you can hold on that long, if necessary. Often, if your case is strong enough, an employer will agree to a settlement outside of court. Those settlements usually occur much earlier than a case would go to court.

Wise Counsel

After you file a claim or lawsuit, an employer is prohibited by law to retaliate against you because of the lawsuit. But you are not protected from discipline if you do something wrong that is not related to the suit. So don't act foolishly thinking you have immunity.

Close Up

A **contingency,** in the legal context, is taking a case on the chance that you will win, with the intention that the legal fees will be paid out of the settlement.

But again, consider what you know about your boss and the company. Some are more reasonable than others. Some might not want to set a precedent of paying off an employee in such a dispute. It pays to do some research to try to find out if similar cases have occurred and what the results were.

When You Feel There Is No Other Choice

Once you have consulted whatever agencies or legal resources are necessary, you will have a good idea of just how strong your case is. If, after researching the situation thoroughly, you still feel that you have been unjustly harmed by a performance appraisal, and you are certain you have what it takes to fight such a battle, you might want to strongly consider filing a lawsuit. Employers who abuse employees should not be permitted to get away with it.

You have to feel very passionately about the situation to take this difficult step. But if you are certain about the facts and your own ability to stick out a legal battle, it might be the best recourse. Consider consulting with an attorney to get his or her opinion, in any case.

The Least You Need to Know

➤ Try to use professionalism in dealing with a hostile boss.

➤ When all else fails, make every attempt to politely end the appraisal conversation and consider other options.

➤ Carefully strategize your next move after an unsatisfactory appraisal.

➤ If you lose your job or a salary increase as a result of a performance appraisal, consider speaking with someone from an appropriate regulatory agency or attorney and then possibly taking legal action.

➤ Taking legal action is difficult, time-consuming, and expensive—make sure to consult with an attorney or someone from a regulatory agency to assist you in thinking it through before you file a lawsuit.

Part 5

Building a New Performance Appraisal Plan

Now that we've painstakingly gone over the various components of a performance appraisal program, you might ask why we are going over it—starting from scratch—again. Well, it has been our experience that many companies have a program in place that just isn't working. There is some desire to redesign a program but maybe not a lot of expertise to do so. And those who are assigned to work on this project—be it a human resources department or a team of other managers—don't really know where to begin.

The next several chapters are written to address that situation and give you a road-map to redesign a plan that will work for your specific company. There is no one plan that will fit every situation. It would be so much easier if there was a "plug-and-play" appraisal program that you could simply buy and start using. And in all honesty, there are many such programs that you can purchase off the shelf or through the Internet. But we don't think you will be happy with a plan that was not written with your company in mind.

Your appraisal program should be a custom plan for your particular situation. If it's not, you probably will be trying a different plan every few years as each plan is tried and fails to hit the mark.

Chapter 18

Every Building Needs a Foundation: Building Your Framework

In This Chapter

➤ Establishing your philosophical reasons for performance appraisals

➤ Doing the appropriate research

➤ Designing a plan to call your own

➤ Making sure your plan passes legal scrutiny

Perhaps some performance appraisal plan has been in place that just hasn't set your company on fire. Don't be disheartened—the majority of companies are in a similar position. Performance appraisals almost always are considered a painful and much-procrastinated—but necessary—evil.

Can you change that long-standing reputation? We think you can—with planning and thoughtful design. Your new system can't be designed overnight, and if you are looking for that kind of system you might as well check to see if your local stationery store carries boilerplate performance appraisals.

But if you're willing to spend a bit of time and effort, you just might find a system that not only works, but that people will look forward to using and use in a timely manner. That in itself is a major accomplishment for most companies.

Whether you are starting from scratch or redesigning another performance appraisal plan, there are certain principles that apply. The tangible part of the plan or program, the part of it that will be seen by everyone in the organization, is the actual performance appraisal form that you choose to design or use. The form should be a reflection of the program you have designed using the philosophy and values the company identifies.

Who Are You?

Time to wax philosophical again. Do you know what your company philosophy is? Often, even though it is not formally articulated, a philosophy is fairly obvious. Take a look at how people—predominantly employees, but often customers as well—are treated at your place of work. If there are enforced policies dedicated to the respectful treatment of people in your company, you can sense that the philosophy is to value and take good care of its human assets. If people are treated like cogs in the giant machine of your company, if they are considered easily expendable and turnover is high, that is the opposite extreme—not a people-friendly philosophy.

Wise Counsel

Your philosophy has to be real, not just words. If your company just pays lip service to a philosophy, you are living a lie. Your employees will know it and resent the contradiction between what you say and what you do.

Your company might lie somewhere in between. It is important that you identify how your company values its human resources. Performance appraisals so intimately affect the employees that a system that fits will have to reflect the company's overall philosophy about those employees.

Just as your company probably has a mission statement, make sure that there is also a philosophy statement regarding the treatment of staff. If your company philosophy is not apparent, make an appointment to talk to the CEO. In order to design this program—or a compensation program to pay fairly and competitively, you need to have a corporate philosophy. If you have a company philosophy that identifies dignity and respect, retention and promotion as important then you have the main components in place to treat your workers as valuable (human) assets.

Close Up

COLA stands for cost of living adjustment. COLA raises typically are a once-a-year, across-the-board wage increase and usually are related to the Consumer Price Index. Some companies give them annually, some do not.

Will a Raise Be Involved?

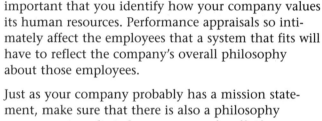

Once you have identified a philosophy, it's time to formalize whatever is the purpose of your performance evaluations. Yes, there are the obvious reasons—but will performance appraisals also be related to salary increases? Will there be a merit increase program tied to the results of the appraisals? You also should find out your company's method of giving salary increases; some companies offer a *COLA* on an annual basis and no other increase. Other companies give a merit increase that has a COLA built into it, for example, everyone gets a two-percent COLA and has the potential of getting up to three percent based on the results of their performance appraisals.

Once you have established the reason or reasons your company is interested in doing performance appraisals, you will have to incorporate those priorities into your system. Performance appraisal formats can be designed differently depending upon their purpose. For example, if merit increases are related, you probably will want to have a scoring system that will translate a performance score into a level of increase.

Similarly, if used for promotional consideration, a scoring system should show why one person was chosen over another. And certain regulatory requirements might call for a completely different method of evaluating and scoring.

Here are some common reasons for doing performance appraisals:

➤ Determination of salary increases

➤ Evaluation for promotional consideration

➤ Identification of training needs

➤ Method of job feedback

➤ Regulatory requirements

➤ Having a recorded history of performance is critical when and if you need to make a decision to terminate employment based on inadequate performance

Research Your Company's History Regarding Appraisals

What has been tried previously? What has worked and what hasn't? If your company has been around for any length of time, reviewing the personnel file of a long-standing employee will accomplish this research fairly easily. There you should find samples of whatever—if any—performance feedback method has been in place since that person was hired.

Talk to employees who have been with the company for several years to get their recollections and opinions on feedback systems. Find out if anything was received well, what bombed, and the reasons why. Record all the information that you receive. You might hear different information depending on the level of the employee interviewed, but all of it is valuable.

Empowerment Zone

Your long-term employees are a gold mine of information. Always take the time to mine this kind of historical treasure. It is amazing how many times businesses repeat the same mistakes, partly because no one has kept track of the past.

Design a Custom Format

Once you have determined your philosophy, your purpose, and what has or has not worked in the past, it's time to design a format. You've got to be pretty familiar with your company to do this. Some elements to consider include the following:

➤ How many employees does your company have? If it's thousands, a more brief form might make more sense. Think of the monumental job of administrating a complex, multipage form for thousands of employees.

➤ How many employees report to each manager? Don't just consider the corporate office—think about all the locations your company might cover. You might have the most brilliant form ever created, but if it's long and time-consuming, it just won't work for managers with too many direct reports. They won't do them consistently—trust us on this. Managers often complain they do not have adequate time to do elaborate reviews, especially when they have a lot of direct reports. Be realistic. If your managers are fairly overwhelmed on a day-to-day basis, where are they going to find the time to do an adequate job? You might need to look at how you allocate the proper amount of time to do a more complex evaluation. That's where getting feedback from those who have to do the process is invaluable.

➤ Is your company goal-oriented—or not? We have shown our bias toward a belief in goals, but be honest. If goal setting is not a priority at your company, that knowledge will assist you in determining your format.

Empowerment Zone

You might talk to people who are fond of the subjective formats—the ones in which it is quite simple and fast to simply check off boxes on a form, without adding any comments. It's understandable that they would like something that is quick and easy—but did such a form meet your purpose for having appraisals?

➤ Have you developed performance standards for the various jobs in your company? Do people honestly know what is required to meet expectations? Has that been shared with employees?

➤ Have current job descriptions been completed for all positions? Have they been updated on a regular basis?

➤ How sophisticated are your managers and supervisors? Will a new form confuse and frustrate them? Does your current form confuse or frustrate them?

➤ Who are your employees? Does it make sense to have different forms for different levels of employees?

➤ Is your staff ready for self-evaluation?

There are a lot of variables to consider before designing a form. Remember that your basic goal is to design a form that people will understand and actually use.

Creating Performance Standards

Having performance standards in place will make the appraisal process much easier. So if you do not have standards established, now would be a good time to do so. Standards basically define what is acceptable performance for any given job. They often are used in production-type jobs where it is normal to expect employees to achieve certain "numbers," as in number of phone calls taken, number of customers served, number of cold calls made, and so on.

In Chapter 6, "First Things First," we discussed the beauty of a well-written job description. Job descriptions, you might remember, are documents that detail all of the duties and qualifications required of a certain position. Performance standards take those same duties and define the minimum level of acceptable performance for each of them.

Empowerment Zone

Having clear performance standards that have been communicated in a department can help reduce potential conflicts about salary and promotions. Those who meet all the measurable performance standards can be easily compared with those who do not. It saves you from an accusation of playing favorites.

Defining Production

Performance standards can be developed for any job. As you get into different types of jobs, the standards might call for demonstrable skills or behaviors rather than numerically quantifiable units of production.

For example, standards of performance for a health care provider might include some of the following:

➤ "Demonstrates knowledge of current nursing practice in assessing patients' nursing care."

➤ "Demonstrates familiarity with all health and safety regulations to provide a safe environment for patients, families, and co-workers."

Quantifiable Measurement

With some jobs, it's quite easy to come up with quantifiable units to measure. For example,

➤ Claims examiners must process a minimum of 100 claims per day.

➤ Data entry clerks will process a minimum of 130 orders per eight-hour shift.

➤ Customer service representatives must handle a minimum of 45 client calls per shift.

Employees who receive clear standards of what their targets are on a daily basis will know what is expected of them. Their performance can be easily measured, and fair comparisons can be made. Of course you do need to compare apples to apples. For example, in comparing the standards expected of sales representatives, it would be unfair to compare the sales numbers of those selling individual products, with those selling large group products, if large group sales was considered more difficult and time-consuming.

From the File Cabinet

Make sure people in the same jobs really do have the same responsibilities. When we consulted about staff turnover at a large call center, our investigation turned up individual differences in seemingly similar jobs. One of the call representatives told us she could not do as many calls as her co-workers, explaining that she was one of only two Spanish-speaking reps among 70. She received all of the Spanish-speaking clients, many of whom were new immigrants. Her calls on average lasted about one third longer than many of the other calls.

Close Up

An **outcome** is the result, consequence, or aftermath of some work or effort. This commonly used buzzword often indicates the desired end to a job's basic function; for example, an outcome of good nursing practice is a higher percentage of well patients.

Other methods of measure include accuracy percentages such as

➤ Receptionist will answer phone on third ring 90 percent of the time.

➤ Food service workers will load trays according to patient menu with 95 percent accuracy.

➤ Sales associates will maintain an 85 percent customer satisfaction rating.

It is quite easy to come up with measurable outcomes for some jobs, while others may approve more difficult. However, there are measurable *outcomes* that can be found for any job, even executive jobs. The following list is a nonexhaustive list of possible criteria that could be considered for a number of jobs:

➤ Quantity

➤ Quality

➤ Accuracy

➤ Timelines

➤ Satisfactory standards of practice

➤ Utilization of professional procedures

➤ Staying current with new information

➤ Customer satisfaction

➤ Co-worker satisfaction

Obviously the criteria you measure will depend upon your industry. See if you can't look at your own job and find ways to articulate measurement language to gauge your own performance.

Will It Stand Up in Court?

Unfortunately, there isn't one guaranteed foolproof design that will always withstand legal scrutiny. However, recent court decisions point to the following factors to ensure that you have a legally defendable performance appraisal system:

1. Managers and supervisors received written instructions and specific training in how to utilize the appraisals correctly.

2. Actual job content was used in determining what was evaluated on the appraisal.

3. Performance expectations had been reviewed in advance with the employees.

4. The appraisals were designed to evaluate behavior rather than personality traits.

5. The form was thoroughly discussed with the employee and the employee had a chance to add his or her own comments, if desired.

Just the Facts

Consistency is crucial in performance appraisals. There have been some high-profile court decisions—with high financial damages—levied against companies showing inconsistent practices in evaluating, and awarding increases in pay or position to, employees. Review of evaluations done of managers by their superiors makes good practice. Make sure there are no patterns that suggest one group is treated differently than others.

Whatever design you decide to use, another very important factor is being consistent in your use of these forms. If compensation and promotional decisions result from these appraisals, you must evaluate everyone fairly and consistently. Should an employee doubt that people were rated fairly and you end up in a court of law, the forms are discoverable. Don't take chances—play fair.

Improvement Plans

Another very useful section to add to your performance appraisal form is an improvement plan. Closely related to goal setting, an improvement plan helps you to suggest ways to help an employee attain a higher level of performance. Things that could be mentioned in an improvement plan section include

Close Up

An improvement plan is a written document that details the necessary steps required for someone to achieve the desired level of performance.

➤ Shadowing another more experienced employee in the unit for a period of time.

➤ Attending in-house or external education sessions.

➤ Working with a neighboring department for a day or two to learn how interdepartmental functions are related.

➤ Practicing good guest relations with difficult people.

➤ Repeating all or part of the orientation program for that position. (This assumes that the original orientation took place.)

Writing Goals

Every appraisal form should have a section to establish goals for the coming year. Your form might suggest ways to assist employees in linking their goals to department and corporate goals.

Goals keep us all going in the right direction. If they are well written they can inspire many employees to bigger and better things, regardless of their position with the company. Find out what motivates an employee, and put it into goal language. After a while you will find it easier to do this, and it actually becomes fun. Although you should be prepared with ideas for goals, of course, you will want to include the employee in the actual goal-setting process.

Solicit and Use Employee Input

If you truly want your new performance appraisal to be accepted and valued by your employees, you need to include them in the design process.

Do you truly value your human capital as much as your financial capital? Then prove it by valuing their feedback and input in this and other processes.

Form focus groups and discuss with employees what kind of feedback they want to receive. Questions to ask include

➤ What does useful feedback look like?

➤ What performance criteria would they include on a performance appraisal form?

➤ What ideas do employees have about measuring performance and fairness?

➤ What does a good job or performer look like?

➤ How do employees currently know when they have done a good job?

➤ What do employees like or dislike about the current system?

➤ How would employees suggest training people on how to use the performance appraisal program?

By including employee input, you might find that the job of redesigning a program isn't as difficult as you might think.

The Least You Need to Know

➤ Clearly articulate your company's philosophy before designing a performance appraisal system.

➤ Decide what your purpose is for having performance appraisals in the first place.

➤ Research what has or hasn't worked in the past.

➤ Customize a plan to meet your company's individual needs.

➤ Keep your appraisals legally defensible by using the format consistently.

➤ Utilize employee input to ensure your plan is accepted.

Open House: Sharing the Plan

It doesn't matter what style of form or program you design, if you don't get staff buy-in, it's not going to be very successful. Too many times companies try to force employees to accept an appraisal program that they resent or that they simply don't understand. Maybe the executives understand it (or not), but the line employees think that it is just more pointless propaganda.

Getting employees to accept an appraisal program involves gaining their trust, which may or may not be a challenge for your company. Trust among management and workers is a noble goal worth striving for—and you can't believe how much more productive your company can be if trust exists. But once again, trust is just a meaningless word unless your actions are consistent with your words. For example you can't talk about having a company policy that requires everyone to be treated with dignity and respect and then swear at your managers if you don't like something that they did.

Employee Buy-In

Companies that are very entrenched in hierarchy often make the mistake of not listening to and valuing the opinions of the line employees. There is a kind of corporate snobbism that develops and people jealously guard their titles and their turf to the exclusion of any real relationship with the staff. It creates the kind of "Us" and "Them" environment that often diminishes productivity and morale.

Just the Facts

An NLRB Case (Electromation, 1992) handcuffed employers from having formal employee-involvement committees since it seemed akin to company-dominated collective bargaining. There is an act before Congress called the Teamwork for Employees and Management (TEAM) Act that will change all that and allow greater formal employee involvement.

Sitting in their ivory towers, as line employees perceive it, executives create programs that may have some intellectual appeal but are not very user-friendly. Managers don't want to take the time the programs require, and if they do, employees are not motivated by them. Worse yet, many consultant- or management-driven initiatives end up creating resentment, because staff and many members of the management team feel that something has been imposed on them. And finally many of your managers and employees find some evaluation systems long, unmanageable, and pointless. They look at the forms and wonder how it really reflects an individual's actual contributions to the organization.

You have a much better chance of getting a program that works if you get input from all constituencies—include all levels of staff from executive to line employee. Only then will you get a rounded picture of what the company needs. Then utilize the suggestions that come from staff. Of course, not all ideas may be feasible, but some will be. There is probably a better chance that one of your line employees will come up with a better solution than most outside consultants. *The best consultants are able to utilize the employee feedback* to come up with the most fitting solutions.

When employees know that they helped to create a program, they have a vested interest in supporting it. And when you have told them that their input is valuable, and then actually use that input, it goes a long way in establishing trust. This technique works on other programs as well. Employees will be more likely to buy in to programs they have contributed to.

No Surprises

Just as performance appraisals should not contain surprises for the person being appraised, a new appraisal program should not be presented as a surprise to your company. Of course, if you have sought employee input from the beginning of the planning process, there will be less chance for surprises.

A sure way to "turn off" a staff is to introduce a new program that has been purchased or designed outside the organization and then introduced suddenly. And it happens all the time. However, we know from experience that the "surprise attack" will be viewed as the next corporate fad that has little or nothing to do with the real people working there.

When you are designing a new program, talk about it at staff meetings, publish it in the newsletter—don't keep it a secret. If you are not talking about it, it gives the impression that there is some reason to hide it. Being cryptic does nothing for establishing trust.

Everyone Gets Evaluated

In the spirit of fairness and trust, your program should be designed for everyone in the company. To deliver appraisals only to the line staff smacks of elitism, if not discrimination. Also in our experience managers are often times the most poorly supervised in terms of their administrators really knowing their work performance issues. As you go up to administration, VP levels and above it sometimes is even less accountable. If this happens you do get a disconnect from the company's philosophies and goals when it comes to management that line employees see, and come to resent. The entire organization must buy in to your program. If it is only utilized on a part of the employee population, it loses its credibility.

Not only should everyone be evaluated using the same program, mangers and others who are giving appraisals to others should be evaluated on their ability to deliver quality appraisals. The evaluation instrument should be a powerful motivating tool, but it will be so only if it is used properly.

Management Training

This is probably the most important part of designing and introducing a performance appraisal system. No matter how exquisite the plan looks on paper, if it is delivered poorly it becomes another worthless, and potentially harmful, piece of paper.

Also, don't forget the possibility that a poorly delivered performance appraisal could lead to litigation from a disgruntled employee. Spending a bit more time in training managers will be much less costly than fighting a legal battle. Refer to Chapter 2, "To Appraise or Not," where we go into the legal considerations involved.

Coaching, giving feedback, and evaluating staff—these are the most important aspects of a manager's job. And obviously these skills play a big part in delivering performance appraisals. If managers are not effective in these areas, they should receive training to help them become effective. If they do not respond to training, it's time to seriously question whether they should be managers.

From the File Cabinet

Some managers routinely consider internal education on a new program to be a waste of valuable time. They usually find a way to be absent from meetings introducing the program, citing more urgent matters to attend to. Or if they do attend because the program is mandatory, they pay scant attention to the presentation.

These managers are so set in their ways that when it comes to giving appraisals to their staff, they'll do it the way they've always done it, ignoring any advice to the contrary.

Having been appraised indifferently again, their direct reports have lost all belief in the new system, regardless of how it had been introduced to the company. A program is only as good as the people who deliver it.

Listed below are topics you should include if you are planning management training on delivering effective performance appraisals.

Empowerment Zone

An important element in any manager's own performance appraisal should be how effectively he or she gives feedback to staff. Superiors should pay close attention to each manager's department and listen to the opinions of staff. This means they (the superiors) have to be involved, but not intrusive, to their direct reports' (the manager's) departments.

➤ The philosophy behind the program: improvement and motivation for the company.

➤ How the program was designed: for what purpose (hopefully members of the management staff were included in the design phase).

➤ How to use the form: how to properly complete and score, if appropriate.

➤ How to give feedback in a positive manner: role play practice should be required.

➤ How to be consistent in giving feedback: how to use behavioral examples.

➤ How to focus on performance and not personality.

➤ How to coach for improvement.

➤ How to make wage and promotional decisions using performance data.

➤ How to discover weak spots and then how to use other resources to correct them.

Don't expect the training to be over in 30 minutes. Depending on the number and expertise of your managers, you should anticipate up to a full day of training. The cost of management training will be far less than a discrimination claim resulting from a manager's improper evaluation of an employee.

The training should be given annually, at orientation for new managers, and as updates when changes occur. You must consider the training ongoing to ensure that your managers will handle their responsibilities in a professional manner that will reduce the possibility of litigation.

From the File Cabinet

One manager we worked with thought she was such a good manager that she would rarely attend inservices to improve management skills, especially one given by the EAP which tended to focus on interpersonal skills. Over the years most of her employees came through the EAP program, many of them complaining about her unrealistic expectations, lack of support, and erratic behavior. Many of these employees would ultimately leave in disgust, or ended up taking long medical leaves. Not once was this manager evaluated on her ability to motivate, lead, retain, and support her staff.

It's very telling that weak managers tend to attribute their inability to get the job done on weak employees. They blame staff and take no responsibility for their inability to coach and motivate.

Confidentiality

In every company we have worked with, there is a common thread—people talk. People compare evaluations and compare salaries. Not all people, of course, but a significant number do so. Is there any way to ensure that they won't?

Keeping employee performance appraisal information confidential is typically a matter of good business practice and company policy. If you want to make a copy of your performance appraisal and

Just the Facts

The information in an employee's own review is his or hers to share or not. If you as a manager, or anyone else with access to the review, were to share that information with other staff members, however, this would violate confidentiality.

share it with everyone, there is nothing but your own good judgment to stop you. Whoever maintains the personnel file which might contain your current and past appraisals may share it only with internal people who have a business reason to see it, such as managers making decisions about promotions or discipline. Other than that the contents of a personnel file are to be shared only by subpoena. Many other things that might appear in a personnel file are protected by law—such as medical information.

Wise Counsel

The contents of personnel files, including performance appraisals, are discoverable by subpoena. So if an employee feels a co-worker received a better appraisal unjustly and takes the matter to court, the appraisals of all people named in the suit must be provided to the other attorney. What you put in an appraisal may end up more public than you intended.

Empowerment Zone

If your system is fair, objective and consistently carried out, there will be very little reason to oppose the sharing of information about performance appraisals. You can let people know that sharing their reviews may encourage jealousy or competitiveness among their co-workers.

Shhhh!

There may be no guaranteed way to prevent employees from sharing information. You can get a pretty good hold on it, however, if that concept is emphasized in the training. If a company treats all employees with trust, there is less of an inclination to be looking at someone else in a competitive manner. In companies where there is no trust, employees are suspicious and want to know if they are being cheated somehow.

The best way to encourage discretion is to treat employees fairly and respectfully, be honest with them, and ask them to handle their appraisals as prudently as possible. The possible consequences of sharing of performance appraisal information range from hurt feelings to something more serious. Though there is no way to force employees not to compare their appraisals, we don't recommend it. You can also tell employees that these are not popularity contests or contests of any kind. They are meant to give meaningful feedback to each person on what they have achieved and ways to improve and grow professionally. Having said we don't encourage sharing them, if you are factual, behavioral, even handed, and consistent in how you rate employees who do the same jobs you will have nothing to defend. As said before you may have to spend some time with employees who feel like they are as good as someone else and did not get credit for it.

Who Gets a Copy?

Once the performance appraisal is completed, delivered, and signed, then where does it go? And who, if anyone, should get a copy?

➤ The official document—the original document—the original document—should be placed in an employee's personnel folder, which is typically kept in a secure place, such as the human resources department, for example.

➤ Employees should also be given a *fully-executed copy* for their own records.

➤ The manager may want to keep a copy in his or her own files on each employee to utilize for reference purposes when giving follow-up feedback.

Close Up

A **fully-executed copy** is a complete copy of the original document, with any changes, added comments, and other information, as well as all signatures in place.

Those Compulsive Sharers

Unfortunately, even the most careful and trusting of companies may have a breach in confidentiality from time to time. It's going to happen and it probably isn't good form to discipline someone if you suspect it.

Confidentiality is overestimated in many areas. There are far fewer laws against sharing of information than many people think. Different kinds of professionals have licensing or ethical obligations but they often are not legal in nature. You also don't want to impose restrictions that are difficult to supervise and enforce.

Just the Facts

Should a performance appraisal be subpoenaed, the attorney issuing the subpoena would be provided a fully executed copy.

However, there should be few repercussions if your performance appraisals have been completed well and consistently. If all comments are backed up by behavioral examples that are real and observable, it will be more difficult for an employee to complain about fairness. There are no guarantees it won't happen, but the odds are in your favor.

Again, we go into the danger of discriminatory practice in Chapter 2.

Rebuttals

It's an employee's right to write a rebuttal if desired. Don't forget the courts like to see that you have given your employees freedom to exercise that right, so let them! Also you hopefully will learn something from it and it may help you to supervise them in the future. You may also see areas where you can prevent misunderstandings related to performance issues.

However, make sure you listen to the reasons for the rebuttal and read the document carefully. If you end up agreeing with the employee's comments, you may want to change the questioned rating on the appraisal form, rather than let the rebuttal appear separately. This kind of arrangement should be discussed with the employee and agreed to with signatures.

If you do not want to change the appraisal, then let the rebuttal stand as an addendum to the appraisal.

Once a Year Is Not Enough

Chapter 21, "Keeping It All On Track: Performance Management," describes how to implement an ongoing feedback program. If you don't want to be that formal about it, suffice it to say you will make your own job, and your employees' jobs, much more satisfying and productive if you give feedback more frequently than once a year. For example, if someone needs advice to do something more efficiently, it's better to tell him or her sooner than wait until an entire year has elapsed.

Casual Feedback

Giving feedback on an ad hoc, unscheduled basis can encourage better relationships. Employees know that you are actually paying attention and observing their performance. Compliments are good, but any feedback is flattering if it is offered in a positive way.

One Minute Manager Techniques

Ken Blanchard's *The One Minute Manager* shares persuasive arguments for on-the-spot feedback. Why wait until you have a meeting scheduled? If you see something that merits feedback, give that feedback now. Such spontaneous feedback encourages another technique that is good for the supervisor as well as the employees. It's MBA—or management by walking around. The only way you are going to see those moments deserving spontaneous feedback is if you are out and about, not glued to your desk all day.

From the File Cabinet

One manufacturing company we worked with had a executive plant manager who was at the office every day at 6:30 A.M. and did not leave until well into the second shift, around 8:30 P.M. He was pretty direct in his feedback to managers and employees. In our data gathering it was very clear: Every employee from the general manager on down to the janitors knew that this executive manager knew about every single area of the plant, respected his feedback, and valued his involvement and knowledge of what they did. We did, however, give him some feedback on the way he delivered his feedback, which often was too rough or intense.

Don't Keep Secrets Until Appraisal Time

Yes, we're going to emphasize this point again. If you are giving regular feedback throughout the year, there should be no surprises during an annual appraisal. The meeting will basically be summarizing things the employee should already know, as they have been mostly covered through the year. It makes it much easier on both of you.

Timing Annual Appraisals

You've got several choices, and there may be arguments for any of them. But our recommendation is to scatter them throughout the year. That way, managers won't be faced by having to do a great number all at once. Your managers will thank you for this arrangement. We talk about the timing of appraisals in more detail in Chapter 1, "Report Cards for the Working Class."

Employees for the most part seem to expect annual feedback on the anniversary of their date of hire. Be sure that you communicate the timing of appraisals when you orient new employees and when you roll out a new program.

The Least You Need to Know

➤ Without employee acceptance and buy-in, your chances of success are low.

➤ Communicate the same thing to everyone, from the top down, and manage the program consistently.

➤ Effective management training is the most critical aspect of ensuring a successful program.

➤ An employee has the right to offer a rebuttal if desired.

➤ Give feedback more often than once a year.

Chapter 20

Tinkering and Remodeling: Improving the Plan

In This Chapter

➤ Adding sophistication to your appraisal program

➤ How to avoid playing favorites

➤ How often does your plan need a tune up?

➤ Identifying and dealing with problems

Once your plan is up and running, don't think that your job is over. Remember that an ongoing feedback system, which includes an annual performance appraisal plan, is a moving, ever-changing program that should be reviewed regularly. In the information age most things are moving so fast; you don't want your program to become obsolete as fast as your PC does.

After all the hard work you have put into your program, you might think it's time to take a break for a while. But jobs change, management changes, and your plan must be adaptable to such changes. What can you do to ensure you have a plan that will adapt to the inevitable changes of today's corporate world? This chapter will give you some advice on keeping your plan current.

Aside from reviewing the plan to make sure it's still working, you might want to add components as you feel your organization is ready for them.

Self-Evaluation

Some appraisal programs include self-evaluation at the very beginning of the process. The effective use of self-evaluation is seen as a way of building on the two-way conversation concept.

Empowerment Zone

Most companies utilizing self-evaluation will give employees a form to complete about a month prior to their annual evaluation. That way their self-feedback can be submitted and reviewed by the supervisor to assist in completing the annual appraisal.

The concept often does not go over well for reasons that we have mentioned previously:

➤ Employees tend to rate themselves harder than they have to.

➤ Employees feel that managers are asking them to do the manager's job.

➤ It can create the feeling of "If I'm so valuable, how come you don't really know what I am doing?"

➤ Some managers don't use the self-evaluation wisely. They merely sign it and make it the official evaluation without any input of their own.

➤ Some employees simply won't complete self-evaluations.

Still, it's possible to gather valuable data from the proper use of these instruments. And if you feel your company is ready, and that you can carefully explain the use and value of self-evaluations, you might want to add this component to your program. Just make sure it does not become the whole program.

We talk about company readiness in more detail in Chapter 26. However, in a nutshell, your company is ready when there is enough trust between management and staff that communication is open and comfortable.

Rather than giving the employee the same form to complete that the manager has completed, we suggest designing a different format that will elicit more information from the employee. A sample form utilizing open-ended questions is shown in the following figure.

Peer Evaluation and 360-Degree Evaluation

After introducing self-evaluation, there are other steps you can take to enhance your appraisal program. Among the options open to you are peer evaluation and 360-degree evaluation. We go into these techniques in more detail in Chapter 26, "Peer-to-Peer and 360-Degree Feedback."

Employee Self Evaluation

(Please answer each question on the form below. If you need additional space, feel free to add another piece of paper.)

1. What goals have you been working on during this evaluation period?

2. During this evaluation period, did your goals stay the same as you planned or did they change?

3. What do you consider your accomplishments during this period?

4. Were your accomplishments consistent with your goals, or different?   Please explain.

5. What accomplishment or achievement are you most proud of?

6. What were the disappointments or frustrations you faced?

7. What goals, if any, did you fail to achieve?

8. What were the reasons for your not achieving the goal(s)?

9. How can your manager help you to achieve your goals?

10. What things do you need from the company?

11. What are your goals for the coming year?

12. Other Comments?

This sample employee self-evaluation asks employees to respond to questions about their perspectives on the jobs they are doing. The questions can be easily modified to fit specific needs.

Customer Feedback

Whether you work in what is traditionally considered a service industry or not, every business has customers that it serves. There is every reason to offer customers the chance to offer feedback on your services. The best reason to do so is that you can learn where you are succeeding with customers and perhaps why you are losing some. However, you must make it easy, accessible, and anonymous for them to do so. In the past year or so we have seen examples of this by a large health maintenance organization, a heating and air-conditioning company, hotels, and a home construction company. Some customers are very vocal and will give feedback whether it is formally solicited or not. However, having a method of regular customer feedback as part of your standard procedures will give others an opportunity to give you feedback that you may never have received otherwise.

From the File Cabinet

For the past 15 years we have run employee assistance programs that have a built-in evaluation as part of the process. Clients are given a form with stamped, addressed envelopes to help get a higher rate of returns. It is always exciting and a bit threatening when each year we compile this data. Each clinician can see how he or she has been reviewed by clients and how the program is rated overall. Getting honest feedback has helped most of the people involved to gain more satisfaction, motivation—and a bit of humility, too. We can't think of a better way of finding out how you are doing.

Here are some ways to keep it simple and make a successful customer feedback program:

➤ Use clear, simple language and keep it short.

➤ Make a drop box or stamped, addressed envelope available with the form—or direct customers to the e-mail feedback address.

➤ Make the form available at the time of service and ask employees to encourage customers to fill one out before leaving. People don't want to look at more mail at home.

➤ Let customers know you really use the feedback to improve services, and to fairly evaluate staff.

Gorden & Associates
2131 San Pablo Avenue, Pinole, CA 94564 (510) 547-8830
5435 College Avenue, Suite 107, Oakland, CA 94618 (510) 547-8830

EMPLOYEE ASSISTANCE PROGRAM
EVALUATION QUESTIONNAIRE

Name of employer_____

INSTRUCTIONS:
Although most questions can be answered by placing a check mark, some questions may ask for more extensive information. We encourage you to write any additional comments you may have. Please do **NOT** put your name on this questionnaire. We ask for your candid opinion about your experience at the EAP.

1. How did you hear about the EAP?
   Brochure ( )   Orientation ( )   Co-worker ( )   Supervisor ( ) Other ( )

2. How soon after your initial phone call were you contacted by an EAP counselor?
   Same day ( )   1 - 2 days ()   3 - 5 days ( )   over 6 days ( )

3. How long did you have to wait for your first appointment?
   0 - 3 days ( )   4 - 7 days ( )   7 - 10 days ( )   over 11 days ( )

4. After your first appointment, how comfortable were you about using the EAP?
   Very comfortable ( )   Somewhat ( )   Not very ( )   Not at all comfortable ( )

5. Please rate the overall effectiveness of the EAP.
   Excellent ( )   Very good ( )   Good ( )   Fair ( )   Poor ( )

6. Please rate the degree to which you feel the program ensured privacy and confidentiality.
   Excellent ( )   Very good ( )   Good ( )   Fair ( ) Poor ( )

   Please comment if you had concerns about how the EAP handled confidentiality:
   _____
   _____
   _____
   _____

7. If there were no EAP, would you have gone anywhere else for help with your problem?
   Yes ( )   No ( )   Unsure ( )
   Comments:_____
   _____
   _____
   _____

8. Who was your EAP counselor?

9. Would you recommend the EAP to others?
   Yes ( )   No ( )   Unsure ( )

10. Comments or suggestions about the program or your counselor.
   _____
   _____
   _____
   _____
   _____
   _____

11. Sex: Female ( )   Male ( )

12. Length of Employment:

   Less than 1 year ( )   1 - 5 years ( )   6 - 10 years ( )   11 - 15 years ( )
   16 - 25 years ( )   Over 25 years ( )

13. Number of sessions:

This is a sample of a customer evaluation used at Gorden and Associates.

209

Consistency

When using any of the more advanced methods of performance appraisal, it becomes more difficult to be sure your appraisals are consistent. Some people might be very good at participating in these other appraisal styles, whereas others might be extremely resistant. And if you are in the position of having to force people to self-evaluate or otherwise participate, it's better not to.

When people strongly feel that they do not want to participate, you must face the fact that your organization might not be ready to utilize these methods. More education—or just more time to let trust develop—might be necessary.

However, many times the reluctance to use the new techniques comes from lack of training. Consistent staff education is always appropriate when introducing new practices. Give the employees lots of examples and lots of time to get their questions answered. Stress the importance of their buy-in and consistency factors so they realize that their participation is a company expectation.

Periodic Auditing

After spending six months or more designing an appraisal system and rolling it out to your company, you will feel a great sense of relief that the project is finished. However, your program is not going to stay current and effective unless you audit it occasionally to see if it is still working.

From the File Cabinet

A large company we worked with was using four or five different evaluation forms for staff all over the company. The communication of revised forms had been so scattered that many departments were still using forms that officially had been obsolete for several years. Conducting an audit of personnel files and evaluating the performance review forms was an eye-opening experience.

How Often

We recommend doing some spot auditing annually. This would require checking the personnel files of a handful of employees to see if appraisals exist and if they have been completed accurately. Of course, if you find no appraisals at all, you have a bigger problem on your hands!

A more thorough audit should take place every two years. In two years' time a lot can change—including job titles, functions, and lots of the incumbents in positions all over the company. Ongoing training of new employees should keep the procedures fairly consistent—but your forms or some of the content therein might need to be revised as jobs change.

Who Does It?

Most often this is a job that is delegated to the human resources department. HR staff have access to all the personnel files, and hopefully have devised a method of ensuring that all appraisals are completed in a timely manner. HR would know how compliant managers have been with follow-ing required timelines. If you are a smaller company it will probably fall to you, the boss, but consider using a few motivated employees as well.

Empowerment Zone

Most of the larger HR offices that have an HRIS (Human Resources Information System) will use the computer to track evaluations. Usually the program will have a field that calls for the date of an employee's most recent evaluation. It is updated when a new evaluation is received.

Oh, Say Can You See ... What to Look For

Naturally, you want to make sure the appraisals are being done in a timely manner. But there are many other components you want to take a look at to make sure your system is attaining the desired results. Start with the managers who are using the forms and ask the following questions:

➤ Are the forms—and is the system—useful to you?

➤ Are the forms easy to follow and complete?

➤ Do the forms encourage two-way feedback?

➤ How have the appraisals been received overall by your staff?

➤ Have goals and improvement plans been set and monitored?

➤ Has there been measurable improvement as a result of the appraisals?

➤ Has there been follow-up on action plans ?

After using the program for approximately a year, managers should have something to say about how well it is working for them. Be sure to document all of their feedback about the program to utilize when tinkering with your form.

Close Up

Used in this context, a **focus group** is a sample group of employees who are chosen to represent the entire employee population in order to discuss a chosen topic. In this case a focus group might consist of a few managers and a few line employees from various departments throughout the company who will meet and discuss their perceptions of the performance appraisal plan.

Communication

The best way to audit the continued effectiveness of your program is to ask everyone about it. Continue your practice of open communication with all levels of employees—not just the managers—and simply ask them what they think is working or not working.

Asking a mixed group of employees and managers—from various areas of the company—and forming a *focus group* to discuss the system often is a very productive way of handling the audit. Appoint a recorder to write down all the commentary about the program and have human resources or the appropriate management group review the comments. Then use those comments while you tune up your performance appraisal system.

How About a Survey?

If your company is large and focus groups are not feasible, an employee survey often is an effective way to obtain staff opinion on various aspects of the organization, or how well the organization is doing including utilizing its performance review program. When distributing a survey, you should let every employee know that they have an opportunity to let their voice be heard. A relatively brief survey could be fashioned to encourage the staff to let you, or whoever is in charge of the program, know their satisfaction level with an appraisal program. A survey can be distributed with paychecks on payday to get the best response.

Your survey might look something like this:

Dear Employee:

Please help us evaluate the current performance appraisal system by answering the following questions and returning this survey to Human Resources in an interoffice envelope no later than (date):

1. I have been given a performance appraisal in the last year. Y N

2. Rate the form according to the following scale: _____

        A.   Encourages useful feedback between myself and my supervisor

        B.   Is acceptable, but needs some modifications to make it better

        C.   Unsatisfactory

Explain:_____

3. The things I like best about the form are:

4. The things I would change about the form are:

Signature (optional):_____

When evaluating the data received from such a survey, you will be looking for trends or similar responses from a number of people. The isolated criticism—or even compliment—is not as relevant as the comment that is repeated by many.

When the Problem Is Management

If as a result of your research with your employees you find that there are problems with your system, you will need to find the actual cause of those problems. Is it the program or is it the people who are delivering the program? If employees feel comfortable enough to be honest, you might find out that the biggest problem with your system is the manner in which some managers deliver appraisals to their staff.

If none of the managers are doing an effective job with the appraisals, it's fairly safe to assume there are major problems in the design of your program. However, if some are doing a good job and some are doing an unsatisfactory job, it might point to some remedial training.

Using the information gathered from employees, try to identify the areas in which they are experiencing the most difficulties and plan a training program around those areas.

Performance appraisals do require a lot of time and effort. But considering their importance in the overall success of your business, they are well worth that time and effort.

Wise Counsel

The most important follow-up you can give your staff following an employee opinion survey is to report on your findings. Summarize what you have learned, and report it back to the entire staff. You can include the response as a memo in the paycheck, include it in the employee newsletter if there is one, or send memos to all.

Empowerment Zone

If some managers "got it" while others did not, think about encouraging the well-trained managers to share their success tips with those needing more time. Often managers will accept the advice from their peers more readily than they will accept it from "trainers" or human resources personnel.

The Least You Need to Know

➤ If your company is ready for them, self-evaluation and other more advanced evaluation formats can help you to gather useful feedback.

➤ Service organizations should consider using customer evaluations as part of their appraisal programs.

➤ Consistency is a must when administrating a performance evaluation program.

➤ You will need to conduct ongoing audits on your appraisal program to ensure that it stays current and viable.

➤ Seek feedback from every level of your organization when auditing the program; then share and use the information that you gather.

Chapter 21

Keeping It All On Track: Performance Management

In This Chapter

➤ What is performance management?

➤ What components might you include?

➤ Is your company ready?

➤ What happens if your company isn't ready?

What do we mean when we say "performance management?" It actually involves following many of the suggestions we've made in this book. Performance management as we define it is a formal system of continuous feedback. It's more than obvious that we advocate the technique of frequent feedback; some companies actually have taken the next step—they not only suggest continuous feedback, they make it a company-wide policy.

Whether a blanket policy of this method will work at your company depends on several factors. The most important thing to remember, however, is that if you implement the plan and announce it to your staff, you—and the entire supervisory staff—must follow through. If you don't, you will be looked at with suspicion and distrust. A real performance management system requires lots of open communication. Can you honestly say that your company is ready for this? Read on and see.

Design in a Nutshell

The once-a-year appraisal method often is referred to as a traditional feedback method; *performance management* therefore is something different from traditional. The words "continuous feedback" can be rather formidable if you have never considered this form of management. Exactly how continuous do we mean? Like all day, every day?

Close Up

Performance management is a formal system designed to provide continuous feedback between employers and employees, rather than the once-a-year approach. Performance standards are established for each job and employees are coached with continuous feedback to reach or exceed the standard.

How Often Is Continuous?

How often you sit down for a formal feedback session depends upon your individual preference. Typically the systems we have seen in process have at least two, and no more than four, formal feedback sessions per year. By formal we mean making an appointment to sit down privately and discuss progress toward goals.

In reality we are always giving continuous feedback. Whenever you choose to remark positively, negatively, or ignore work behavior, this is feedback. When you are too busy to meet with your direct reports this is taken by them as feedback. When you come in each morning and rush to your desk without acknowledging the receptionist or co-workers, this is feedback. The feedback may not be intended, but be sure it is having an effect on behavior. So if you think about continuous feedback as the effect of your behavior, policies, and management style and work environment on your employees' behavior; learn to make sure you are using it effectively to improve performance and morale in your place of work.

Designing a Plan

Just as you must take the time to plan a traditional performance appraisal plan, you must also take the time to adequately research and design a system of performance management. We've provided a list of some of the bases you should cover during this planning process.

➤ Before undertaking the plan, the company should articulate its most important goals and values; for example, why does the company exist and what is it trying to accomplish? (One of the values established should address the company's attitude toward its employees.)

➤ Goals that are related and complementary to the company's goals should be agreed upon with all employees. Spend time learning the motivations of your staff to find ways to link goals.

➤ Decide on the number of formal appraisal sessions that will be scheduled between each supervisor and employee. You might tie these sessions into quarterly returns or bi-annual company performance.

➤ Employees and managers should agree upon the performance standards on which employees will be evaluated. In other words, what does success look like? Would someone from outside the company who was watching people work be able to pick out the behaviors that you are trying to measure or encourage?

➤ Educate managers and employees on how the program will work. Emphasize the two-way conversation part of the program. Employees must be encouraged to give feedback to the boss as well.

➤ Develop forms to be utilized for feedback sessions, if desired.

➤ Roll out the program to the company and monitor its consistent application.

➤ If there is a gap between actual performance and the established performance standard, identify training needs and provide appropriate training.

➤ Help employees learn how to identify resistance, or personal blocks to engaging in desired performance or behavior.

There are a number of ways that you can make feedback continuous. You do not have to micromanage by following every employee around to

Empowerment Zone

Keep in mind that if your supervisors have trouble giving appraisals once a year, it will take a major paradigm shift for them do more appraisal meetings per employee per year. If you are committed to making this change, you must realize that you will have to allocate time for assessments, education, and training of your managers on how to manage these meetings.

Just the Facts

Using different types of reinforcement schedules with different types of behaviors is important. Try continuous positive reinforcement for very new behaviors, and differential reinforcement when the behaviors have been well established; this will keep people invested and feeling that their efforts to change matter. We all want to feel noticed and rewarded for our efforts.

give frequent feedback. Instead you should find ways to make yourself available to employees. Some ways of doing that are

➤ An open door policy to make it clear that you are available for impromptu meetings or discussions as needed.

➤ Brown bag lunch discussions to go over how the company is doing and how the employees' contributions are helping to attain goals.

➤ Taking the time to notice and reinforce what you want to see more of. If you see someone going the extra mile, acknowledge that person.

➤ Try to find out what kind of behavior from you as a manager is positively reinforcing to your employees. One person may respond well to praise, another to some flexibility in their schedule needs, and a third to your giving them more autonomy.

Empowerment Zone

Try not to confuse being available with micro-managing. When you are walking around the department, focus on encouragement, not scrutinizing every detail of what employees are doing. With open, trusting communication there should be no need to micro-manage.

From the File Cabinet

The most effective positive reinforcement for Beth was for her supervisor to check in with her in the morning to give her assignments and to check in at the end of the day to see how her work went. The feeling that she was trusted to do her job was what made Beth happy at work. Then Beth got a new supervisor who checked on employees often throughout the day, thinking people would like this and also to learn how people did their jobs. After staff meetings, the new supervisor realized she had to let her staff know she needed more contact to really orient herself to the job. Effective performance management identifies the reinforcements for each person, and then deliberately applies them to each situation and person.

There might be many other creative ideas to keep the feedback going. When you truly keep the employees informed about how their progress impacts the company's progress, real teamwork and loyalty are often the result.

A technique you might try is to keep a feedback log on all of your employees that simply helps you keep track of dates and kinds of feedback given. You could keep this on a computer spreadsheet or just a manual log.

Employee Name	Hire Date	Feedback Date	Documented? Yes/No	Type of Feedback

Here is an example of a feedback log that you might keep for your direct reports. It could be kept on your computer or could be simply a manual log that you can access and update quickly.

Encouraging Collaboration

One of the best features of an ongoing performance management program is that it removes much of the top-down judgment aspect of traditional appraisal, and makes feedback a collaborative situation. Instead of employees waiting a year (or more) to hear the verdict of an autocratic manager, they will have ongoing discussions that will enable them to make changes when necessary and get encouragement when they need it most. Managers will hear feedback that might help them become better managers.

It really is the ultimate win-win for managers, employees, and the company.

Components of a Performance Management Program

Any or all of the levels of feedback we have discussed can be utilized in a performance management plan. If your company is ready for performance management, it probably is ready for the more sophisticated feedback methods. These include

1. **Self appraisal**   Employees should be able to appraise themselves prior to their formal feedback sessions with you. As your appraisals will be focused on goals,

it should be possible for them to report on their progress and whether any problem is hindering their efforts to accomplish their goals. You might want to provide a basic outline form for them with four to six open-ended questions.

2. **Peer appraisal**   A team that is utilizing the open communication technique in a mature manner is ready to give evaluations of teammates. Keep in mind that before you start such a program, employees should receive education in giving feedback that is both behaviorally based and constructive. We describe this technique more fully in Chapter 26, "Peer-to-Peer and 360-Degree Feedback."

3. **360-degree appraisal**   A great way to start this program is to ask all your staff to review you first. You can discuss this at your formal feedback sessions. Once they are comfortable being able to appraise you, the program can be opened up to co-workers in other departments, customers, and so forth. Again, refer to Chapter 26 for a more in-depth look at 360-degree appraisals.

Empowerment Zone

Tone and phrasing are everything when giving feedback. Watch your tone for whining, sarcasm, judgmentalness, and other undermining messages. Instead of saying, "I hate the way you never help out your co-workers," try "I would like to see more teamwork, like your offering to fill in on the phones when your co-worker goes on break."

In order to ensure you have a comprehensive program, it is important to be consistent in asking employees if you or the company can do something that will improve their jobs or work environment, and to provide ongoing educational opportunities to keep staff up to date and motivated toward improving their skills will also make your plan more complete.

Another good suggestion when designing your plan is to customize forms for feedback that encourage the two-way conversation, utilizing a series of questions regarding goals—whether they have been met, if they should be changed, and so forth.

Advantages and Benefits

There are many advantages to using continuous feedback. We have mentioned most of them throughout the book. By communicating frequently with your employees you have a much better chance of building a team of people who are not only loyal, but also accountable for their work. Employees who take pride in the fact that they personally impact the success of the company will be more productive. People really do want to know where they stand in your estimation. Not keeping them in the dark helps them to relax, change, or re-examine where they need to be.

Quarterly Self Review

GOALS

1. Describe your goals for the current quarter

Increase sales by 10% over same quarter last year
Increase contact list by 30 new potential contacts

2. Did your goals change or stay the same during this quarter?

Stayed consistent

ACCOMPLISHMENT

1. Describe your performance versus your goals

Sales are going well. I'm over my goal of 10% with 12% increase this quarter over last year.
I'm below my goal on contacts. Sales negotiations took more time than I had anticipated.
I plan on making that up next quarter.

2. What other objective(s) did you achieve over your goals?

Closing the Richardson deal felt like a major accomplishment. They had presented a number
of challenges and I thought it might take longer to close them if at all. But it was worth the time
and effort. In the future I think they will be a good client for us.

3. What are you most proud of?

See above – the Richardson deal.

SETBACKS

1. Did you experience any setbacks or frustrations this quarter?

Emma's resignation as a sales associate was a big disappointment for me. She was one of
my strongest team members and I'm sorry we couldn't find a way to convince her to stay.

2. What goals (if any) did you fail to reach? Why?

I didn't quite reach my goal on new contacts. Losing Emma certainly played a part in that.
Our team has been short staffed since August. I have interviewed some new associates and
we should have a replacement hired within the next few weeks.

EXPECTATIONS

1. What are your expectations for the next quarter?

Fourth quarter has always been my strongest quarter, so I expect to do quite well over the next three months.
I expect to catch up on new contacts from last quarter and to make an additional 30 contacts by quarter's end.
I am aiming for sales of 15% higher than the same period last year. And, of course I'm expecting to hire another
sales associate and have him or her trained by end of quarter.

2. How can your manager help you achieve your goals?

Consistent support and feedback is important. I like the fact that she isn't always looking over my shoulder, but
I appreciate our bi-weekly meetings to discuss progress.

3. Is there anything you need from the company?

We needed updated materials on the Series Q Product line. Some design features have changed, but the materials
don't reflect the changes.

OTHER COMMENTS

I want to commend the production department on improving their speed of product delivery. It really has gotten better
in recent weeks.

---

*A feedback form walks an employee through a series of questions that then
can be reviewed in a sit-down meeting with the manager. The manager also
can fill out a form and respond to the same kinds of questions.*

Just the Facts

The 1997 National Study of the Changing Workforce in America asked employees what they feel are the most important reasons for staying at a job. 85 percent cited "open communication" as one of the most important reasons for staying where they currently work.

Wise Counsel

The worst thing you can do with the subject of continuous feedback is to announce to the staff that it is implemented, and then to never follow through, or ensure that managers are complying. Not doing what you say you will do is a bad practice.

For employees, the benefits of continuous feedback can include the following:

➤ More involvement with the company's goals

➤ Opportunity to have their opinions heard

➤ Being recognized for accomplishment

➤ Feeling of value to company

➤ Identifying continuous opportunities for learning and development

➤ Possible rewards built into actual results

➤ Work environment built on trust

Companies might also enjoy many benefits from continuous feedback, including

➤ Productive, enthusiastic staff.

➤ Improved or better employee retention.

➤ Being perceived as an employer of choice, which may make recruitment easier and more productive.

➤ Combined goal orientation, with everybody headed in the same direction.

➤ Clear expectations that result in more accurate work.

➤ More involved, experienced management.

➤ Opportunity to identify obstacles to productivity and take action before damage occurs.

➤ Better accountability when there is a non-performing employee.

The Right Stuff to Make it Work

In the right company, a well-designed and consistent performance management system can be extremely powerful. When it is up and running, employees will be participatory and will tell others about it. It will be easier to recruit new people to the company.

Which Companies Are Right for Performance Management?

If the company is small enough and new enough to introduce performance management as a policy, the process might be quite successful. Size can play a part in that the program will take a lot of monitoring in the early stages, and if there are too many employees spread over a large area or areas, your ability to monitor is diminished. If you are a larger company you will need committed directors or other senior managers who will help to monitor and teach this new way of doing things.

Companies who are not so new but have a strong tradition of open communication also are likely candidates for performance management. Some companies might already be utilizing many of the components of continuous feedback, but have never formally put a label on what they're doing.

Often companies who adopt a performance management program are organizations that also believe in the concept of continuous learning. These companies provide training at all levels and establish the kind of culture that rewards employees for learning and developing. In-house learning opportunities are frequent, and outside education supporting the business is subsidized and encouraged.

From the File Cabinet

A large company we worked with faced the typical challenge of getting all of its employees evaluated. Company leaders, along with an expensive consultant and a team of managers spent months designing a performance management program that included quarterly feedback sessions. Human Resources assisted with the roll out for more than 2,000 employees in 10 locations. Four-hour training sessions were given to all managers.

Within the first year of the new program, 75 percent of managers were unable or unwilling to meet their commitment of four feedback sessions per year. The human resources department was too busy with new projects to continue training new managers for the program. Employees soon were scoffing at the notion of performance management, and the program quickly dissolved.

When the Timing Is Wrong

If you and your company are still taking baby steps toward implementing performance feedback of any kind, it might not be advisable to spring a formal performance management program on your staff. Unless your management team is experienced in feedback, imposing a continuous feedback system almost certainly is doomed for failure.

Many companies should be glad to simply get a system of regular annual appraisals in place. Once everyone is on board with annual appraisals, and they have been monitored successfully for at least two years, you might want to layer in some of the other components.

Here are some signs that your company probably isn't ready for performance management:

➤ Performance appraisals are rarely completed in a timely manner (if at all).

➤ Managers claim to be too busy to talk to employees regularly.

➤ Staff meetings are frequently canceled because everyone is too busy or no one has suggested any agenda items.

➤ Top administration manages from an "ivory tower" and doesn't communicate with line staff.

➤ "Us" and "them" mentality is obvious everywhere.

➤ Turnover is high.

➤ Morale is low and trust is nonexistent.

➤ Managers are inexperienced, timid, rigid, or unable to lead by example.

➤ Little or no communication is available to staff about how the company is doing.

➤ There is little or no orientation toward goal setting.

➤ There is little or no emphasis put on education and development.

Just the Facts

A survey done in 1997 for the Society of Human Resources Management illustrated the high cost of turnover. To replace a manager or employee with very hot skills costs two to four times the annual salary of the person being replaced.

Empowerment Zone

Running a successful meeting isn't as easy as it sounds. Try varying the pace and mixing questions and answers with reports on various aspects of the department or company. Get feedback on how you run meetings and ask for suggestions on how to meet specific needs. You might need to gain new speaking and facilitation skills, but the results are well worth the effort.

These characteristics are distressing, and also could be signs that a company may be experiencing challenges in financial, leadership, retention, and other important areas. Unfortunately, many companies share at least a few or more of these problems. However, it is never too late to take strides toward changing the situation.

To Change a Bad Situation

We've said it before and we'll say it again: Practice MBWA— management by walking around. Talk to your employees, listen to their opinions, and take the first small steps toward open, two-way communication. You might be surprised at all the good and productive ideas that come out of those conversations.

You will go a long way toward improving trust at your company if after getting opinions from your employees you actually act on their suggestions. Prove to them that their ideas are valued within the company. This will start the process of earning the trust of your staff. And with trust comes loyalty. It isn't difficult to achieve if you give it a chance.

The Least You Need to Know

➤ Performance management can be designed in a number of ways, but basically it is a formal plan of continuous feedback.

➤ A well-designed performance management program can help your company become more successful, with employees who are motivated and accountable.

➤ If feedback of any sort is a problem, you are not ready for performance management.

➤ Before performance management is attempted, trust should be developed between management and staff.

Part 6
Measurement Matters: Types of Appraisals

The next several chapters will show you some ideas for designing your performance appraisal forms. We try to cover several of the popular types of forms that we have run across in the corporate world. There probably are hundreds of individual designs being utilized in various places.

The choice of which instrument to use has a lot to do with the kind of organization you work for. For example some industries might have regulatory requirements that must be covered in an appraisal. Also the size of the company, number of employees, and kind of work being done can impact your choice. Just let your fingers do the walking through some of these samples and see if one, or a hybrid of more than one, feels right for you and your company.

Chapter 22

Check Please: Fill in the Blanks

In This Chapter

➤ The basic, one-page, check-the-box type form

➤ When this format is a good choice

➤ When another format might be better

➤ Deciding on the rating scales to use

By far the simplest form of performance appraisal is the fill-in-the-blank form. These also probably are the most commonly used forms. The reasons are obvious: They are brief (typically one or two pages) and they can be completed rather quickly. Managers who have great numbers of appraisals to complete can get this kind of form done more quickly than the other lengthy forms that require narrative text.

Some models tend to be too character-trait–based, but there are some that incorporate behavioral measurement in the form as well.

What's the Score

The typical fill-in-the-blank form will call for the appraiser to rate an employee's performance according to a ratings key. Ratings usually are numeric codes that are equivalent to levels of performance.

Following the ratings key will be a list of performance descriptors, each of which should be evaluated by the manager and given a rating number.

The simplest of these forms calls for no documentation to explain why an employee receives whatever rating is checked. Without documented performance examples, the form easily can be criticized for invoking a subjective opinion from the manager. If the manager likes the employee better than someone else, what is there to stop him or her from rating him or her higher than someone else?

Basic Performance Review

Employee's Name:_____ Department:_____

Job Title:_____ Date Hired:_____ Time in Current Job:_____

Supervisor's Name: _____Supervisor's Title:_____

Length of Time Covered in Appraisal:_____

Importance of Evaluation Factor: Rate the importance of each factor in terms of its effect on overall job performance:

3 – Critical
2 – Very Important
1 – Somewhat Important

Rating Key: Please rate the employee according to the following definitions:

E –	**Clearly Outstanding.**	Exceeded all job expectations.
A –	**Above Expectations.**	Met all expectations and exceeded many of them.
M –	**Met Expectations.**	Met all position expectations, exceeded some of them.
B –	**Below Expectations.**	Failed to meet or only partially met expectations. Improvement needed.
U –	**Clearly Unsatisfactory.**	Performance is unacceptable.

<table>
<tr><td align="center" colspan="2">**Evaluation**</td><td align="center">**Importance/Rating**</td></tr>
</table>

1. **Job Knowledge.** Evaluate use of information, procedures, equipment, etc. necessary for job.

2. **Quality.** Evaluate the accuracy, completeness, and follow-through of work.

3. Planning/Organizing. Consider areas such as varying work demands, meeting goals, etc.

4. **Productivity.** Evaluate the volume and timeliness of work.

5. **Initiative.** Consider self-starting ability, resourcefulness, creativity applied to duties.

6. **Cooperation.** Consider relationships with other employees.

7. **Dependability.** Consider punctuality, attendance, meeting deadlines, etc.

8. **Customer Service.** Consider relationship with other departments, external customers.

Overall Rating: _____

Employee Signature:_____   Date:_____

Supevisor's Signature:_____   Date:_____

The basic performance review form employs a very simple, fill-in-the-blank technique. Managers are instructed to rank the importance of each factor, and then to evaluate each one. It would be advisable to add a second page to the form to enable the manager to back up his ratings with behavioral examples.

Annual Performance Appraisal

Name of Employee Being Reviewed:___Mindy Samuels_____

Manager's Name:_____George Rockwood_____

Review Period Start Date: _7__/__1_/_99

Review Period End Date: _6__/_30__/__00_

Rating Key:

NA –Not Applicable

1 – Unsatisfactory	Unable to perform required tasks. Requires too much supervision.
2 – Marginal	Meets some requirements. Needs improvement in quality of work and completing tasks on time.
3 – Meets Requirements	Quality of work consistently meets requirements and tasks are completed on time.
4 – Exceeds Requirements	Consistently goes above and beyond goals and objectives required for the position. Exceeds requirements for quality and quantity.
5 – Exceptional	Significantly exceeds requirements and expectations. Always accomplishes results far beyond what is required. *Note: usage of this rating is highly limited.

JOB PERFORMANCE:

	NA	1	2	3	4	5
Works effectively with their team to achieve set objectives. Profits from constructive criticism.	NA	1	2	3	x4	5
Capable of required job skills and knowledge.	NA	1	2	x3	4	5
Demonstrates effective use of skills and training.	NA	1	2	x3	4	5
Behaviors consistent with company policy.	NA	1	2	x3	4	5
Has the ability to learn and use new skills.	NA	1	2	x3	4	5
Keeps current with changes and trends in the technical knowledge required for the position.	NA	1	2	x3	4	5

Comments:

Mindy is a reliable employee who meets all performance expectations. She is a very strong team player.

Another approach to the basic style of appraisal leaves some space for comments after each area of performance is described. There also is a space for goal setting and improvement planning.

RESPONSIBILITY AND RELIABILITY:

Responds effectively to assigned responsibilities.	NA	1	2	x3	4	5
Communicates effectively, promoting productivity, understanding and respect. Keeps others informed.	NA	1	2	3	x4	5
Meets attendance requirements.	NA	1	2	x3	4	5
Delegates subordinate relationships and development in an appropriate manner.	NA	1	2	x3	4	5
Takes responsibility for actions.	NA	1	2	3	x4	5
Demonstrates foresight in recognizing potential problems and develops solutions.	NA	1	2	3	x4	5

Comments:

Mindy is an excellent communicator – better than most. I know she will keep the team informed of any news. She is extremely responsible, I can count on her to follow through. She is very good about suggesting solutions when problems come up.

PROBLEM SOLVING:

General problem-solving skills.	NA	1	2	3	x4	5
Offers constructive suggestions for improving work.	NA	1	2	3	x4	5
Generates creative ideas and solutions. Initiates change when necessary. Encourages others to accept change.	NA	1	2	3	x4	5
Meets challenge head on.	NA	1	2	3	x4	5
Acquires and analyzes all relevant information before making decisions.	NA	1	2	x3	4	5
Provides appropriate alternatives when making recommendations.	NA	1	2	x3	4	5

Comments:

Again, Mindy is very good at handling problems and finding appropriate solutions.

FUTURE GOALS AND SUGGESTED IMPROVEMENTS:

    1. Enroll in supervisory training given in the Fall at headquarters.
    2. Continue to improve computer skills.
    3. Design an orientation and training class for new clerks.

EMPLOYEE COMMENTS:

SUMMARY AND OVERALL EVALUATION

Overall rating   NA   1   2   3 x 4   5

Comments:

Mindy is one of our strongest employees. I'd like to see her continue to grow in her position and to strengthen her leadership skills.

I acknowledge receipt of review and my signature does not necessarily indicate agreement.

_____	_____
Employee	**Date**
_____	_____
Direct Supervisor	**Date**

Wise Counsel

If you plan to rate someone at the "needs improvement" level, plan on having constructive ideas for how the employee can improve his or her performance. Don't just leave the employee with a marginal rating and no suggestions for change or improvement.

Empowerment Zone

Research has shown that employees are more ready to accept a performance appraisal if they have had a chance to discuss their performance freely. Regardless of the form you use, plan on listening to employees' perceptions of their performance as well as telling them your own.

Some forms, such as the example with comments, also include an acknowledgement statement above the employee's signature. It is written to encourage an employee to sign the form even if he or she disagrees with the evaluation. It is a good idea to have such a statement on your signature page. However, even though the statement is there, some employees still might not want to sign. If an employee refuses to sign, you may want to request another manager to come in, sign the form, and serve as a witness and state that the employee refused to sign. Be forewarned.

When These Appraisals Are a Good Idea

Our advice to any company considering using these check-the-box formats is to proceed with caution. Unless managers are given very explicit training on how to add comments to justify their ratings, there is some risk that these will be considered too subjective. If you are using the performance appraisals to make decisions on promotions or increases, the more detail the better. We're not necessarily saying these are problematic to use—but they do have to be used wisely.

This format might be a good idea for large companies with many people doing similar kinds of activities. If a supervisor has 20 or more direct reports, the prospect of checking the boxes certainly is more appealing than that of completing long narrative reports on many people. In the case of large numbers of employees doing similar work—for example in a factory—a custom form could be developed that rates the employees according to factors that are very specific to the job. Ultimately you still could check off boxes rather than writing text. But the boxes could rate people according to actual data, measured in terms of productivity.

When These Forms Are a Bad Idea

A standard check-the-box form is not a good idea for jobs that are constantly changing, professional jobs, or jobs that have strong potential for upward mobility. There simply is not enough information for someone else to evaluate whether a promotional decision was just.

A better option might be a hybrid form that gives you some opportunity to expand upon your ratings. You can be very clear about what level of performance you see in someone. But ask yourself if someone outside the company—an arbitrator or judge, perhaps—could understand your reasons for the ratings you chose.

Rating the Ratings

There are countless different rating scales you could use when designing your performance appraisal format. We have illustrated some within this chapter. The most simplistic are simply a list of traits and/or responsibilities and boxes that ask you to choose between the highest rating—sometimes described as "Excellent" or "Outstanding," perhaps some middle range—sometimes referred to as "Good" or "Acceptable" and the lowest range—often referred to as "Poor" or "Unacceptable." Often there are a number of selections (five is typical) for example:

5. Excellent

4. Above Expectations

3. Acceptable

2. Needs Improvement

1. Unacceptable

When More Is Not Necessarily Better

Some companies have expanded the choices to seven categories that result in scales that might look something like this:

➤ Clearly Outstanding—Consistently performs above expectations

➤ Excellent—Often exceeds expectations

➤ Very Good—Sometimes exceeds expectations

Empowerment Zone

Frequently reviews will have a signature line for the next level up, such as the supervisor's supervisor. This shows that the appraisal has been reviewed by another set of eyes for fairness and consistency.

Empowerment Zone

From our point of view and experience we find that most employees appreciate a more individualized appraisal of their work—something that identifies more of their individual strengths. Even negative feedback is more useful if it is more specific to the individual and is offered in a way that provides an outline with specifics for how to change.

➤ Meets Expectations—Consistently meets expectations

➤ Needs Improvement—Meets some expectations, but not all

➤ Marginal—Meets minimal expectations, requires additional coaching

➤ Unsatisfactory

The number of selections in your rating system is entirely a personal decision. Some managers find a certain comfort in having more rather than fewer choices. Perhaps they feel it's easier for them to motivate an employee by showing more levels to aspire to. Our experience has shown that more choices actually might make the performance appraisal meeting more difficult, rather than easier.

How will you justify which employee is "Very Good" and which is "Excellent?" How will you communicate your reasoning for deciding that the employee "sometimes" or "often" exceeds expectations? You will have to have some number or quantitative measurement to differentiate between "sometimes" and "often." And you will have to explain to your employees why you chose one rating over another.

One problem you will have with almost any of these rating systems is that people will somehow translate them into grades of some sort. Once this is done you have another problem that is prevalent with school age kids and carries over into work and many other parts of life in our society. "Expectation inflation" might be a good way of describing this phenomenon. No one wants to feel they are average. Getting a pass, a "C", being told you are an average-looking guy, may be received by many people as insulting.

Advertising in particular plays on the theme of being unique, fantastic, beautiful, extreme, and almost any other exaggerated image that comes to mind. So when people see the words "meets expectations," they often feel disappointed. For an extreme of this many of you may have noticed in the recent Olympics how only gold medals got the real coverage, while many athletes seemed disappointed and looked as though they felt they had failed by getting a silver medal. This is one reason you have your work cut out for you as a manager and as a company when trying to educate people on what you really believe your ratings measure in performance evaluations.

Fewer Choices, Fewer Arguments?

In recent years companies have reduced the number of ratings choices because of the difficulty in justifying why one rating was selected over another. A system that we see very frequently is a rating scale with only three choices. Those choices are typically something like:

➤ Exceeds Expectations

➤ Meets Expectations

➤ Does Not Meet Expectations

From the File Cabinet

Judy, a serious, no-nonsense person, had worked as an administrative assistant for three years. When it came time to receive her annual performance appraisal, Judy was confident she would get top ratings.

Her boss, Mary, valued Judy as a hard-working employee. At the appraisal meeting, Mary evaluated Judy as "Excellent" in two categories and "Above Expectations" in all of the others, and sincerely thanked her for the job she was doing. Judy was flabbergasted and hurt. She demanded to know why she had not received "Excellent" in every category. Mary tried to explain her reasons for making the selections she had, but Judy rose from her chair, announced she would be filing a formal grievance, and left the office.

Although fewer choices might leave less room for argument, this kind of design requires lots of education—for both managers and line staff. Perhaps because of conditioning we received in school, many of us are accustomed to thinking of the middle range, in this case "meets expectations" is liking getting a "C" on our report card. In our minds it reads you're okay, but just barely okay.

Used in this instance "Meets Expectations" is something much better than a "C." Managers and employees must be educated that meeting expectations is a very good thing. To get a "Meets Expectations" means that you are doing everything correctly—in the manner it's supposed to be done. So if you receive the score "Meets Expectations" in every category, you are doing everything the company wants you to do.

In order to receive "Exceeds Expectations" your performance has to be above and beyond what the company expects of you. The criteria for getting this score could be tied to extra projects, substantially exceeding productivity measures—some consistent behaviors that far exceed that of other workers. Those behaviors that exceed expectations should be described fully on the performance appraisal form.

In the same way, to receive "Does Not Meet Expectations" the worker would have to fall below productivity levels expected of all workers. And the behaviors that fall below the expectations would have to be described on the form.

How Brief Do You Want to Get?

Another rating scale being used is actually the same as many universities and colleges use when rating students in some courses. Just as schools use a "pass" or "fail" system, some companies use a system with just two choices:

➤ Meets Expectations

➤ Does Not Meet Expectations

Basically in this kind of design, a worker either is doing the job or is not doing the job. It leaves very little wiggle room. The advantage of such a system is that it will reduce the arguments of those who think they are better than everyone else. The disadvantage is that it might not be viewed as motivating. Those people who clearly are outstanding will get the same score as those who just meet the minimum expectations. Again, using this method will require your careful education of managers and staff so that they accept or at the very least understand the concept. It seems to work at universities, so why not in the workplace? While it may work well in many university settings, it may not be nearly as successful in your workplace.

The Least You Need to Know

➤ The "check-the-box" form of appraisal is the simplest to use and one of the most common appraisal forms.

➤ There is a danger that these forms may illicit more subjective than objective ratings from those using them.

➤ Adding more information to justify ratings is always good advice.

➤ In the right circumstances, these forms work well—but not every company has the right circumstances.

➤ Carefully choose the style of ratings system to use on your performance appraisals and be sure to educate management and staff on how it is properly used.

Chapter 23

Appraisals Everyone Loves to Hate

In This Chapter

➤ How to accommodate regulatory requirements

➤ How to quantify nearly everything

➤ Making a difficult format functional

➤ How to measure anything quantitatively

For the majority of companies, performance appraisal design and implementation can be customized for a particular situation. There is at least one industry that we are aware of, that has stricter requirements when it comes to what must be included in a performance appraisal. A regulated industry can't fool around with such requirements and stay in business successfully.

Regulated industries usually impose rules to cover serious safety issues. There might be mandatory procedures to protect the workers and those they work with. Most enforce their regulatory requirements through their standard operating procedures. If a safety procedure is violated, an employee and the company itself can be fined—or even closed if the violation is severe enough.

One regulated industry, health care, actually mandates what kinds of things should be covered in a performance appraisal. If you are in a regulated industry, you will know it and probably are well aware of what is required. Health care workers should be familiar with the requirements imposed by the JCAHO (Joint Commission on Accreditation of Healthcare Organizations).

In general, you still will need to follow most of the same principles of completing and delivering a performance appraisal. The regulations will apply to how the criteria are written on the actual appraisal form. This chapter explores a regulated industry, specifically health care, and what it takes to do performance appraisals "by the book."

Toeing the Regulatory Line

Although you might have your heart set on utilizing a simple, basic format, if you work in health care you might be forced to comply with certain *regulatory requirements* that prevent you from doing so. If a hospital wants to be approved by the Joint Commission on Accreditation of Healthcare Organizations (JCAHO), it must comply with many, many prerequisites. Being approved by JCAHO means that the hospital has met all of the standards of care necessary to provide patient safety and acceptable service. Without such approval, it is difficult for hospitals to remain open.

Among the many mandatory elements imposed by JCAHO is the requirement to make performance appraisals "competency-based." In other words, the appraisal instrument must show that health care workers are competent in all the areas necessary to perform their jobs. In this case, JCAHO also defines which competencies must be demonstrated by which workers.

Hospital staff are required to pore over several large books that describe all the requirements, including competencies, that are necessary. When JCAHO first started mandating the content of a health care performance appraisal, they used the term "criteria-based." By using that term they required that the standard level of performance be built into the language of the performance appraisal. In other words, not only did you have to list the duty, you also had to define the minimum acceptable level of performance. As time went on, JCAHO replaced the term criteria-based for competency-based. By doing this they are mandating that the competencies required for each health care position be stated on the performance appraisal. The minimum acceptable level of performance is a demonstration that the employee is competent. So in effect, the concepts of criteria-based and competency-based performance appraisals have been combined.

Close Up

Regulatory requirements are rules that govern certain systems or industries and mandate strict compliance with defined standards and applicable state and federal laws.

Empowerment Zone

Keep in mind that any good performance appraisal also should show that a worker is competent in all the areas necessary to do his or her job, whether an outside agency requires that you show that or not.

Competency means the knowledge, skills, abilities, and attributes required to perform a position in an acceptable or competent manner. People often confuse competency with knowledge or skill. Competency is not acquired simply by going to school or receiving training in a particular area. Competency is a measurement of an individual's ability to perform a certain task.

For example, doctors are trained in medical school to do many procedures. But how can you evaluate whether a physician is truly competent at performing the procedure? Would you want a doctor who went to classes in plastic surgery but has done very few surgeries to reconstruct your face? Components other than training must be considered, including experience, proven ability, and the judgment to know if he or she was able to operate successfully or not.

Empowerment Zone

Companies not subject to regulatory requirements also might want to use competency-based performance appraisals. If they are well written, they are a very good method of appraising performance and are perceived as legally defensible.

"So what?" you might ask. What makes this any different from any other appraisal? The biggest difference is that each position probably will have a unique performance appraisal. Because different jobs require different competencies, it's difficult to come up with a form that will cover them all.

From the File Cabinet

When the JCAHO requirement for criteria-based performance appraisals first came to light some years back, those of us working in health care started the process by painstakingly rewriting everyone's job descriptions to ensure all the correct criteria and competencies appeared. Then we basically turned the job description into a performance appraisal by adding a scoring element and space for behavioral examples attached to each criterion. Some of the appraisals turned out to be 10 pages long!

Among the many things we learned from that exercise is the old advice called KISS— "Keep It Short and Simple." Job descriptions and performance appraisals should be as concise as possible. Very few managers kept up with completing 10-page appraisals and the system was painstakingly revised.

Close Up

Quantitative measurement means measurement that's able to be measured. In performance appraisal terms, it means looking at any job duty and defining how you will measure whether or not it has been done correctly and how well it has been done.

Competency-based performance appraisals require, among other things, *quantitative measurement*. And measuring something that normally is not thought of in numeric fashion can require a lot of creative thinking. But performance appraisals that are effective usually do require quite a lot of thinking and planning.

Although some people might look at regulated appraisals as a more difficult assignment, you also could look at them as being easier, in that the rules are more clearly defined. Of course this limits your design possibilities to some extent. However, there are many creative ways of dealing with the requirement, including the practice of attaching an actual job description to a brief appraisal form. If the job description is written using the quantitative language, why recreate the wheel by repeating that language on a performance appraisal form?

Empowerment Zone

To accurately measure whether someone is competent in a job, you need clear, understandable standards against which you can compare actual performance.

Quantitative Measurement—What Is It?

Numbers people thrive on things that have quantitative elements to them. That's why having some good numbers people to help you define measurement on this type of performance appraisal is not a bad idea. And as we covered in Chapter 18, "Every Building Needs a Foundation: Building Your Framework," you might have to work at putting measurable language on all of the items that are considered competencies. It can be done, but it does require that you do your homework on defining the standards that comprise acceptable performance.

With well-written performance standards, you should be well on your way to creating measurement language for any competency in any job.

Among the resources you might find to assist you in writing measurement language, we found an excellent one online. The Web site www.zigonperf.com/performance.html offers free measurement resources for hard-to-measure work and teams. Jack Zigon, President of Zigon Performance Group, provides a site rich with measurement language for many job titles. It's a great place to start if you are embarking on a competency-based project. Jack Zigon's web site is listed in Appendix D, "Resources."

Performance Evaluation

Employee Name: _____   Department:_____

Job Title:_____   Assigned Shift:_____

Supervisor's Name:_____   Date of Hire: _____

Supervisor's Title:_____   Period of Appraisal:_____

Patient Care	Meets	Does Not Meet
1. Demonstrates ability to assess patient condition and treatment according to accepted performance standards	☐	☐
2. Administers prescribed medications with 97% accuracy	☐	☐
3. Handles initial admission and assessment within acceptable timing & accuracy guidelines	☐	☐
4. Follows patient care plan according to acceptable and agreed upon performance standards	☐	☐
5. Adheres to all rules of patient safety and advocacy per established standard	☐	☐
6. Assesses changes in patient condition and takes appropriate action according to acceptable standard	☐	☐

This is a small section from a competency-based performance appraisal for a health care position.

JCAHO and other regulatory agencies are focused on successful *outcomes* of acceptable performance. In patient care, the obvious positive outcome is recovery of a patient, a reduction in the amount of time needed for a patient's stay in the hospital, or reduced cost by careful utilization of resources. The outcomes resulting from a health care provider's care then become important measurements of success in an employee's performance.

When requirements are specific, you are forced to define the parameters of acceptable performance. In our sample form we show a ratings system of either meeting or not meeting the required standard. A "meets or does not meet" standard often is the easiest to explain—and usually is fairly apparent to employees.

Close Up

An **outcome** is the consequence of a particular action. In the case of health care, a positive outcome could be the result of treatment that improves a patient's health; a negative outcome would be one in which a patient's condition worsens.

Empowerment Zone

The more choices available in a scoring system, the more you leave yourself open to argument. It is difficult to explain the difference between various levels. Having only two choices—either you meet the standard or you don't—leaves little room for disagreement.

Measurable standards can be established for any job, for example:

➤ Reports are submitted with accurate results (measured by numbers of errors reported by end users).

➤ Returns are filed accurately (measured by absence of assessed penalties).

➤ Staff has demonstrated familiarity with compliance factors according to quality assurance standards.

➤ Counselors demonstrate knowledge and compliance with reporting laws. (Chart review to assess this.)

➤ Teacher had one hundred percent compliance with turning in complete attendance data.

➤ Manager reported quarterly sales for each sales associate.

➤ Sales associate turnover is under ten percent.

➤ Monthly status reports are submitted by the tenth of the following month.

➤ The phone is answered within a certain number of rings.

➤ A specific percentage of customers are satisfied when surveyed on a quarterly basis.

➤ The number of labor grievances goes down over a certain time period.

➤ Sales negotiations result in cost savings.

➤ The percentage of repairs returned for unsatisfactory quality declines.

➤ The percentage of food wasted because of improper handling or cooking declines.

What measurements are common in your industry, company, or job? Use the space below to try to describe your own job in quantitative terms.

Duty/Task	Measurement
1.	
2.	
3.	
4.	
5.	
6.	
7.	
8.	

If There's a Harder Way of Doing Something ...

Having lived through several reviews by a regulatory agency, we used to feel that requirements were imposed just to make our lives miserable. However, in retrospect we have learned that with proper understanding and interpretation, a regulatory agency can give you the kind of information you need to make objective evaluations of performance. The rigors you experience actually force you to remove the subjectivity from the process of evaluating employee performance. Few people like being told what to do; but in this case the results, or outcomes, might be quite positive.

Having actual numbers or other proof of each task's completion forces a more objective evaluation. The old saying that the numbers never lie may or may not be true. But using this approach, you compare scores that are actually tangible, making it harder to play favorites on the basis of personality. It also gives employees something concrete that they can look at to understand how their actual performance fared compared to a company goal, and their fellow workers. Here is another example of this. You have an agency that provides worker retraining for unemployed or welfare clients. If you manage caseworkers, and are trying to move clients from your work training program to full-time employment, and your agency is charged with achieving 75 percent success to maintain federal funding, this is your threshold for meeting the minimum standard. If some of the caseworkers achieve 85 percent results, this may be the "exceeds standard" rating, while if you achieve 90 percent success from a few caseworkers, this may justify giving these workers an "outstanding" evaluation. Having something verifiable and measurable makes evaluating employees a much clearer and fairer process.

The reasons for imposing a regulatory method of evaluation, such as JCAHO's, have been studied and reviewed by many people who know what they are doing. Experts have studied the outcomes of successful and not-so-successful organizations, and are using that data to create the best system they can. So like it or not, regulations are not a bad thing. Regulated performance appraisals actually can protect your organization and make it stronger.

Strangely enough, the more you are forced to think in those quantitative terms, the easier it will become. Soon you will be making quantitative analyses of everything—at which point you might drive your friends and family crazy!

Wise Counsel

If you ever wind up in litigation for discriminatory practice, having properly utilized, competency-based performance appraisals will help your case immeasurably. Judges like to see these kinds of instruments as ways for evaluating the work of people doing the same or similar jobs. It makes their own jobs a little easier, too.

The Least You Need to Know

➤ Your industry might require a regulated method of performance appraisal that you must learn to utilize.

➤ Performance standards are necessary and form the backbone of these regulated performance appraisals.

➤ Regulated performance appraisals are designed for positive outcomes and can help you more than hurt you.

➤ Practice makes perfect when it comes to creating quantitative measurements.

Chapter 24

Balance Is a Happy Medium

In This Chapter

➤ How to achieve a balanced format

➤ Setting mutually agreed-upon goals

➤ Adapting to changes

➤ It's all in the delivery

Somewhere between the most subjective forms and the highly regulated forms there is a happy medium. What constitutes the criteria of a happy medium? We think it's a format that requires participation and discussion of both parties, but that is clear and straightforward enough that it can be completed in a reasonable amount of time.

Can you achieve the perfect form for your company? If perfect means that everyone is happy with it, that's a difficult goal to meet. It's a fact of life that someone somewhere will always disagree with your ideas no matter what. So let go of the notion that you will have 100 percent support. Simply having a form that the majority of managers will use accurately is what you should be aiming toward. We'll show you a few examples of some *balanced forms*. You can decide if they are formats that you can use or customize to fit your needs.

What Will Work For You

Our experience has shown us that overly long and overly complex forms frequently are not used properly, if at all. There still are important things you want to accomplish, and you can do that in a concise manner. Given the time constraints of most supervisors and managers, more brief usually is better.

Close Up

A **balanced form** is an even distribution of measurable performance factors and areas that encourage discussion and seek agreement.

Empowerment Zone

More brief is not always better. But our experience has taught us that managers are more inclined to complete a brief form than a long one. The more brief the form, the better the chance that most, if not all, managers will honor their commitments to evaluate all of their employees.

Brevity Can Be Attractive

The trick to keeping an appraisal form brief is being able to attach a job description and job standards. The manager is expected to review the job description and evaluate whether the employee has met expectations for each duty on the description. If expectations are unmet, or if they have been exceeded, the form requires and has space for an explanation. Behavioral examples are called for to adequately explain why someone is above or below the norm.

This kind of form has a number of advantages:

➤ It's brief and a lot less intimidating than a longer form.

➤ It's clear and easy to understand.

➤ It evaluates an employee using an individual job description.

➤ It evaluates everyone based on the company's expectations for all employees.

➤ It requires documentation for scores above or below the "meets expectations" mark.

➤ Fewer rating choices might lead to less argument.

➤ It has a section for goal setting.

➤ It has room for employee comments and encourages the use of attachments if necessary.

➤ It makes clear that an employee's signature does not imply agreement.

Performance Summary

Employee Name:__Jane Doe___   Evaluator:__Amanda Johnson_____

Dept;__Sales____Job Title:_Sales Assistant   Dept.:_Sales__ Job Title: Sales Manager

Appraisal Period: From_6/99 To__6/00   Date Appraisal Given:__7-13-00_____

Section I: Job Description (and/or performance standards) attached with each item marked "M" for meets expectations, "N" for needs improvement, or "E" for exceeded expectations. All "E" and "N" ratings require documentation in Sections III & IV.

Section II: Company Performance Expectations
(Discuss definitions with employee, write performance examples on this or on an attached piece of paper.)

		E	M	N
1. TEAMWORK	1.	X		
2. ORGANIZATION/TIME MANAGEMENT	2.	X		
3. QUALITY/ACCURACY OF RESULTS	3.		X	
4. ADAPTABILITY	4.		X	
5. INITIATIVE	5.		X	

OVERALL RATING (Including both job description and Performance Expectations above.)

         E   M   N

         ☐ x- x☐   ☐

Section III: Job Duty Performance Standards Exceeding Expectations/Areas of Strength

1.   Providing back-up and support to Sales Executives at presentations to new employers. Jane is extremely professional & reliable, responsive to questions and never fails to make a positive impression. Sets a standard for the other sales assistants.

2.   Research and follow-up of client questions and problems. Jane is unfailingly polite with clients. She has been commended by a number of clients in her tenacity to solve problems and correct mistakes. Clients request her by name when they call with questions.

3.   Positive vendor relations. Jane consistently maintains good relationships with all of the product vendors. Several of them have commented to me that she is efficient and pleasant, even when the stress is running high. Being able to successfully handle this diverse group of personalities is commendable. Again, Jane sets the standard for others in her classification.

Section IV: Job Duty Performance Standards that Need Improvement
      (including timeframe for meeting standards)

1.   Jane needs to practice asking for assistance when needed. She often spends many overtime hours trying to get all the sales packets prepared for the next day's presentation. If she would let me or another assistant know she needs help, the project could be done during regular business hours.

Section V: Additional Goals for Next Performance Summary/Other Professional Development Objectives

1.   We agree that Jane will take a lead role in doing open enrollment presentations in the coming year. She would like to handle some of the presentation on her own and I support her initiative. We will have her going out on her own by October.

2.   Jane agrees that she would like to learn about other products in our sales line. She will attend classes in the life insurance area with the goal to get her sales license in life and health.

3.   Jane would like to move from Small Group to Large Group Sales. We have agreed that she will begin to move into that area, and work part time with Lois Lane in Large Group beginning in January.

Employee Comments (optional):

**Additional Evaluator and Employee Comments are optional; please attach.
Employee signature does not necessarily indicate agreement.**

Employee Signature:_____   Date:_____

Evaluator Signature:_____   Date:_____

This appraisal form is quite brief—only two pages.

249

Brief forms have their disadvantages, too, such as

➤ You would need to have job descriptions and performance standards already written for all your jobs.

➤ Your company must have articulated performance expectations that are mandatory for all employees.

➤ It requires that you trust your managers to evaluate job duties accurately—in other words, the "halo effect" still could occur.

For a company that already has completed job descriptions and announced overall expectations, this form is a pretty good balanced style of appraisal.

The Secret to Completing a Performance Appraisal Quickly and Accurately

If you have to trust your memory on the many factors needed to cover each employee's performance appraisal, completing those appraisals could be a frustrating and time-consuming process. The key to making the process much quicker and easier is to be prepared—and the best way to be prepared is to keep a performance diary. For each of your employees, keep a folder in which you can put notes throughout the year when you notice good or not-so-good performance. Of course the folders you maintain for your employees should be kept in a confidential place to prevent any improper disclosure of information.

Wise Counsel

When developing the questions for your form, have three or four people read each question and make sure each has the same interpretation of what that question asks. This is the only way to ensure that people using your form are doing the same thing, or interpreting the meaning of the questions the same way.

Some organized managers make a list that has headings to guide them through the process.

		Audrey Employee	
Date	Incident	Comment	Follow-up
2/13	Client Rogers called irate about incomplete order	Audrey calmed him down, used great people skills to meet his needs	Rogers called me to commend Audrey.

It actually takes very little time to set up a system such as this. And not only will it make your life easier at appraisal time, but it also will give you an opportunity to give and document feedback in a more timely manner. Your employees will be happy that you have noticed and commented on their performance—even if it is constructive criticism. Employees like to know that you are paying attention. Additionally, if follow-up is needed, you have the documentation to help jog your memory.

This is another example of how putting just a little bit more time on the front end can save you lots of time on the back end of the appraisal process. It's quite similar to doing another task that most people hate and therefore procrastinate—doing your income taxes. If you keep a box or folder with all of your receipts for the year, you don't have to spend hours trying to collect all your paperwork to do your taxes.

Empowerment Zone

Choosing the performance expectations that apply to everyone can be tricky. It's best to get the opinions of others before you set them in stone. This is an area in which it would be wise to talk to your employees.

Yes, it takes a bit of organization and discipline, but these are qualities that you might be evaluating in your staff; it would be a good idea for you to practice them, too. If you do not have performance diaries started on each of your employees, why not start them right now?

A good technique would be to review your notes at the end of each day—just take five to ten minutes to review in your mind the highlights or memorable moments of the work day. Adding just a line or two on a performance diary takes a small amount of time each day and will help you immeasurably later on. If this seems too much to handle, even weekly or bi-weekly reviews of events will be incredibly helpful when it comes time to do a performance evaluation, a formal or informal counseling session, or a disciplinary action.

Another Balanced Approach

Another approach to a balanced form is a more comprehensive performance review. This style of form requires that you review duties and accomplishments and document them on the form. The next page defines performance expectations for employees and specifies which areas should be evaluated.

Employee Name: _____Natalie St. James__ Employee Number: ___96-034_____

Department: __Administration__ Job Title: __Executive Secretary_____

Supervisor's Name: _Simon Schwartz_____ Supervisor's Title: ___Operations Director____

Date of Review: __4/28/00_____ Period Covered: From_3/99_ To_3/00

1. **Major Job Responsibilities:** List most important duties and responsibilities for this employee.

   a. Provide administrative support to the operations director.
   b. Supervise staff of two office assistants
   c. Assist in support of management staff reporting to the operations director, including the managers of sales, billing, purchasing, receiving, security
   d. Supply inventory for all departments reporting to the operations director
   e. Chairs the Social Committee which plans the staff Christmas party and picnic
   f. Provides training on in-house computer program to other support staff as needed

2. **Accomplishments:** List any major accomplishments made by the employee this year.

   a. Completed revision of administrative manual--a huge undertaking. Revised 100 pages of data to ensure compliance with changes in laws. Reformatted into a very readable style.
   b. Successfully handled a difficult disciplinary problem with one of our office assistants. Was extremely professional and supportive, reached an amicable solution.
   c. Christmas party was the most successful that the company has had—Natalie was commended by CEO for her excellent planning.

3. **Performance Expectations:** Evaluate employee's level of performance in each area according to the ratings below.

Rating Scale:

1 = **Unacceptable** – (Does not meet requirements)
2 = **Needs Improvement** (Meets some but not all requirements)
3 = **Meets Expectations** (Consistently meets all requirements)
4 = **Exceeds Expectations** (Consistently exceeds some expectations)
5 = **Outstanding** (Consistently exceeds all expectations)

More comprehensive, this four-page performance review form uses a ratings scale with five possible choices. When you have more ratings, you must be more careful to justify how you select the levels of performance. This is one of those times when it's extremely important to be consistent in your ratings.

Performance Expectations	Comments Describe how performance compares with expectations, strengths and areas for improvement.	Rating **1, 2, 3, 4**, or **5**
Job Knowledge & Skills Ability to get the job done; assists others when requested; keeps informed of latest developments.	Natalie knows her job very well. I can depend on her to complete her assignments on time. She is very good at working with others in the department, and offers assistance quite willingly. I would like to see her learn more about the industry and suggest she take an evening class to do so.	4
Communication Uses effective communication techniques; listens and responds clearly; prepares reports clearly and accurately, etc.	Natalie has excellent communication skills. She is always polite and helpful, listens to others and responds appropriately. She asks for help appropriately if she doesn't know the answer. Her reports are always top notch —very professional and accurate.	5
Cooperation Works effectively with others, including co-workers and customers.	Natalie has to interact with a large number of people every day. Most of my managers have complimented me on how efficient and effective she is. She is always willing to help others out if needed.	4
Planning & Follow-Through Completes tasks thoroughly; utilizes appropriate guidelines & policies; meets timelines, etc.	I can trust that Natalie will complete her tasks on time. She is very good at planning her time and she knows how long most projects take. She is proficient at following guidelines. She is rarely late with a deadline.	4
Initiative Results oriented; shows desire for excellence; works without supervision; exhibits positive attitude, etc.	Natalie showed great initiative this year by undertaking and completing the administrative manual project. She worked without supervision on the project. It was difficult and time consuming and she never complained.	5
Accuracy Performs high quality work; manages time well; schedules priorities effectively, etc.	Natalie's work is usually excellent. I rarely find errors. She has a very good judgement about priorities	4

Decision-Making Makes appropriate decisions; obtains essential information; offers alternative solutions, etc.	Natalie makes decisions when needed, although she sometimes seems reluctant to make decisions without authorization. Her position gives her the authority to make those decisions.	3
Leadership Promotes teamwork; leads by example; resolves conflicts effectively; delegates responsibility effectively; coaches and trains team members, etc.	Natalie has been very effective with her duties supervising the office staff. She solved a disciplinary problem and others look to her for training.	4
Overall Performance Summary	Summary of accomplishments and strengths, as well as areas for improvement. It has been a very good year for Natalie. She has grown in her position, taken on new responsibilities and handled them well. I would like to see her work on her decision-making ability and expand her supervisory duties to new hire interviews.	Overall Rating 4

Goals for the Coming Year

1. Performance goals

    A. Increase industry knowledge
    B. Attend class in interviewing and selection
    C. Train staff in upgrade of in-house system

2. Areas for Development

    D. Work on decision-making process; I agree to assist her in this goal
    E. Work more collaboratively with the purchasing department

Employee Comments:

Employee Signature:_____ Date:_____
(Your signature does not necessarily signify agreement.)

Supervisor Signature:_____ Date:_____

Mutually Established Goals

Having a section on your form to establish goals for the future is good for a number of reasons, not the least of which is that it implies the employee will be working with you for another year. And if the goals are attractive enough and challenging enough, the employee probably will stay at least that long. You need to find ways to keep strong performers interested and stimulated or some other company might steal them away.

Naturally you want the goals to be in sync with the company goals. An effective way to start this process is for both the appraiser and the appraised to think about goals in advance and come to the meeting prepared to discuss them. You can prime employees by passing out a list of the company's goals for the coming year and asking them to find ways to relate their personal goals to the company's goals. You also should complete this exercise in terms of how each employee can meet departmental—as well as company—goals. You might start this part of the process by asking the employee, "What or how would things be different if you were successful in meeting your goals for the year? How would I, or you, or someone who saw you each day see or measure this change?"

From the File Cabinet

One manager we worked with wanted to have better communication and relationships with her employees. When we asked her how she or others would know if this was happening, she replied, "Well, if I would spend more time getting to know my staff personally, it might help." One step toward the goal was to eat in the main cafeteria, sitting with different employees at least two days a week. Another goal was to institute weekly staff meetings in which at least part of the time was devoted to acknowledging successes and problems that needed group solutions, and giving employees the opportunity to ask management about present concerns in the department. Most of the resulting changes could be counted or observed by someone watching her during the day.

When you get to this part of the performance appraisal discussion, you can share both of your suggestions for goals. Unless someone is way off base, you probably will find a number of goals that can be blended effectively.

Really listen to what your employees are saying when they articulate their desired goals. If the goals are unrealistic, try to find a way to take "baby steps" in the right direction. You are the boss and your opinion is final—but if you totally shoot down someone's ideas, you might be hurting that person's motivation. Besides, it is easier to hold people accountable for goals that they have had a part in setting.

Make Your Form Adaptable to Changes

Because a performance appraisal is supposed to be a two-way conversation, make sure your form can handle any changes that might be brought about by your meeting with the employee. If everything is written "in stone" or at least in ink, it will be more difficult to accommodate changes.

Empowerment Zone

Do not simply hand goals to an employee without getting his or her input and opinion first. Resist the urge to be that controlling. Find ways to work with the employee's goals and to help the employee work with your ideas.

From the File Cabinet

A very effective boss taught us a technique for completing performance appraisals. She completed any form entirely in pencil. When other facts came up in conversation, she added comments in pencil (or erased comments if necessary). At the end of the appraisal, she would make a copy of the penciled appraisal and give it to the employee to make sure everything was agreeable. When the employee agreed with what was written, she had the form redone by computer. Then she met again with the employee, who would sign the new final copy. It took a little longer to do it this way, but she always reached agreement on performance appraisals with her employees.

You might come into the meeting with your comments in note form and complete the appraisal during the course of the meeting. Depending on the length of the form, however, that might not be feasible.

As we just mentioned, under no circumstances should you write in the goals before you have discussed them with the employee. Writing them together, as you summarize them in the employee's words, can be very powerful and persuasive. Don't shortchange the time it might take to do this. Some employees find this exercise quite easy because they are naturally goal-oriented. Those who are not goal-oriented might find it more difficult and will need more coaching from you. Either way it will be worth the effort.

Empowerment Zone

Really be open to your employees' suggestions, ideas, and views of the situation. Obviously you are the boss and can make the final decision, but being collaborative and truly open will only make this process smoother.

The Delivery Matters Most

No matter what form or technique you use to complete a performance appraisal, the most powerful tool in the process is your manner of delivering the information to the employee being appraised. With a sincere, warm, and honest approach, any form, no matter how simple or complex, will be a winner. The form, after all, is just words on paper, which can be interpreted in different ways depending on the tone you read into them.

Don't let the employee interpret a tone that isn't there. Deliver the message that you want to get across in the manner in which you want it to be heard. The appraisal can build this employee up to do bigger and better things, or it could get him or her to give up on trying to do anything meaningful.

Your sincere, disarming delivery will encourage the employee to communicate in a similar manner. When you are both relaxed and the conversation is real—that will be a balanced, satisfying meeting. Agreements are reached much more easily in that kind of atmosphere.

So the bottom line on a balanced delivery is to not let the form get in your way or force you to communicate in a forced, unnatural manner. Put the form aside and speak from the heart. If need be, you can look at the form a moment and refresh your memory of where you are going. That will be the most effective performance appraisal that you and your employees can experience.

The Least You Need to Know

➤ A balanced form is one that allows for individual performance to be documented as well as rated.

➤ Brief is not necessarily better, but it will be accepted more readily.

➤ Let your employees set goals; then find ways to blend their goals with the department and company goals.

➤ Make sure your form can be modified as a result of the performance appraisal meeting.

➤ Your warm, thoughtful delivery is one of the most important and effective elements of a performance appraisal.

Could You Put That In Writing?

The typical performance appraisal appears on some kind of form; one that probably is used for everyone else in the company. However, there are times when something different might be appropriate. The memo or *narrative* type of performance appraisal is just as effective—maybe even more so—if it truly documents performance using behavioral examples.

Make Mine a Letter: The Narrative

It's not hard to figure out that the narrative form simply is a letter or memo from supervisor to employee. A narrative performance appraisal summarizes the supervisor's evaluation of the employee's work and documents the goals for the coming year.

Close Up

A **narrative** is a manner of telling a story or giving an account in writing or speech. A narrative appraisal is writing the appraisal in text form.

The Casual Approach

Narrative appraisals can be quite informal. They often are used when a manager becomes an employee's supervisor in the middle or toward the end of an appraisal period. If the employee has worked with a manager for only a brief period of time, the manager might not have enough information to give a complete appraisal. In such a situation, it is appropriate for the manager to write a document that summarizes the circumstances and what is known about an employee's performance.

It is not uncommon for one manager to take over for someone who leaves, only to find that no documented reviews are on file for any of the employees. With no history to draw from, the narrative format might work well for at least the first round of appraisals.

The narrative format typically requires a bit more time to complete because you need to write text—you are not just checking off boxes. However, some managers like to add narrative commentary to almost any appraisal and will find the narrative appraisal quite natural. Writing in narrative form also allows for a great deal of specificity, or the ability to detail specific examples of this employee's work performance and behaviors. Most workers really appreciate feedback that is truly specific to them.

From the File Cabinet

One manager inherited her department from a long-term manager who had not done any performance appraisals for six years. The new manager had to start from scratch with each employee, as the former manager had neglected the process entirely. Some employees were unhappy about being reviewed by someone so new, but the new manager wisely used the process to build her knowledge of how the employees saw themselves and how they felt their jobs should be done. She interviewed each employee to share her vision for the department as well as to hear their goals for themselves and the department. The new manager summarized in narrative format the content of these interviews, which she then placed in each employee's personnel file. The employees were pleased that some feedback was actually placed in their files—at long last!

Dressing Up

Some companies prefer to use narrative performance appraisals for all employees. When this is the case, the narrative often has been formalized into a standardized form or format to follow. Such a form doesn't give boxes to check but instead requires that you write a description of what went right and wrong during the year for each employee.

Narrative Performance Appraisal

Employee Name: _Jason Webb_____   Employee #:____xxx345_____
Title:__Delivery Driver Department:__Transport_____

Supervisor Name:_Max Hanover Supervisor Title:_Transport Mgr

Date of Appraisal:___5/6/99 Period Covered: From5/98 To 5/99
Review goals set at beginning of appraisal period. Address the following areas in narrative format as accurately as possible:

Major Accomplishments:

Jason successfully met his goal for the year of achieving a 90% on time delivery average. This is up from 78% last year at this time. I know he worked extra hard to make that number.

Jason has also greatly improved his customer service skills over last year. The company has received no complaints from clients this year, which is an improvement over last year's results.

Met Expectations:

Last year I had a problem with truck maintenance. Jason has made an improvement this year. The truck has been left in clean condition on weekends. He has made sure the relief driver starts his shift with a full tank of gas.

Jason's attendance was very good this year. There were only three absences on his record for the year.

Breakage was kept at the company standard. Jason is careful with loading and unloading.

Areas Needing Improvement:

It's important that Jason works on controlling his temper with the night supervisor. He seems to get stressed when he's tired and has a hard time taking directions without complaints. He has worked hard to improve his customer relations, I would like to see him make the same effort with his co-workers.

Overall Rating – please check one

[ ] Exceeds expectations—Consistently above requirements
[x] Meets expectations—Consistently met requirements
[ ] Requires Improvement—Sometimes met, but not consistently
[ ] Unacceptable—Does not meet minimum requirements

Comments:

Overall, I'm very happy with Jason's progress this year. He really worked at the goals we agreed on last year. He has improved a lot over the year and with more experience will be one of our best drivers.

Identify goals and developmental activities:

Now that he has mastered Routes A & C, learn routes D & F
.
Work on good communication skills with co-workers

Take class on "Handling Hazardous Materials" to become qualified for other routes.

Employee Comments:

Employee Signature:_____ Date:_____

Supervisor:_____ Date:_____

This example shows a format that a company provides for managers to complete a narrative appraisal. Rather than the blank sheet of paper approach, the form leads managers through a series of performance-related questions. Managers write a narrative response to each question.

The narrative appraisal requires well-written comments about an employee's successful or unsuccessful accomplishment of expectations. As in most appraisal formats, it makes the assumption that employees have been made aware of what is expected of them.

A narrative format is somewhat harder to change, once completed, without rewriting the entire form or memo. But as with any other form, you will want to formalize goal statements after the appraisal conversation with the employee.

Does Style Matter?

Narrative appraisals can be written in almost any style you feel appropriate. Many appraisals address an employee in the *third person*, and you can feel free to do that as well.

This very simple example shows a third-person narrative appraisal. It is written in memo form and although a copy will go to Emily Employee, the original will go into Emily's official personnel file. So in effect, the appraisal is written to a file.

Memorandum
March 27, 2000

TO: Emily Employee

FROM: Brad Boss

RE: Performance Appraisal 11/99-3/00

This memo is written to evaluate the performance of Emily Employee over the past year. Emily has worked for XYZ Company for less than just a few months, however I can make the following general comments about her performance to date:

She has shown great initiative in becoming acquainted with the department and her staff. The staff has shown progress under her leadership.

Her team members on the management team have found Ms. Employee to be responsive, experienced and cooperative.

She has spent time to become familiar with the company and its policies.

In summary, in the four months she has been working for me, I am quite pleased with her progress and look forward to the coming year of our working relationship.

Another perfectly acceptable style would be to write it as a *first person* letter directly to the person. This approach might make it easier to use a warmer, more natural way of writing as if you were speaking.

Ms. Emily Employee

Manager, Production Department

XYZ Company

Dear Ms. Employee:

As all performance reviews take place during the month of March, this letter is written to serve as your review over the past four months of your employment.

Although we have worked together for just a brief period, I have been very pleased with your rapid progress. The comments I have received from the production department have been very positive, and I can see that you have already established an open relationship with your staff.

The members of the management team have found you to be a welcome asset. They have trust in your opinions and advice. Several have commented that you have assisted them successfully on projects.

Although I might expect a learning curve with your learning a new company, I have been impressed with how quickly you have absorbed our procedures and protocols at XYZ.

Ms. Employee, it is a pleasure working with you. Your first few months have exceeded my expectations. I look forward to the coming year.

Sincerely,

Brad Boss

Director

This example shows a letter format of a narrative appraisal. As it is a letter, it is written in the first person directly to Emily Employee. The original will be placed in Emily's personnel file, and she will ultimately receive a copy after she has reviewed it and added any of her own comments.

When the Narrative Format Works Best

As we mentioned previously , new supervisors who have less than a year of experience with employees might find the narrative format ideal for their feedback.

Another situation in which this kind of appraisal works well is in small companies. With few employees, it might not be practical to design a form for performance appraisals. A letter or memo is much easier and makes much more sense. Because there are fewer employees, the manager is able to take the time to write an individual letter to each employee. And in small companies, it's likely the jobs are quite distinctive and might not fit into a convenient, one-size-fits-all format.

Empowerment Zone

When asked to complete a performance appraisal, some managers we are acquainted with invariably take out a blank sheet of paper. They believe no form is necessary and that everyone deserves an appraisal in narrative, text format.

Empowerment Zone

A good way to utilize the narrative appraisal is to have the appraisal discussion with the employee first, then follow with the written appraisal after all the agreements are made.

If you are a person who enjoys writing in a narrative style, this might be the best kind of appraisal for you to use. It will enable you to say whatever you want without having to conform to checking boxes. Of course, you can always add an extra sheet of paper to any performance appraisal to add narrative comments. As stated before, using additional narrative comments helps you to individualize your performance evaluations to a greater extent than a check-the-box-only form.

Naturally, as with other formats, you have to remember to use behavioral examples when describing performance. The narrative format gives you more space to go into behavioral descriptions than other formats might. Managers may have to be coached not to resort to focusing on personality traits. (Refer to Chapter 11, "Script or Ad Lib?" for reminders about using behavioral language.)

When the Narrative Format Is a Bad Idea

If your company is rather large and you just haven't had the time to design a performance appraisal form, this might not be the best situation for a narrative format. We say "might not" because you might have great relationships and feedback from your managers, and you might be able to count on them to produce this kind of appraisal for all of their employees.

However, speaking realistically, if your managers have a large number of employees reporting to them, it's unlikely they will take the time to write narrative appraisals on all of them. At that point you might be better off with a fill-in-the-blank form, as long as managers have been trained to complete them honestly, accurately, fairly, and consistently.

Any written performance appraisal can be used against you if an employee feels that it reflects some sort of discriminatory practice. As with any other appraisal format, managers must use caution to be consistent in their completion to avoid any potential legal problem later on. Were a manager to complete a lengthy complimentary narrative appraisal on a favorite employee and not complete appraisals for others not in favor, there is a potential for trouble of a legal nature. So whether you use a narrative format or any other format, consistency and fairness are crucial.

We know from experience that the vast majority of overworked managers will not do a good job on individualized appraisals. Sure it sounds good, but it probably won't happen. And why tempt fate? If you want to tempt fate, and it really is important to your company to develop a more narrative format, make sure you give your managers the time and support to do a good job on this. One manager told us he spent up to four hours on some of his individual reviews.

A Word of Caution

Something to watch out for with the narrative format is over-familiarity. Yes, we want you to be warm, real, and sincere in your comments, but this is still a professional letter that will be part of an employee's permanent record. You might have established friendly relationships with your direct reports and might be tempted to use your normal speaking style in the performance appraisal. That's okay to a point—but other eyes might be reviewing this document. It's advisable to not write anything that might be considered an inside joke or slang.

There are ways of maintaining a warm, open style without becoming overly informal. Although you might be convinced that your staff will appreciate any humor you might add, this is a professional document that carries a lot of weight. Don't trivialize it.

Wise Counsel

The simpler and less time-consuming the format, the greater chance you have of successful participation. Trust us on this one, it's difficult enough to get all managers to comply with any appraisal system.

The Least You Need to Know

➤ The narrative format can be as simple as a letter or memo documenting performance and goals for each employee.

➤ A more formal narrative format might be a form with a series of questions related to an employee's performance and goals.

➤ The narrative format generally works well in smaller companies.

➤ Larger companies will probably have a hard time getting all managers to write narrative appraisals on large numbers of employees.

➤ Maintain a warm, sincere, but professional tone in your narrative appraisals.

Hey guys, How'm I doin??

Chapter 26

Peer-to-Peer and 360-Degree Feedback

In This Chapter

➤ What are these tools?

➤ Are they useful to you?

➤ Trust is the key

➤ Is your company ready for these tools?

We referred to these two advanced methods of evaluation, *peer-to-peer* and 360-degree, in Chapter 20, "Tinkering and Remodeling: Improving the Plan," and 21, "Keeping It All On Track: Performance Management." This chapter will explore them in more detail, focus on some actual examples, and let you see how some other companies have approached them. As with all other appraisals, there is not perfect format for every situation. What's right for one company can be terrible for another.

Peer-to-Peer Evaluation

Some companies ask employees to review their peers—their co-workers—within a certain department. As you might imagine, this step requires a great deal of trust within a department to carry it off well. Because of that, we don't recommend adding this component until you are very sure that your employees are ready for it.

Close Up

Peer evaluation is the practice of having teammates or co-workers within a department evaluate each other, usually using a special format that is meant to draw out constructive feedback.

Empowerment Zone

If your company is structured into teams, another way to introduce peer feedback is to take a team approach—have one work team evaluate another work team. Team performance, not individual team members, is evaluated. It might be a less intimidating way to start.

How do you know when that point of readiness is reached? You make sure you are having regular staff meetings and that you bring up the subject enough times to let people explore their feelings and fears about such a process. Usually when people have opportunities to express their doubts, you can help them to identify which fears might be groundless and guide them to overcome these concerns.

This technique carries the risk that conflicts between employees might play out on the form. However, with a staff that is experienced and mature enough to handle it professionally, it can be very educational to see how peers rate each other. Let's face it, most of the time most people have very little direct feedback from their peers. Usually when they do get it, the feedback comes with anger or irritation or is too sugar-coated. If employees take the time to give thoughtful and reasoned information to each other, most people stand to gain greater insight into their work relationships and performance.

A form can be designed that asks for more narrative feedback depending on the level of employee. For line employees it's probably better to make the form less time consuming.

Any of these forms can be used or customized to fit your situation.

360-Degree Evaluation

This instrument takes the concept of peer evaluation and expands it to other levels within an organization. 360 degrees implies a full circle. This evaluation invites comments from not only peers, but also subordinates, supervisors, self, and perhaps even customers. It is designed to get a well-rounded, "full circle" of feedback.

Not all companies or individuals are appropriate subjects for this kind of feedback. Just as trust must be present for peer reviews, a great deal of trust must be developed before this "multisource" feedback can be utilized properly. Additionally, there will have to be staff education to explain the method, its purpose, and how to give objective and constructive feedback.

Employee Peer Review

Name of Employee Being Reviewed:_____

Reviewer Name:_____

Review Period:_____

Instructions: Circle the appropriate rating for all the areas of performance listed using the key below.

Rating Key:
NA = Not Applicable
1 = Not Acceptable
2 = Needs Improvement
3 = Good Work
4 = Above Expectations
5 = Clearly Outstanding

1. Demonstrates required job skills   NA 1 2 3 4 5

2. Demonstrates ability to learn new skills   NA 1 2 3 4 5

3. Understands how job relates to peers   NA 1 2 3 4 5

4. Uses resources in an effective manner   NA 1 2 3 4 5

5. Follows attendance guidelines   NA 1 2 3 4 5

6. Takes direction from supervisor   NA 1 2 3 4 5

7. Meets their commitments   NA 1 2 3 4 5

8. Demonstrates problem solving skills   NA 1 2 3 4 5

9. Offers suggestions for making improvements   NA 1 2 3 4 5

10. Takes responsibility for actions   NA 1 2 3 4 5

Additional comments:

This is a very simple form that can be filled out quickly. It also leaves room for additional comments, should the person desire to add narrative detail. This particular form asks for the appraiser's name. It also could be left off if you want to protect anonymity.

Peer Evaluation

Please rate each person in your group on the following items. Do not share this evaluation with any other member of the department.

Employee Name:_____

Did not Participate	Seldom Participated	Frequently Participated	Adequately Participated	Always Participated

1. Participation in Team Project

Excellent	Good	Average	Mediocre	Poor

2. Quality of Work

Excellent	Good	Average	Mediocre	Poor

3. Cooperation with others

4. Strengths – List particular strengths this person adds to the department

5. Areas of Development –Suggest areas this person may need to improve upon.

This sample shows another sort of peer format that is designed to evaluate employees who work in a formal work team situation. The form asks employees to evaluate their peers' participation in team projects. It also asks for a narrative response to strengths and areas of improvement.

Peer Appraisal Form

Employee name:_____ Date of Appraisal:_____

Rating Key: **Satisfactory = S**
                          Needs Improvement = NI

Please assign a rating to each of the following factors: **S or NI**

1. **Teamwork**

    Comments:

2. **Quality of Work**

    Comments:

3. **Work Habits/Ethics**

    Comments:

4. **Communication Skills**

    Comments:

5. **Safety Awareness**

    Comments:

6. **Creativity**

    Comments:

    OVERALL RATING

    Comments:

Rather than asking for an excellence rating–style evaluation, this form simply elicits whether the work is okay or if it needs improvement. Documentation is requested to explain why each choice was made. This kind of either/or format leaves less room for hurt feelings over whether a co-worker might rate a person "very good" rather than "excellent."

Additionally, it's best not to include this type of feedback in determining an employee's salary increase because that sort of knowledge might impact someone's totally honest rating. If the reviewer really likes a person or really dislikes a person, that might be reflected in the score. If you want to have it relate to salary increases, making it effect only a portion of the increase, say 25 percent may minimize the possibility that it will impact the integrity of the evaluation.

The form can be designed in a number of ways. A series of open-ended questions is a format that has been used frequently. How detailed it becomes again depends on the readiness of your company to take this advanced step in feedback.

Empowerment Zone

The technique of 360-degree (multisource) feedback most frequently is used with management positions or above. The reason for this is that managers typically work directly with more constituents, and their direct superiors might not be privy to all the points of view that impact performance.

Just the Facts

Frequently the feedback given in a 360-degree evaluation is anonymous—participants do not put their names down as the reviewers. The intent of anonymity is to encourage more honesty about performance and less emphasis on personal traits.

How Useful Are Peer-to-Peer and 360-Degree Evaluations?

Good question. Why would you be looking into these forms of appraisals in the first place? If someone has suggested them as the latest "trend *du jour*," that's not a good reason to initiate this advanced form of appraisal. However, there are good reasons to introduce them to a company that is ready. Possible good reasons might include some of the following:

➤ You have a mature staff that is ready for more in-depth feedback.

➤ Your employee population is relatively small and most of the employees in the designated jobs interact with one another individually or through teams.

➤ There is a high degree of trust among your employees.

➤ Employees have important knowledge when it comes to evaluating supervisors. They're the ones who receive the supervision and know how it effects their ability to do the job.

➤ Employees have requested other methods of feedback.

➤ Because of job circumstances, other employees have more knowledge about workers than their supervisors do.

From the File Cabinet

Although there probably are a wide assortment of formats you could use for a 360-degree evaluation, a very simple, straightforward example helped one company we know to introduce the concept. There was no form—a manager would send a memo to all constituents from whom feedback was sought asking just three questions:

➤ What am I doing that I should continue doing?

➤ What am I doing that I should stop doing?

➤ What am I not doing that I should start doing?

It's quite brief, although it might elicit a longer response. And it seems less threatening than asking others to rate you according to some sort of excellence scale.

If any of these sounds like your company, moving on to peer-to-peer or 360-degree evaluation might be useful and productive. If several of the preceding are true, by all means, introduce one or both of these appraisal techniques. In a company that has a high level of trust, such instruments will help to make the company even stronger. Employees will appreciate that their opinions are sought and valued.

Trust Is the Key

Neither of these advanced appraisal formats will work if there is no trust between co-workers. They definitely are not something to spring on staff unless you are certain that they trust and respect each other as well as senior staff. That does not mean there are not conflicts between people, just that there are basically good working relationships, with a fair amount of maturity showed by most of the staff. You will never have uniform trust among all the employees.

These signals suggest that trust exists at your company:

➤ There is open communication at staff and employee meetings.

➤ There are few conflicts—employees are able to handle interpersonal conflicts on their own.

➤ Disagreements are handled in a professional and nonpersonal manner by the majority of the employees.

➤ There is minimal gossip and rumor.

➤ Attendance is good.

➤ Employees tend to stay a long while with the company.

➤ Employees feel comfortable giving feedback to management staff.

➤ Employees work as a team and are supportive of each other's efforts.

➤ Employees treat co-workers and management with respect.

➤ Managers treat staff with respect.

Ask yourself if this sounds like the environment at your company. If you are uncertain, ask others—ask some employees. Trust doesn't just happen magically. It occurs gradually when people start to feel comfortable and secure with each other. Trust cannot be mandated; it has to be earned. And that might take a bit of time. People will trust you by your behaviors, not just by your words.

Too many times we have seen executives assume that trust exists among their direct reports because no one feels comfortable enough to actually tell the truth. Successfully playing corporate politics does not mean that trust exists among a group of colleagues. Of course if you are unaware of your true work environment, it is possible that you will become more aware by having an anonymous feedback mechanism about the senior staff, which can be used to see where you need to start in terms of building trust.

Are You Ready?

In a trusting work environment, you are well on your way to introducing these new concepts. However, just as with a regular performance appraisal system, you've got to plan on training the participants in how to use these tools.

Your Program Will Only Be as Good as Your Training

All participants of peer-to-peer and 360-degree review should be given formal training sessions on how to use the instruments. Even with a mature, sophisticated staff, do not assume that people just naturally know how to give constructive feedback properly.

Remember that different kinds of people and personalities make up any work environment. There will be some very direct, assertive types who might expect that same direct kind of feedback. There also will be more sensitive people who can take criticism well only if it is couched in a softer or more supportive style. The most effective way to give feedback is in a supportive style. If it is not done in this way, then a lot of people will feel it is punishment, which is a poor long-term motivator.

From the File Cabinet

A company that thought it was ready for "cutting-edge" performance management techniques decided that peer-to-peer appraisals sounded like a great idea. They simply announced to the management staff that they should start the practice with their respective departments. They gave no training to their managers on what the appraisals should look like, thinking that managers can figure that stuff out on their own. Not surprisingly, the plan flopped miserably. The managers felt awkward and unprepared, and the employees thought it was a ridiculous idea. Without training, these kinds of programs are doomed to failure.

The training has to address all the styles and encourage feedback that will be honest but also will be designed to have a positive, not discouraging, effect.

Training should include topics such as:

➤ Is the utilization of peer-to-peer or 360-degree feedback optional or required?

➤ Will the feedback be anonymous?

➤ How can employees give and receive constructive feedback that is meant to support their co-workers?

➤ What part will this play in the overall appraisal system?

➤ What specific areas of performance will be evaluated?

➤ How will the feedback be given to those appraised?

Wise Counsel

Training in how to give feedback properly is not a 20-minute, brown-bag presentation. Take the time you need to prepare your staff for something new. As with any introduction to a new performance appraisal system, your enthusiasm and belief in the system must be evident. This is not an area to enter into half-heartedly.

You can customize the training for your individual situation with your participants in mind. We have found that some companies utilizing these techniques have started the program on a small scale. Participation was voluntary and feedback anonymous. It takes a while for these methods to feel comfortable, so starting smaller seems to

Empowerment Zone

A great way to design a peer feedback form is to ask your employees to design it themselves, with guidance from you. They might have good ideas about what kind of feedback they think would be valuable from their co-workers. They will also give you some insight into what way and how far they want to take this type of feedback.

help. With anonymous feedback, the comments or ratings are averaged or summarized when given to the worker being appraised.

You might want to start out utilizing the techniques on management staff and above at first. Evaluating the trust factor between your managers will be necessary, of course. Then you can include others as you become acclimated to it.

However, if your staff traditionally has no problem speaking up to management and sharing feedback, the program might be a natural extension of your corporate style. You might learn things that you would never have found out any other way.

More Thoughts on 360-Degree Feedback

Some companies have found the following suggestions effective when first introducing 360-degree feedback:

➤ Let the employee choose who he or she will be evaluated by; depending on company size, this could be 6 to 12 people.

➤ Make the individual feedback anonymous.

➤ Have the manager review feedback with the employee instead of just handing the person a piece of paper.

➤ Summarize results. Give an overall feedback picture, don't focus on the one very positive or not-so-positive comment.

➤ Be sure the criteria evaluated are behavioral in nature—you are not looking for personality (traits or) factors.

➤ Use the results for developmental purposes only, not salary increases.

➤ Keep them brief—results are not optimal if someone has an inbox stuffed with appraisals that take up to an hour each to complete.

Be Constructive, Not Destructive

Even if your feedback will be anonymous, try to remember to give *constructive* feedback that is meant to motivate and improve someone. You might think that your comments will be diluted among others' comments, but you have to remind yourself that the desired result of any appraisal is to make the company stronger. If you feel that someone is failing to meet company expectations, try to word it in a way that will support their improvement.

For example, if you feel that someone you are evaluating has a problem with starting and promoting office gossip, you could make a comment like: "Having open, communicative relationships with co-workers is an asset, and one you have developed. There are many times that I have seen you use these interactions effectively. In the future it would be more productive if this quality were to be used for improving work flow or communicating problems that affect your or others' work, and not as has been sometimes observed to draw people into nonproductive discussions about personality issues or nonwork matters."

Close Up

In the performance appraisal context, **constructive** means leading to improvements and advancements. In other words, constructive feedback is meant to build people up, not tear them down.

It's always important to think about the words you use when writing an appraisal in any context. Those who can be professional and candid will be the most successful. It's not always easy, but it is always worth the time it takes to word it in a more supportive way.

---

360 Degree Feedback

Date:_____

(Employee Name) has requested that you evaluate factors of his/her performance using the form below. Please rate each factor according to the following scale:

        E = Excellent
        S = Satisfactory
        ND = Needs Development

A.   Does the above named employee clearly communicate and keep co-workers/customers updated on things they need to know?

B.   Does the employee follow up on questions and concerns in a timely manner?

C.   Evaluate the employee's ability to problem solve.

D.   Does employee honor deadlines and schedules?

E.   Does employee lead by example?

Overall Rating

Additional comments:

This is a very brief 360-degree feedback instrument that is meant to be completed anonymously. The employee to be appraised actually addresses the forms to reviewers that he or she has selected. Reviewers are instructed to return the form to the employee's supervisor who will then summarize the results.

This example shows a very simple 360-degree appraisal format. The reviewer need only answer the questions briefly—or in more detail, if desired. Such a form is much less intimidating than a long form asking for some sort of excellence rating.

TO:_____

FROM:_____

Please answer the following questions as briefly and concisely as possible:

1. What part of my performance as _____ do you think I should continue doing?

2. What part of my performance should I stop doing?

3. What am I not currently doing that I should start doing?

The Least You Need to Know

➤ Peer-to-peer appraisals ask co-workers to evaluate each others' performance.

➤ Using the 360-degree appraisal you get full-circle or multisource feedback from peers, subordinates, customers and others you work with regularly.

➤ Both peer-to-peer and 360-degree appraisals can be very useful if your company is ready for them, has the time and motivation to do them, and is willing and able to provide a thorough training program for everyone involved.

➤ Evaluate your company's readiness or ask others to help you in that pursuit.

➤ Consider starting the new system slowly, using anonymous feedback.

➤ Maintain a professional, supportive tone when giving feedback, even if it is anonymous.

Glossary

Americans with Disabilities Act (ADA)   Federal anti-discrimination law written to protect the rights of qualified workers who are disabled. It pertains to employers who have 15 or more employees. It is enforced by the Equal Employment Opportunity Commission (EEOC) and can heavily penalize companies for intentional discrimination.

anniversary date   Commonly defined as the date of hire, typically the first day actually worked. However, it also could denote the anniversary of a job change or promotion, so there might be more than one anniversary date in a personnel file.

autocratic   The state of being extremely authoritarian and possessing absolute power.

balanced form   A form that is evenly distributed with measurable performance factors and areas that encourage discussion and seek agreement.

behavior   The way in which one behaves; the actions or reactions of a person under certain circumstances.

buy-in   Refers to employees' understanding and acceptance of a new idea or program. Either your employees "buy" it or they don't.

COLA   Cost of living adjustment; a once-a-year, across-the-board wage increase usually related to the Consumer Price Index.

constructive   In the performance appraisal context, means leading to improvements and advancements. Constructive feedback is meant to build someone up, not tear someone down. In a behavioral context, it means the use of positive or negative consequences following the occurrence or non-occurrence of a particular behavior or behaviors.

contingency   In the legal context, taking a case on the chance that you will win, and the legal fees will be paid out of the judgment.

direct reports   The employees whose primary reporting relationship is with you. You probably hired them, and at the very least, you directly supervise them.

discoverable   Information that is considered evidence and can be used in a legal case. A performance appraisal frequently is sought during an investigation or formal discovery process prior to a trial or hearing.

disengage   To release oneself or withdraw from a previous involvement or position; to detach.

Employee Assistance Program (EAP)   An employee benefit frequently provided by employers. The EAP should be staffed by licensed mental health providers who can do psychological assessments and brief treatment with employees.

feedback   In the business context, giving evaluative or corrective information to the other person about an action, event, or process.

filter   The manner through which someone perceives the world after being influenced by factors including ethnic background, family dynamics, environment, and others.

fully-executed copy   A complete copy of the original document, with any changes, added comments, and so forth, as well as all signatures in place.

halo effect   The technique of rating all employees as "good" or "acceptable" in all areas regardless of actual performance.

independent contractor   Someone who is not an employee who is hired to do a specific task for an agreed-upon price, and who can retain the right to control the manner in which they complete the job.

intervention   The act of interceding as an influencing force to modify or hinder some action.

introductory period   A period of time when a new employee is being evaluated for appropriate fit with a job. Commonly this period is 30 to 90 days.

micro-manage   The style of closely supervising employees to the point of always looking over their shoulders as they work. Micro-managers have little trust in the employees' ability to work without constant supervision.

mentor   Someone who acts as a wise, trusting advisor or counselor to another person. A mentor typically shares lessons in leadership with those he or she mentors.

narrative   The practice of telling a story or giving an account in writing or speech. A narrative appraisal is writing the appraisal in text form.

neutral space   An area that is considered safe, such as a location that has no connections to previous emotionally charged or stressful events. If your office is known as the place where people are disciplined (or even terminated), it won't seem like a neutral space.

open-ended question   A question that is designed and worded to elicit more than just a "yes" or "no" answer.

peer evaluation   The practice of having teammates or co-workers within a department evaluate each other, usually using a special format that is meant to draw out constructive feedback.

performance management   A formal system designed to provide continuous feedback between employers and employees, rather than the once-a-year approach. Performance standards are established for each job and employees are coached to reach or exceed the standard using continuous feedback.

philosophy   The set of general principles or laws of conduct you use for practical purposes; usually includes your system of ethics.

positive reinforcement   Refers to a procedure in which some positive event is presented following a behavior that makes it more likely that the behavior will occur again.

proactive   Taking the first step first; showing the initiative to start a project before being asked.

productivity measures   The standards used to compare the quality of work among staff members in a certain area of your company. For example, each employee might be responsible to turn out x number of widgets per hour, and reduce waste and error to five percent.

punishment   The presentation of an aversive event after a behavior, meant to result in a subsequent decrease in that behavior.

reasonable accommodation   Term the ADA uses to describe a modification made to a job in order to permit a disabled person to perform its essential functions. Although designed to require employers to be more flexible, the law does not consider reduced productivity to be a reasonable accommodation. Nor does it expect an accommodation that would create an undue hardship on the employer.

regulatory requirements   Rules governing certain systems or industries that mandate strict compliance with defined standards.

retention   Keeping employees at your company. Using effective retention devices has become critical in keeping companies staffed.

roll out   The formal presentation of a new program or product. Usually a roll out has been designed to have a live presentation with overheads, handouts, full explanations of the product or procedure, and an opportunity to ask questions.

semantics   How things are said; how word meanings can be interpreted differently depending upon how they are used.

separation agreement   A contract to terminate the employment of a staff member under mutually agreed-upon circumstances. Frequently there is a financial agreement in exchange for confidentiality of the terms and other negotiated concessions.

shaping   Reinforcement procedures used to increase or decrease behaviors that you have identified. When you use shaping in the early stages of change you will use positive or negative reinforcement with behavior that resembles or approximates the desired goal behavior. For instance, if an employee who never took the initiative to problem solve on their own suddenly made an attempt to independently solve a problem, you would want to positively reinforce this. This would be true even if the problem-solving attempt was incomplete. Positive reinforcement is an example of a shaping mechanism. The three main mechanisms are positive and negative reinforcement and operant extinction, or in simpler words, ignoring of behavior.

subjective   Affected or produced by the perceptions of the person doing the thinking; in performance appraisals, personal—or existing in the mind of the person doing the appraisal.

third person   The form of addressing the person spoken of with the pronouns "he" or "she."

threat   An expression of an intent to do harm. One threat expert points out that the people who make threats usually are desperate and feel they have very little power. The value of a threat is that it is meant to cause fear and uncertainty.

Sample Forms

This appendix contains a sample performance review template and a sample annual performance appraisal form that you are free to use as is or adapt to fit your company's needs.

Performance Review

Employee:

Manager:
    (Note: All managers who have managed this individual during the current focal review period are responsible for providing review input. *If you are the current manager, you are responsible for collecting review information from the previous manager(s).*

Review Period:

Date of Review:

Ratings

I = Improvement Required
Employees whose performance *INCONSISTENTLY MEETS OR DOES NOT MEET* the requirements of their job in the major areas of objectives and performance categories.

S = Successful
Employees whose accomplishments and performance *REGULARLY MEET* the requirements of their job in the major areas of objectives and performance categories.

VS = Very Successful
Employees whose accomplishments and performance *REGULARLY EXCEED* the requirements of their job in the major areas of objectives and performance categories.

E = Exceptional
Employees whose accomplishments and performance *REGULARLY FAR EXCEED* the requirements of their job in the major areas of objectives and performance categories. These individuals clearly stand out as exceptional employees to peers and management.

Managers: Use the boxes below to rate each goal/objective, each success factor and for the overall rating. In MS Word, go to "View" pull down menu and select Toolbars. Add the "Drawing" toolbar to your Word desktop. Use the paint bucket fill-color tool on the drawing toolbar to shade the appropriate box.

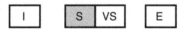

Overview
Managers: In this section, describe overall performance during the review period. For example you can include information about performance relative to the overall context of the business or employee's growth within the position.

Sample performance review template.

Accomplishment Input or Self Evaluation From Employee
Managers: Place input below, in body of review, or include as attachment.

Objectives and Results

I. GOAL / OBJECTIVE –

I		S	VS		E

II. GOAL / OBJECTIVE –

I		S	VS		E

III. GOAL / OBJECTIVE –

I		S	VS		E

IV. GOAL / OBJECTIVE –

I		S	VS		E

Success Factors
Managers: Put your comments below rating to explain how employee performed against Success Factor criteria.

Communication
Keeps others appropriately informed through the use of accurate, consistent, timely, open, honest, trusting and straight forward oral and written communications. Utilizes electronic communications appropriately and with regard to security. Utilizes appropriate methods to ensure open channels of communications at all levels.

I		S	VS		E

Customer Focus

Builds effective interpersonal business relationships with external and internal business partners and external customers through timely provision of service. Demonstrates willingness to go the extra mile to support legitimate requests of others. Provides assistance and consultation.

| I | S | VS | E |

Productivity

Meets commitments and accomplishes all major objectives accurately and on time. Results produced are relative to that expected for the time invested. Strives to work more effectively and efficiently. Establishes and manages priorities effectively.

| I | S | VS | E |

Results Focus

Manages simultaneous demands on resources and time and remains focused on achieving results. Keeps commitments and avoids activity for activity's sake. Establishes challenging and productive objectives, priorities, standards, and responsibilities and moves the company and the business forward. Is resourceful and works well within the system to solve problems. Accepts accountability for own actions.

| I | S | VS | E |

Initiative

Proactively exerts influence over events rather than passively accepting them. Modifies own behavior to respond to obstacles while still achieving own objectives. When appropriate, assumes duties and responsibilities which may be outside of his/her regular job scope and responsibility. Seeks self-development and learning opportunities which enhance current position and allow for advancement and growth. Generates innovative ideas, approaches, and solutions.

| I | S | VS | E |

Teamwork

Demonstrates positive, motivated behavior and provides support as well as accepts guidance from fellow co-workers and management. Gains cooperation and works effectively with others to produce desired results. Fosters cooperation and teamwork. Modifies individual objectives and desires to support the efforts of the team. Exhibits flexibility and adaptability.

| I | S | VS | E |

Summary and Overall Rating

| I | | S | VS | | E |

Employee Development Plan

List developmental activities needed to enhance the employee's job performance, for example training, coaching, adjusting performance objectives, etc. Set a timeline for the training.

Career Enhancement Opportunities

Describe opportunities for job enrichment or career development. Employee may want to increase skills and/or acquire more responsibility.

NOTE TO MANAGERS: THIS IS THE END OF THE INPUT PORTION OF THE EVALUATION. SIGNATURES AND EMPLOYEE COMMENTS FOLLOW. ENSURE THAT PAGE BREAKS OCCUR AT THE APPROPRIATE PLACES PRIOR TO PRINTING BY USING THE "PRINT PREVIEW" OPTION LOCATED IN THE "FILE" MENU. PAGE BREAKS ARE ADDED THROUGH "EDIT...INSERT PAGE BREAK." PLEASE DELETE THESE INSTRUCTIONS PRIOR TO PRINTING.

Signature Section

The employee's signature in this section indicates that s/he has reviewed this performance evaluation. The signature does not imply an agreement or disagreement with the content of the review. The employee may add comments in the Employee Comments section or attach additional sheets if necessary. *These comments are due within five working days from the date the employee receives the review.* The employee is also encouraged to work with management and/ or Human Resources to resolve any issues regarding this evaluation.

_____   _____
Manager Signature   *Date*

_____   _____
Second - Level Review (VP or CEO)   *Date*

_____   _____
Employee Signature   *Date*

_____   _____
Human Resources Signature   *Date*

Employee's Comments: (attach additional page(s) if necessary)

_____

_____

_____

_____

_____

_____

_____

Annual Performance Appraisal

Name of Employee Being Reviewed:_____

Manager's Name:_____

Review Period Start Date: ___/___/___

Review Period End Date: ___/___/___

Rating Key:

NA – Not Applicable
1 -	**Unsatisfactory**	Unable to perform required tasks. Requires too much supervision.
2 -	**Marginal**	Meets some requirements. Needs improvement in quality of work and completing tasks on time.
3 -	**Meets Requirements**	Quality of work consistently meets requirements and tasks are completed on time.
4 -	**Exceeds Requirements**	Consistently goes above and beyond goals and objectives required for the position. Exceeds requirements for quality and quantity.
5 -	**Exceptional**	Significantly exceeds requirements and expectations. Always accomplishes results far beyond what is required. *Note: usage of this rating is highly limited.

JOB PERFORMANCE:

Works effectively with their team to achieve set objectives Profits from constructive criticism.	NA	1	2	3	4	5
Capable of required job skills and knowledge.	NA	1	2	3	4	5
Demonstrates effective use of skills and training.	NA	1	2	3	4	5
Behaviors consistent with company policy.	NA	1	2	3	4	5
Has the ability to learn and use new skills.	NA	1	2	3	4	5
Keeps current with changes and trends in the technical Knowledge required for the position.	NA	1	2	3	4	5

Comments:

RESPONSIBILITY AND RELIABILITY:

Sample annual performance appraisal form.

289

Responds effectively to assigned responsibilities.	NA	1	2	3	4	5
Communicates effectively, promoting productivity, understanding and respect. Keeps others informed.	NA	1	2	3	4	5
Meets attendance requirements.	NA	1	2	3	4	5
Delegates subordinate relationships and development in an appropriate manner.	NA	1	2	3	4	5
Takes responsibility for actions.	NA	1	2	3	4	5
Demonstrates foresight in recognizing potential problems and develops solutions.	NA	1	2	3	4	5

Comments:

PROBLEM SOLVING

General problem solving skills.	NA	1	2	3	4	5
Offers constructive suggestions for improving work.	NA	1	2	3	4	5
Generates creative ideas and solutions. Initiates change when necessary. Encourages others to accept change.	NA	1	2	3	4	5
Meets challenge head on.	NA	1	2	3	4	5
Acquires and analyzes all relevant information before making decisions.	NA	1	2	3	4	5
Provides appropriate alternatives when making recommendations.	NA	1	2	3	4	5

Comments:

FUTURE GOALS AND SUGGESTED IMPROVEMENTS:

EMPLOYEE COMMENTS:

SUMMARY AND OVERALL EVALUATION

Overall rating   **NA   1   2   3   4   5**

Comments:

I acknowledge receipt of review and my signature does not necessarily indicate agreement.

_____   _____

Employee   **Date**

_____   _____

Direct Supervisor   **Date**

How to Say It: Sample Lead-Ins

The following pages have some sample language to help you begin an appraisal conversation, close the conversation, and handle some difficult situations. You can use these for rehearsal purposes, or try to put them into your own words so they sound more natural for you.

Sample Language for Managers

Here are some examples of how a manager might open a traditional performance appraisal meeting:

➤ "We're here to take a look at your performance over the last year. I'd like to start by reviewing the goals we set last year and the progress made toward them; then I'd like to hear your feedback on how the year has gone. And finally, I'd like us to agree on goals for the coming year. So shall we get started?"

➤ "We're here to have an exchange of feedback. I am going to review with you my perceptions of your work over the past year, and I'd like to get your perceptions of how things are going as well. In addition, this could be a time to give me feedback about how I supervise you and what you like or need to be different."

➤ "My intention with this meeting is that we have a conversation about how things have gone over the past year. I'm sure I have some ideas and you have some ideas. Let's share our information in terms of goals and how much has been—and will be—accomplished."

➤ "Our ability to meet company goals is very closely related to how our employees are meeting their individual goals. Our purpose for meeting today is to exchange feedback on how we are doing on accomplishing our goals."

➤ "This is a performance appraisal meeting and I realize that you might be nervous about it. Let me assure you that it is stressful for me, too. My intention is that we make it a two-way conversation so that we both can feel more comfortable."

➤ "It's been a challenging year, and I'm as interested in hearing your point of view as you are in mine. The intent of this meeting is to share perceptions about how to make things continue to progress in the right direction. I want you to know right off that I am impressed with you and the work you have done."

Here are some examples of how a manager might begin a difficult appraisal:

➤ "We are meeting to talk about how the past year has gone. I have some perceptions and I am sure you do, too. My intent is that we share our ideas to find out what went well and what did not go so well over the past year. This applies primarily to your performance but also to my management style and how I can help you to succeed."

➤ "We all know this was a difficult year for members of the department. The intention of this meeting is to exchange ideas about what actually was happening and how we can structure our goals for a positive future."

➤ "As you know, this is a meeting to discuss your performance over the past year. I want to assure you that my intent is to share perceptions, to listen to your opinions, and to arrive at ways we can mutually plan for a productive future."

➤ "I want to start by saying we are going to discuss work performance, and anything that might seem critical is meant to be constructive feedback. I want you to know we care about you as a person, even if we have had some issues with your work this year. I also am interested in your feedback about your performance."

These examples illustrate how a manager might politely disagree with an employee's perspective:

➤ "I hear what you are saying. And I understand how you feel about it. And I would like you to hear what others in the department have said about this situation."

➤ "I appreciate your feelings about this situation. And I want to remind you that we have to take into consideration the feelings of the rest of the department as well. Let's explore what others have said about this."

➤ "I hear that you are upset about this situation. You have a right to feel the way you do. Let's look at how others have perceived the situation. Does this solution meet the goals the company has established?"

➤ "I am very interested in hearing your point of view, but I feel we have moved away from our topic, which is your performance appraisal. Perhaps we could address this issue at another meeting."

➤ "I know it can be difficult to hear feedback that is different from what you wanted to hear. It clearly was a difficult transition for you, and I am concerned about how to help you succeed here."

➤ "Actually this is an example of how difficult it is to give you feedback that is different from your opinion of the situation. My goal is not to upset you or make you feel put down. I'd like to see if you can take this information and think about it and perhaps we could talk about it again in another meeting, after you have had the time to reflect on it."

Here are some ways a manager might bring the performance appraisal meeting to a close:

➤ "Okay, we've reviewed last year's performance, and set goals for the coming year. Is there anything else you'd like to cover before we end the meeting?"

➤ "I know this can be a difficult process, and I appreciate that it may not have been easy for you to hear some of this feedback. I want you to know I am committed to helping you succeed in your present job, especially if I see you working on the areas we identified as needing to improve."

➤ "It's been good to have the opportunity to talk in depth about how things are going. I appreciate hearing your point of view. We have a big year coming up, and I'm confident we can make good progress toward our goals."

➤ "These kinds of conversations are always a little difficult. I'm glad we had a chance to clear the air and share our feedback. I want to encourage you to keep the communication going. By working together we can accomplish a lot. Thank you for your continued efforts and hard work."

Employee's Opening Statement

These sample statements might help an employee open a performance appraisal meeting:

➤ "I appreciate having the time to talk to you one-on-one about how things have been going. I value your feedback and look forward to hearing your perceptions of the last year."

➤ "Thanks for meeting with me. I'm sure we both have a lot of information to share about the past year. I look forward to hearing your comments."

➤ "I am hoping to get more specific goals and ideas of how to achieve them in this meeting. Also I am hoping to share my ideas on what I feel will help me to acquire more skills that are of value to the department."

➤ "I've been looking forward to this meeting. It's been a challenging year, and I'm interested in hearing your feedback. Also I've been formulating some goals for next year that I want to share with you."

These examples show some ways that an employee can initiate a conversation about a difficult appraisal or performance situation:

➤ "I realize this has been a difficult year. I sincerely want to work with you to find ways to make next year a stronger year. Perhaps we can meet on a more regular basis to discuss these kinds of things."

➤ "Thank you for taking the time to meet with me. I realize we have had some disagreements in the past. My hope is that we can discuss the last year professionally and come up with ways to make next year a productive year."

➤ "Performance appraisals are always difficult. I am interested in your opinion and I hope I'll be able to share my comments with you."

➤ "I realize that we have had different ways of approaching and evaluating how I am doing in this company. I am looking forward to your help in defining a more specific way that we can monitor my progress toward mutually defined goals."

Here are some ways an employee can politely disagree with a manager's perspective during a performance appraisal meeting:

➤ "I hear what you are saying. However, I see it differently. May I explain my point of view on this?"

➤ "There are reasons that things turned out the way they did. May I have an opportunity to explain the other side of the story?"

➤ "Last year you told me what your expectations were. It seems to me that you are evaluating me for something outside of those expectations. Can we clarify where this fits into last year's goals?"

➤ "I need to say that I have found that the expectations in the department have not always been consistent. I really would like an opportunity to work together to create a more consistent set of specific work goals and behaviors that are acceptable to you."

Here are some ways an employee can bring a performance appraisal meeting to a close:

➤ "Thank you for meeting with me. It's good to get the opportunity to talk about how things are going and to agree on goals."

➤ "Thank you for your time. I will think about additional comments to write on the form and get back to you next week."

➤ "Thanks for the feedback. I appreciate the open communication and look forward to a great year."

➤ "I know this wasn't easy for me, so it must not be easy for you either. I really do hope this will give us both more incentive to keep communication open during the coming year."

Resources

These are resources that you might find helpful in your quest to design the perfect performance appraisal system. Some of them we consulted while writing this book; others we just know are good places to increase your knowledge on the topic. We tend to be favorably inclined toward resources that share our belief that employees should be treated like the invaluable, highly respectable, and hard-to-replace individuals that they are. The fact that we list them here does not necessarily mean that the following resources are guaranteed to be suitable for your situation. But these are people and resources that we respect and value.

Management Philosophy

Stephen R. Covey, *The 7 Habits of Highly Effective People,* a Fireside Book, Simon & Schuster, 1989—A great resource on positive management practice.

www.Deming.org—The Web site for the W. Edwards Deming Institute, with lots of information about Deming and his "system of profound knowledge."

www.lessonsinleadership.com/blanchard—This Web site provides information about Ken Blanchard, author of *The One Minute Manager*, which has sold more than 9 million copies worldwide. Blanchard is our kind of management consultant. He has written many other books on management that have reached the best-seller list. Some of his best sellers include:

The One Minute Manager, William Morrow & Co., 1982.

Raving Fans, with Sheldon Bowles, William Morrow & Co., 1993.

Mission Possible, McGraw Hill, 1997.

Performance Appraisal Assistance

www.freeworks.com—Free, usable performance appraisal forms, as well as a large variety of other human resources–related forms are available at this great site.

Dick Grote, the guru of performance appraisals, has written the ultimate resource, *The Complete Guide to Performance Appraisals* (Dick Grote, 1996).

Another of his works that is in sync with our philosophy is *Discipline without Punishment* (Dick Grote, 1995).

Performance Management

www.zigonperf.com—A very helpful site full of free performance measurement resources, as well as information about other services to make you a performance management expert.

www.shrm.org—This is the Web site for The Society of Human Resources Management, the international professional organization for human resources practitioners. The site has loads of free information as well as plenty of invaluable resources for members. Members share job descriptions and much more. Membership at the time of this printing is $160 per year.

Other Good Resources

The Seven Principles of Making Marriage Work, John Gottman, Ph.D., and Nan Silver, 1999, Crown Publishers Inc., 201 East 50th Street, NY, NY 10022.

Bandura, A. *Social Learning Theory*, Morristown, N.J. General Learning Press, 1971.

Your Boss is Not Your Mother, Creating Autonomy, Respect, and Success at Work, Brian DesRoches, Ph.D., New York, N.Y., 1995.

Behavior Modification, Handbook of Assessment, Intervention, and Evaluation, Eileen D. Gambrill, Ph.D., San Francisco, CA, Jossey Bass, 1977. Although this is not a business book, it is a very detailed book where you can learn a lot about behavior change, assessment, and evaluation procedures and reinforcement procedures.

Index

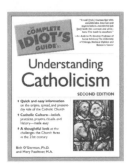
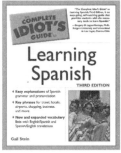

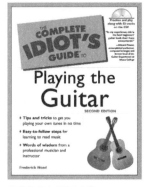

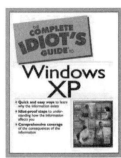